JOHN REIFENBERG

THE PRETRIAL CONFERENCE
AND EFFECTIVE JUSTICE

A CONTROLLED TEST IN PERSONAL INJURY LITIGATION

The PRETRIAL CONFERENCE and EFFECTIVE JUSTICE

A CONTROLLED TEST
IN PERSONAL INJURY LITIGATION

by MAURICE ROSENBERG

with a Preface

by JUSTICE TOM C. CLARK

COLUMBIA UNIVERSITY PRESS
New York and London   1964

MAURICE ROSENBERG is Professor of Law at Columbia University and former Director, Project for Effective Justice (July 1, 1956, to June 30, 1964).

Copyright © 1964 Columbia University Press
Library of Congress Catalog Card Number: 64-8492
Manufactured in the United States of America

To my wife . . .

PREFACE

UNLIKE DRYDEN,* the writer is not accustomed to being a prefacer, and hopes, therefore, to be excused if he exceeds the jurisdiction of the traditional.

The efficacy of the pretrial conference technique has long been in dispute. Its supporters declared it to be the answer to the problem of docket congestion. Its detractors, on the contrary, held it to be but an appendage to the judicial process and a traducer of our adversary system. Indeed as early as 1956, as Chief Justice Weintraub relates it as to New Jersey, "the air was full of claims and arguments, but not the facts and figures to determine which side was right." As "proposals for sweeping changes were pressed upon us," he continued, "we very much needed the guidance that can only come from an impartial, systematic study."

The Chief Justice, being a practical man of action, turned to Professor Rosenberg and his Project for Effective Justice sponsored by Columbia University. The result was the first scientifically controlled test of the effect of pretrial procedures upon the disposition of personal injury litigation in New Jersey. The experimental research that followed led to the adoption of new rules by the Supreme Court of New Jersey governing pretrial in the Superior and County courts of that

---

* "Read all the prefaces of Dryden,
For these our critics much confide in,
(Tho' merely writ at first for filling
To raise the volumes' price a shilling." —SWIFT, *On Poetry*.

PREFACE

UNLIKE DRYDEN, the writer is not accustomed to being a prefacer* and hopes, therefore, to be excused if he exceeds the jurisdiction of the traditional.

The efficacy of the pretrial conference technique has long been in dispute. Its supporters declared it to be the answer to the problem of docket congestion. Its detractors, on the contrary, held it to be but an appendage to the judicial process and a traducer of our adversary system. Indeed as early as 1959, as Chief Justice Weintraub relates it as to New Jersey, "the air was full of claims and arguments, but not the facts and figures to determine which side was right." As "proposals for sweeping changes were pressed upon us," he continued, "we very much needed the guidance that can only come from an impartial, systematic study. . . ."

The Chief Justice, being a practical man of action, turned to Professor Rosenberg and his Project for Effective Justice, sponsored by Columbia University. The result was the first scientifically controlled test of the effect of pretrial procedures upon the disposition of personal injury litigation in New Jersey. The experimental research that followed led to the adoption of new rules by the Supreme Court of New Jersey governing pretrial in the Superior and County courts of that

---

*Read all the prefaces of Dryden
For these our critics much confide in,
(Tho' merely writ at first for filling
To raise the volume's price, a shilling) .—SWIFT, "On Poetry."

state. Rather than the mandatory requirement, the rule was relaxed making pretrial optional in negligence cases.

The Pretrial Conference and Effective Justice records the manner in which this experiment was conducted and the findings of the researchers. It is a landmark in judicial administration, offering, as Chief Justice Weintraub described it, "a sound, fruitful approach for solving problems in the administration of justice." And, as the Chief Justice continued, "the day is not long off when the courts and legislatures will regularly turn to empirical research to answer questions of the kind we faced with pretrial five years ago."

For those of us who are interested in the modernization of the courts—and that should include every citizen—this book charts a course that can be followed with profit in every jurisdiction, namely, the use of empirical research in obtaining answers to procedural problems facing the courts.

I cannot close without a personal word concerning Professor Rosenberg. Most of us see things as they are. He does this with remarkable insight, but he also dreams of things as they should be. And, what is more, he does something about them with both skill and foresight. For three years I have worked closely with him both at the Seminars and the National College of State Trial Judges sponsored by the Joint Committee for the Effective Administration of Justice. He gave generously of his time and talents in these important projects among the state trial judges. He is truly an extraordinary man whose efficacious methods have left a tremendous imprint upon the administration of justice in the trial courts of our country.

Tom C. Clark
Associate Justice,
Supreme Court of the United States

September 9, 1964
Washington, D. C.

ACKNOWLEDGMENTS

CONSTRAINTS of custom even more than of space will explain why the names of many persons who labored mightily on this book are mentioned here with far more brevity than is their due. First it should be said, though, that the whole venture owes its beginning, middle, and end to the Walter E. Meyer Research Institute of Law, Inc., and The New York Foundation, Inc., for their generous financial grants to support the study in all its parts.

Early in the work the Project's staff of lawyers, as novices in experimental social research, found it essential to consult with the Columbia University Bureau of Applied Social Research for technical guidance, and that close liasion continued over the years required to complete the study. The Bureau's director, Dr. Allen H. Barton, has been a friendly and lucid source of expert counsel on many of the perplexing problems of method. Dr. Gene Levine, research associate at the Bureau, helped substantially in formulating the research design. Dr. Helmut Guttenberg, also of the Bureau, was a patient and stalwart guide through the labyrinthine data processing.

The vital and novel aspect of this study as a scientifically controlled experiment in law research is a tribute to the justices of the Supreme Court of New Jersey and in particular to Chief Justice Joseph Weintraub. Their unique readiness to take reasonable steps to modify procedural rules on an experimental basis, without injury to the litigants' rightful interests, made possible whatever of value flows from this study. Besides demonstrating rare open-mindedness in thus permitting their own rules to be put under closest scrutiny by outside investigators, they enlisted the indispensable interest and help of other New Jersey judges, and of court personnel and lawyers. Most of these who were involved in the study were more than generous with their energies, and accepted with good grace the large burden of completing batteries of forms used by the Project to record the test data. Edward B. McConnell, Director of the Administrative Office of the Courts in New Jersey, was an unfailing source of help in many respects, and helped particularly in arranging the study and in supplying essential statistical materials. His deputy, Mortimer G. Newman, Jr., also merits our gratitude for his energetic aid.

Many members of the Project's Advisory Committee made helpful comments and suggestions upon successive drafts of the manuscript and to them too go warm thanks. The two distinguished chairmen of the Advisory Committee, first General Edward S. Greenbaum and then Allen T. Klots, Esq., gave unstinting support to the staff; and Professor Hans Zeisel of the University of Chicago Law School was exceptionally generous with his helpful comments and advice.

From the title page are absent several names whose contributions were very great indeed. Most recently, Project staff attorneys Mrs. Audrey L. Goldberg and Mr. Robert B. Levine have given their entire and devoted attention to the completion of the manuscript. Earlier, Robert H. Chanin, then a staff attorney, had poured prodigious efforts into the analysis and preliminary draft work. Earlier still, his predecessor, Mrs. Myra Schubin, did important work on the design and administration of the test forms. Without the devoted labors of those four this report would not have ripened, and grateful acknowledgment is made to each of them. In addition, Dr. Vernon K. Dibble, presently associate director of the Project, and Professor Michael I. Sovern, who formerly held that post, made helpful contributions to the work. Berton Pekowsky, a Project research associate, rendered extensive service in connection with statistical work and data analysis. Many former law students were among those who contributed to gathering, processing, and analyzing the data. Miss Erna Pospischil worked with great diligence and skill on the secretarial tasks related to preparation of the manuscript.

MAURICE ROSENBERG

April, 1964

CONTENTS

Preface by Justice Tom C. Clark, United States Supreme Court	vii
Acknowledgments	ix
Introduction	1
I. The Pretrial Conference in Perspective	5
II. The Controversy over the Effectiveness of the Pretrial Conference	12
III. The Methods and Materials of the Study	16
IV. What Pretrial Apparently Does and Does Not Do	23
V. New Jersey Judges Speak Their Minds about Pretrial Conferences in Personal Injury Cases	71
VI. Clinical Views of the New Jersey Pretrial in Action	93
VII. Techniques and "Artistry" in Pretrial	106
VIII. A Pretrial Conference Program for Personal Injury Cases	113
Notes	133

Appendices
- A. New Jersey Rules of Civil Practice Relating to the Pretrial Conference — 171
- B. Recent New Jersey Appellate Court Decisions Regarding Pretrial — 177
- C. Forms Used in the New Jersey Study — 184
- D. Credibility of the Findings — 208
- E. Pretrial of Civil Cases in the States — 210
- F. An Audit of the Effects of Transferring "Undersized Cases" from the "Larger" to the "Lesser" Courts — 218
- G. Applicability of the Findings to Cases Other than Personal Injury Actions — 226

Bibliography — 230

Index — 245

TABLES

IN TEXT

1. Good Trial Presentation More Frequent in All-Pretried than in In-Part-Pretried Group — 34
2. Good Trial Presentation Less Frequent in Not-Pretried Cases — 35
3. Good Quality Evidence More Frequent in All-Pretried than in In-Part-Pretried Cases (Judges' Reports) — 37
4. Index of the Quality of Evidence at Trial — 38
5. Good Quality Evidence Less Frequent in Not-Pretried Cases — 38
6. Absence of Trial "Surprise" More Common in All-Pretried Cases — 40
7. Trial "Surprise" More Common in Not-Pretried Cases — 40
8. Comparative Settlement Frequencies — 48
9. Not-Pretried Cases More Commonly Produced Short Trials — 52
10. All-Pretried Cases Did Not Settle Earlier than In-Part-Pretried Cases — 55
11. Not-Pretried Cases Settled Early More Commonly than Pretried Cases — 55
12. The All-Pretried and the In-Part-Pretried Cases Produced Recoveries with Equal Frequency — 60
13. Plaintiffs Recovered in Not-Pretried Cases with Same Frequency as in Pretried Cases — 60
14. All-Pretried Cases Recovered More than In-Part-Pretried Cases — 61
15. The Not-Pretried Cases Recovered Less Money — 62
16. Pretrial Judges' Estimates of Plaintiff's Recovery, Assuming Defendant Liable — 63
17. Constant Frequency of Judges' Agreement with Juries' Liability Verdicts — 65
18. In Not-Pretried Cases Judges More Frequently Agreed with Juries on Damage Verdicts — 66

IN NOTES

A.	Distribution of Type of Action by Test Groups	147
B.	Type and Complexity of the Test Cases	147
C.	Duration of Pretrial Conference	147
D.	Distribution of Cases That Recovered Something by Amount Recovered	149
E-1.	Trial Duration of Cases That Went to Verdict	149
E-2.	Trial Duration of Cases That Commenced Trial	149
F.	Frequency of Motions for New Trial	152
G.	Type of Cases in the B and C Groups	156
H.	Type of Pretrial Processing Had No Consequences for Settlement	156
I.	Duration of Trials and Appeals	157
J-1.	Trial Duration of Motor Vehicle Cases Was More Commonly Short in Not-Pretried Cases	158
J-2.	Trial Duration in Non-Motor Vehicle Cases Was More Commonly Short in Not-Pretried Cases	158
K.	Jury Trials Took Longer than Non-Jury	159
L.	Number of Judge Hours Annually Devoted to Pretrial Conferences in Personal Injury Cases	160
M.	Type of Processing Had No Effect on Whether Plaintiff Recovered Anything	162
N.	All-Pretried Cases Recovered Less than In-Part-Pretried	162
O.	Not-Pretried Cases Recovered Less than Pretried	162
P.	Not-Pretried Cases Recovered Less Money than Pretried	163
Q.	Pretried Cases Settled at Different Rates	163
R.	Cases Estimated by Judges to Have Large Potential Recoveries Were More Durable	167

IN APPENDICES

F-1.	Durability of Transferrable Cases	221
F-2.	Transferred Cases Reached Trial More Often than Cases That Were Not Transferred Although Normally Eligible	221
F-3.	Defendants Won More Verdicts in Transferrable Cases than in Transferred Cases	223
F-4.	Transferrable Cases More Frequently Recovered over $3,000	223

FIGURES

1. High Quality Trials Were More Common in the All-Pretried Group   41
2. The All-Pretried Group Did Not Produce More Frequent Settlements   46
3. The All-Pretried Group Did Not Produce More Short Trials   51
4. Estimated Saving of Judge Time from Converting to Optional Program for Pretrial in Personal Injury Cases *(based on certain assumptions)*   57

THE PRETRIAL CONFERENCE
AND EFFECTIVE JUSTICE

A CONTROLLED TEST IN PERSONAL INJURY LITIGATION

INTRODUCTION

FOR several decades the custodians of American justice have shown growing awareness that due administration is as vital as correct adjudication for the integrity of the legal process. Increased attention to administration in the civil field has begotten novel procedures and methods to expedite proceedings, clarify issues, marshal evidence, and neutralize disparate skill in advocacy. Among the new devices, the pretrial conference procedure ranks as one of the most controversial.

Its dynamics are simple: generally speaking, under this procedure, when a case is well on its way to trial, the court calls a conference that the lawyers must attend but that the clients need not and rarely do attend. The judge then holds a formal preview, usually along stylized lines, of the matters trial might unfold. Very often the conference results in a formal order in some degree intended to map the course of subsequent steps in the case, especially including the trial, should one prove necessary. "Pretrial"[1] departs from a steady tradition that the lawyers, not the court, shall supply the impetus to move the litigation forward, assemble the evidence, and sift the issues. Instead, it gives the judges the initiative for managing the suit.

This book is a report of an effort to measure by systematic empirical research the impact of the pretrial conference of New Jersey upon the processing of personal injury cases in its Superior and County courts during 1960–62. Throughout the United States, personal injury cases are the most numerous of civil suits, probably absorbing in all states the bulk of the energies of the trial courts of highest noncriminal jurisdiction. The processing of these cases is of central importance.

This study came about as a result of a campaign by an important segment of the New Jersey bar to modify the rule that a pretrial conference must be held at a certain point in every personal injury case filed in the state's major courts. A specific proposal for change was offered in May, 1959, but at Chief Justice Joseph Weintraub's request its sponsors deferred pressing it pending a full-scale study of the effects of the existing pretrial procedure in personal injury cases. A controlled official experiment was the chief means of conducting the study. The launching of the controlled experiment signaled an awaited break-through in legal research aimed at improving court processes. It brought into being a research effort built, in part, on suggestions advanced by other investigators of the administration of justice in American courts.[2]

Planning of the study was done by the Columbia University Project for Effective Justice[3] in 1959, and the test procedures were installed early in 1960. Two years were required for the test cases to run their courses and be disposed of. Then the data on them were gathered, tabulated, and analyzed. The results are intended to produce insights into how the pretrial conference has performed, and to provide clues as to how its functioning can be improved for the future.

The test itself necessitated a temporary suspension of certain rules, including the rule prescribing a mandatory pretrial conference in virtually all civil cases, in order to set up statistical controls. The program is believed to be a unique application by court authorities of experimental scientific methods to aid in evaluating the work of a major rule of civil procedure.

Data from the controlled test furnish the main source of information for this report; in addition the report draws upon extensive firsthand observations of the actual conduct of scores

INTRODUCTION

of pretrial conferences by many New Jersey judges. It draws also on the legal literature, including court decisions wherever they are relevant. Finally, it analyzes the verbatim transcript of a three-day seminar conducted for New Jersey judges at Princeton, New Jersey, September 5–7, 1962, on the pretrial conference in the light of the Project's then tentative report.

I. THE PRETRIAL CONFERENCE IN PERSPECTIVE

THE stylized pretrial conference is a latecomer to American judicial administration and civil procedure, having arrived on the scene only about twenty-five years ago.[1] Yet it has already been hailed as "the salvation of the administration of justice in the Twentieth Century."[2] Pretrial has been cast in a large role, both in relation to other modern procedures designed to improve the administration of justice and to the basic controversy over the proper functions of judges and courts in the common-law system of litigation.

Pretrial conference procedure has drawn very wide attention because at least on paper (its champions say in practice as well) it comes to grips with two critical present-day problems in the administration of civil justice. One is that of excessive delay in trials, a condition afflicting many important courts of the nation. The other is the stubborn problem of improving in essential ways the fairness of the litigation process in order to avoid decisions that are the product either of intricacies of procedure or ineptitude of counsel. As it grapples with these matters, pretrial finds itself in the eye of a great storm—the debate over whether the adversarial motif in American civil litigation must give ground to some extent to an intensified pursuit of "objective truth" and more perfect case-by-case justice.

Before trying to evaluate what the New Jersey pretrial conference in fact achieves, it is important to note precisely what it has sought to achieve.[3] In New Jersey the avowed purpose of pretrial is to program the case for trial, on the assumption that the time and energy to do this will be well spent whether or not the trial materializes. To see why its sponsors take that view, a bit of perspective on common law litigation is useful.

In a modern procedural system such as that of New Jersey and of other states influenced by the federal model, the pretrial conference is one of four major procedural devices utilized in the before-trial stages, the others being pleadings, motions, and discovery. The theory of the system is that the formal, written *pleadings* are relatively unimportant in staking out the boundaries of the controversy or informing the other side and the court of the matters to be proved at the trial. Hence, the theory goes, they can be quite general and uninformative and readily amended. *Motions* have important functions in a small fraction of the cases, but they are less important than they were in earlier days or in other systems, when they led to many final adjudications on the basis of technical deficiencies in a party's pleadings. By contrast, the *discovery procedure* is critically important in modern systems, for it absorbs the slack left by loose pleading and takes on the major burden in the trial preparatory stages of the case.

Finally, there is the *pretrial conference* itself. New Jersey is the pioneer and archetype among jurisdictions that hold that the pretrial conference should dovetail with discovery.[4]

In substance the New Jersey rules were modeled on Rule 16 of the Federal Rules of Civil Procedure,[5] but they provide for a mandatory instead of a discretionary pretrial conference and are more specific and comprehensive than Rule 16. The text of the rules appears in Appendix A.

Rev. Rule 4:29 of New Jersey's court-adopted rules of civil practice provides for a pretrial conference to be held in the courtroom for the purpose of formulating a pretrial order covering sixteen specified subjects. Counsel must meet beforehand and agree upon as many of the items as possible. At the conference they are to be ready to enter into discussion or consideration of such items as a concise statement of the nature of the action; the parties' positions as to facts affecting liability; damage claims; admissions as to the extent of damages; limitations on the number of expert witnesses; specification of the legal issues; further discovery in exceptional circumstances; filing briefs; estimating the length of trial; and fixing the date on which the case will be called for assignment to trial. Either during or after the conference the pretrial order is to be prepared and signed in open court. To the extent that the order is inconsistent with any pleading, the latter is superseded.[6]

The New Jersey rules contemplate that discovery will be completed and that trial will usually be imminent by the time the conference is held.[7] The conference will thus be the occasion to find out which issues are actually in dispute, and which are not; and which pleas need to be amended, which claims or defenses dropped, and which questions clarified. In this view, the major purpose of the pretrial conference is to map the course of the trial by sharply delineating the legal and factual issues. Such a view is vigorously pressed by Justice William J. Brennan, Jr., architect of the New Jersey rules, who has said:

the overriding, primary, almost exclusive function of the pretrial conference is to further the disposition of the cases according to right and justice on the merits...[8]

Another leader of the pretrial movement, Alfred P. Murrah, Chief Judge of the United States Court of Appeals for the Tenth Circuit, maintains:

Pretrial procedure is a common sense method of sifting the issues and reducing the delays and expense of trials so that a suit will go to trial only on questions as to which there is an honest dispute of fact or law.[9]

A third federal judge who strongly supports the procedure argues that it prepares the trial judge and counsel "for the best possible trial" and assures that "neither surprise nor technicalities win the battle."[10]

The Federal Rules and those of most states also adopt the premise that the pretrial conference is designed mainly to develop and clarify the issues so that they can be resolved in a way that reflects the merits of the case.[11] In their view the pretrial conference is squarely oriented toward improving the trial process.

Some other states, such as New York, are of a different persuasion. They hold that the prime purpose of the conference is to dispose of the case without trial: to get it settled. They stress settlement as the main object of the pretrial as a means of helping their busy courts avoid trials whenever feasible to keep from capsizing in the flood of their business. Of course, these states do not admit to any less concern for deciding cases in accordance with the merits. They take the position that any settlement to which both sides assent will necessarily be based on the merits.

The rejoinder from New Jersey is not that settlements are unwanted there or that they do not result from pretrial, but that "the contribution of the conference to a settlement can never be the reason for the conference. . . ." Settlement, if it comes, is "merely an incidental, although, of course, valuable result of it."[12]

From the time in 1948 when New Jersey introduced the mandatory pretrial procedure, its rules have explicitly relegated settlement to a subsidiary importance by declaring that the "matter of settlement . . . shall not be mentioned in the [pretrial] order."[13] The 1959 *Manual of Pretrial Practice*,[14] in accord with the Brennan view, stresses that settlement is "not the primary end sought" by pretrial, but a "valuable by-product." Nevertheless, the New Jersey rules do authorize and approve settlement discussions. Rev. Rule 4:29-3 (b) requires that counsel "come to the pretrial conference prepared to discuss settlement and have their clients available in person or by telephone for this purpose." Oddly, Rev. Rule 4:29-5[15] by its title and content suggests that there are to be two different confrontations between judge and counsel, one a "Pretrial Conference in Open Court" and the other a "Settlement Conference in Chambers."

Despite these ambiguities, in essence the New Jersey pretrial conference setup, as outlined in the rules and *Manual*, is that 100 days after the complaint is served and as the trial date approaches, counsel are called by the court to a pretrial conference for which they must take preparatory steps; the conference is designed chiefly to map the course of trial, if there is to be one; and settlement, if it results, is a welcome by-product of this process. Appellate court decisions in New Jersey have not disturbed this view of the chief function of the pretrial conference.[16] Inferentially the higher courts have rejected the suggestion of some authorities that the pretrial conference is to be used for "poor man's discovery," a belated chance to get on-the-spot information of the type normally obtained by interrogatories or depositions. The whole idea of conducting discovery at the conference is at odds with the design of the rules to complete all such work before the conference date.

Sometimes it appears that the dispute over trial orientation versus settlement orientation is a quibble involving only a question of emphasis. In our judgment there is more to the quarrel than verbal shadowboxing. As we try to show later, a pretrial conference oriented toward trial requires types of preparation, inquiry, and activity quite different from those required in a settlement-oriented proceeding.[17]

To be sure, some of the items on the conference's agenda serve both ends, but others serve only one and not the other. For example, the pretrial order, so climactic and vital in a trial-oriented conference, has no serious role in a settlement conference.

There is still a third use of the pretrial conference, not widely practiced in this country except in particular types of cases but important nonetheless. In some jurisdictions the pretrial conference follows directly after issue is joined in the case and is used to blueprint and supervise the course of discovery and motion procedures in the preparatory phases of the cases. In the Southern District of New York, "protracted" cases receive this type of treatment.[18]

The controversy over whether pretrial should aim chiefly to delineate issues and shape the case for trial, or to promote settlement, is by no means its only controversial aspect. Pretrial conference procedure has been a battleground of clashing philosophies about the proper role of the judge in common law litigation. The diverse attitudes can be arrayed along a scale marked "active judge" at one end and "passive judge" at the other, with an active judge frequently adopting stances such as these: He is not content with the attorneys' vague replies to questions he poses at the pretrial conference, but will probe and pursue in an attempt to obtain particulars instead of generalities.[19] He will tend to insist on full disclosure of the names of trial witnesses, to limit the number of experts the parties may call, and to take steps to assure that all documents are marked that can be marked in advance of trial. If he detects unpreparedness by counsel, he tends to take up the slack in a rather compelling way. On the other hand, a passive judge will tend not to insist or press in any of these respects.

Because the pretrial conference confronts the judge with so many choices as to the intensity of his participation, and does so in an atmosphere less inhibited than at the trial itself, it is an unmatched ground to test competing views as to the judge's due function in a civil litigation. In New Jersey the appellate courts have spoken plainly on this question, declaring that the pretrial judge must take an active and forceful role at the conference and must "compel" the litigants to reveal their positions and expose the issues.[20] No doubt the pretrial judges take these admonitions seriously but that does not deter some from expressing a contrary philosophy of their role[21] or from being less than forceful in their insistence that litigants reveal positions and clarify the issues.[22] This laissez-faire approach seems clearly at odds with the statement at page 3 of the *Manual of Pretrial Practice* that the function of a pretrial judge "is actively to guide and direct the conference to produce a pretrial order which will strip the case to its essentials as they have been defined herein and will clearly set forth the legal contentions of the parties upon the issues to be decided at the trial."

Next the lawyers enter the fray. Many of them reject pretrial for undercutting the adversary system.[23] They contend that the lawyers for the parties should control the proceedings, including the decision to settle the dispute or take it to trial.[24] They believe the judge's job is to rule on the issues brought before him, not to take charge of the proceedings by means of pretrial. Justice will be served best in this view by permitting the adversary attorneys to be the prime movers of the litigation throughout its course.[25] Otherwise, they say, the inept or slothful lawyers will benefit, with the court's help, at the expense of their skilled and diligent adversaries.[26]

The last great dispute swirling around the pretrial conference is not concerned with theoretical or jurisprudential issues, but with the simple question, Does it work?

II. THE CONTROVERSY OVER THE EFFECTIVENESS OF THE PRETRIAL CONFERENCE

WITH the adoption in 1938 of the Federal Rules of Civil Procedure the pretrial conference procedure received a strong impetus and spread rapidly to over three fourths of the states.[1] By 1959 this momentum was spent. Signs of disaffection appeared in California and led in 1963 to a retrenchment in the pretrial system.[2] Similar signs appeared in New Jersey, which had not only embraced the procedure but had made it mandatory as far back as 1948, and which since then had been regarded as a model of vigorous and effective pretrial. There and elsewhere some of the rising opposition was pitched to the theme already noted—that in the common law system it is not a due judicial function to take so active a hand in managing the cases, and to do so usurps the lawyers' prerogative.[3] But the main opposition was based on the view that even if pretrial is sound in theory it fails on pragmatic grounds because as conducted by many judges it is a useless ritual, a waste of time for the lawyers as well as the judges.[4] Reaching as it does to the heart of the matter, that contention calls for a closer look and a listing of specific pros and cons.

Those who favor the conference procedure claim it makes justice swifter and better.

In saying pretrial makes the litigation process more efficient, they mean that fewer judges are needed to keep abreast of the court work than would otherwise be necessary.[5] In saying it makes justice work better they mean it contributes to more just results, either by increasing the litigants' mutual knowledge[6] (thus allowing them to compromise their dispute closer to its true merits), or by improving the trial process (which also in turn furthers the prospects of a better decision).[7] These contentions can be put in more specific terms: Pretrial enhances court efficiency because both the prospect and the actual process of the conference promote settlements, so eliminating trials that comprise the major drain on the judges' time.[8] In turn the judge is freed to attend to other cases, so that the same number of judges can dispose of a larger volume of cases and reduce the backlog. The step-up in settlements is not, it is insisted, the product of judicial coercion but only the natural consequence of more detailed mutual knowledge of each side's strengths and weaknesses, for then they are in a better position to weigh the risks of trial and arrive at a realistic compromise.[9]

The conference is also claimed to reduce the time required by the cases that do reach trial, in part by inducing more jury waivers,[10] thereby cutting the frequency of longer-running jury trials, and in part by simply condensing the trial.[11] This occurs, it is contended, when the issues in dispute are clarified and facts are stipulated, so that irrelevant or repetitious or cumulative evidence is avoided.[12]

Pretrial's champions make the further claims that in many cases it accelerates the date of settlement by leading to a compromise at or shortly after the conference,[13] and that this avoids potential work for the courts; also that by deemphasizing pleading niceties, time otherwise wasted on motions designed to polish these papers is saved.[14]

They say that the procedure has the collateral advantage of permitting the backlogged courts of major jurisdiction to shunt some of their business to the less delayed inferior jurisdiction courts by providing for screening and transferring "undersized" cases at the start of the conference.[15]

In its other aspect pretrial claims many champions as a procedure that promotes "justice." The late Federal Judge McIlvaine put it in these terms:

> Frankly, if pretrial procedures as we practice them had no effect on congestion, and I have some doubts as to its effect on our own docket in personal injury cases for reasons I will mention later, I would still be among its strongest supporters for I feel that it aids in achieving justice.[16]

As conducing to "better justice," the pretrial's partisans urge that the conference improves the conduct of litigation all along the line by assuring better prepared judges and counsel,[17] by eliminating maneuver and surprise tactics at trial and by simplifying and clarifying the proof.[18] The mere imminence of the conference is said to speed discovery efforts, leading to earlier preparation of the case.[19] Finally, some of its friends say that pretrial tends to avoid unjust settlement by furnishing a judicial forum in which the parties may negotiate on a plane of equality, free of false tactical worries such as that it shows "weakness" to be first to mention the possibility of settlement.[20]

The opposition camp denies that benefits result from pretrial on any of these scores—court efficiency, fairer process, or more just dispositions.[21] They argue that issues are clarified at the conference only if the judge takes an active role by coaxing or insisting; but if he does either, he undermines the adversary process. The conference either duplicates the work of the pleadings, motions, and discovery procedures[22] or else lets the judge intrude improperly in the process. According to this camp, lawyers are in a poor position to resist a judge's request for stipulations, admissions, and disclosures at a conference, because they fear incurring his displeasure for this case and future ones. On the other hand, if the judge at pretrial hears admissions, sees the lawyers' private files, takes positions and commits or involves himself, it will often be unfair for him to sit in judgment in the case at the trial.[23] In a county with only one or two judges this may confound the course of justice.

Furthermore, critics say, pretrial conference lets a poorly prepared lawyer borrow the benefit of his adversary's work. This may dampen his own efforts at proper preparation.[24]

Personal injury cases have been singled out as particularly unsuited for universal pretrial, the chief argument being that the issues in them are generally simple and need no elaborate restatement at a formal conference.[25]

Clearly, these arguments touch vital questions. Despite this and despite the fervor of the debate, neither camp has produced more than fragmentary evidence to back its claims.[26] It was the aim of the present study to gather and interpret basic data that will shed light on the disputed issues. It was not the aim of the study to try to answer the question of whether inroads on the traditional adversary system are desirable or undesirable in general. Whether it is sound to water down the old advocacy, the "close-to-the-vest" approach in civil litigation, to curb tactical secrecy, is essentially a question of policy, which the research done in New Jersey can slightly illuminate but cannot come close to answering.

The authorities in New Jersey became convinced that the contrasting estimates of the effectiveness of their pretrial system required facts that could be obtained only by a deliberate, large-scale research program, and not by unaided armchair analysis no matter how open-minded. They therefore requested the Columbia Project's aid in a systematic study of how the system was functioning and gave unprecedented cooperation to assure that the research could be conducted without some of the handicaps that had consistently blunted efforts to do research on law in action.

III. THE METHODS AND MATERIALS OF THE STUDY

PAST efforts at fact inquiries to gauge the impact of the pretrial conference have yielded equivocal data because of problems of method. The usual approach has been to gather statistics and opinions on what happened after the pretrial procedure was introduced in the court under study. But even those who have conducted such inquiries have recognized the fatal weakness of this method, namely that it does not disclose whether pretrial, the factor being examined, is responsible for the results observed, or to what extent. Since many factors and variables, often changing from year to year, impinge upon the operation of court processes, research efforts in which these factors continue to assert unknown influences on the process cannot serve as predicates for decision. The data produced are more likely to be interesting than reliable. This difficulty is not limited to the problem of evaluating pretrial. Any effort to test the impact of law in action encounters similar problems.[1]

Thus, the "before-and-after" approach and "side-by-side" comparisons, although useful as research techniques, have distinct limitations, and by far the most satisfactory method of researching law in action is to introduce a scientific "control" at the beginning of the program.[2] With the active aid of the Supreme Court of New Jersey, an officially controlled experiment was possible in this research. The Project designed a test program that would determine what the pretrial conference does or does not do in personal injury cases by controlling its application. Personal injury cases were selected as the subjects because their volume and nature made them the largest question mark in the pretrial picture. The test was limited to injury cases alone in order to keep out unknown factors that might confuse the findings or make the results ambiguous. The proposal was that the Supreme Court of New Jersey issue a special order applicable to personal injury cases in the Superior and County courts, relaxing the across-the-board feature of the mandatory rule so that during the period of the test there would be a compulsory pretrial only in each alternate case and none in the other cases.[3] The purpose of setting up the test in that way was to produce two groups of cases that would be alike in all relevant ways except for the single factor of exposure to pretrial. The concept was that as the exposed group and the unexposed group of cases made their way through the court process any observed difference in performance and results in the two groups would reflect the impact of the pretrial conference. In research parlance the not-pretried group would serve as a "control" for the pretried group. From the research standpoint this plan would have been the ideal one to measure in the simplest and clearest way the impact of the pretrial conference on cases subjected to it.

However, the Supreme Court of New Jersey thought it necessary and wise to relax the experimental design to a certain extent. The rule actually promulgated in late 1959, effective in January, 1960, departed from the ideal design sketched above by providing as to the group of cases not scheduled for pretrial that if either attorney or both attorneys expressed a desire for a pretrial conference one would be held in that case.[4] The lawyer-chosen cases would then be entered on the pretrial conference docket and would proceed to a conference exactly as if they had been set down on the mandatory pretrial list from the beginning. In other words they would be integrated into the same schedule, processed by the same judges, and handled in exactly the same manner as the mandatorily pretried cases. This modification in the test design had certain consequences for the analysis and interpretation of the findings, and we discuss them later in this report.[5]

The test was conducted in seven New Jersey counties, which based on available statistics, were thought to handle a good cross section of the civil litigation of the entire state. The counties were Essex, Hudson, Morris, Passaic, Sussex, Union, and Warren, some of which are urban while others are rural, some with backlogs and growing trial delay, others with light, up-to-date calendars.[6] Together they processed in the test period about 50 per cent of all the civil law cases disposed of in the New Jersey Superior and County courts.[7] In order to assure useful results from a technical viewpoint, on the advice of the Columbia University Bureau of Applied Social Research, it was decided to draw a systematic sample of 3,000 cases.[8] To obtain the sample, the procedure now described was followed.

Starting on January 4, 1960, as all personal injury cases on the calendar of the Superior and County courts in the seven test counties reached the point at which they would normally be scheduled for a pretrial conference, they were randomly segregated into two groups.[9] Cases 1, 3, 5, 7, etc., were sent regular notice of pretrial and the usual procedure of holding a conference was followed. Cases 2, 4, 6, 8, etc., were, on the other hand, not scheduled for the conference as a matter of course. Instead, a special form was sent to the attorneys in those cases announcing that the mandatory pretrial conference requirement had been lifted, but that a pretrial conference could be requested if desired. It included the statement:

> To assist the Supreme Court in this experiment it is earnestly requested that you determine, as objectively as possible, whether this is a case in which you would ordinarily request a pretrial conference

METHODS AND MATERIALS OF THE STUDY

if our regular rule made such conferences optional. The value and reliability of this study depend upon your sincere cooperation.

(A specimen form designated "Pretrial Test Form B" is included in Appendix C, which contains the test forms.) As a result of the test, three separate groups of cases emerged:

The (hypothetically) odd-numbered "A" cases which were all set down for a compulsory pretrial conference, here called "mandatory" or "all-pretried" or by cognate expressions,

The (hypothetically) even-numbered "B" cases which were not scheduled for and did not have a pretrial conference, here called "not-pretried" cases; and

The (hypothetically) even-numbered cases which were not scheduled for a pretrial conference but were given one at the request of one or both counsel for the litigants (so becoming "C" cases) and here called "optional" cases. The not-pretried B cases and the optionally pretried C cases form the "B+C" group and are collectively called "nonmandatory" or "lawyers'-choice" or "in-part-pretried" cases.

This alternating plan continued for more than six months, in effect placing the odd-numbered cases in the mandatory group and the even-numbered cases in the nonmandatory group. By September, 1960, when slightly more than 3,000 cases had been exposed to the alternating procedure, this phase of the test ended and the courts returned to the system of mandatory pretrial in every case.

The information concerning the cases was derived from several sources: to the extent possible, from regularly kept court records; from the court clerks' entries on special record sheets provided by the Project; and from judges and lawyers who filled in extensive forms specially designed to keep track of what happened in the test cases until they were terminated.[10] The information obtained from these sources was transferred to punch cards and tabulated on IBM machines. Sociologists and statisticians assisted in the collection and processing of the data.

THE TEST CASES

The next few pages provide essential background for reporting the study's results. They frame the context of the controlled experiment and describe the "population" that was tested. The data are assembled at this point for convenient reference, should the reader wish to return to them from time to time in this report.

Each year in the New Jersey Superior and County courts about 19,000 personal injury cases are "added to the calendar," according to our best estimates.[11] They comprise about three fourths of the civil law business of these trial courts. The ratio shrinks to 12 and 14 per cent for the civil appeals in the Appellate Division and the Supreme Court respectively.[12]

In all, 3,142 cases were included in the test. After weeding out 188 intruders that did not belong in the test case population, or that were defective for other reasons, there remained a basic sample of 2,954 cases.[13] We have, for simplicity, rounded that figure to 3,000, except when rounding would compromise accuracy in special contexts.

If the optional procedure had not been introduced, the test groups would have comprised two subgroups of about 1,500 cases each, but as it actually turned out, nearly one half the nonmandatory B cases opted for a conference. The result was that the A group contained 1,495 cases, nearly 51 per cent of the test cases, the B group nearly 26 per cent (758 cases), and the C group nearly 24 per cent (701 cases). When only one party opted for a pretrial conference (as usually happened), it was much more frequently the defendant. Plaintiffs opted alone in 32 per cent of these cases, defendants in 68 per cent.[14]

METHODS AND MATERIALS OF THE STUDY

Two thirds of the cases in the sample arose from motor vehicle accidents. Most of the rest are what may be called "public liability" or "premises" accident cases, with 10 per cent of the total "miscellaneous" in origin.[15] Three fourths of the cases involved more than two parties and are classified as "multiparty" cases in this report; and just over half—57 per cent—of the cases are for a like reason termed "multiclaim" cases.

The most common type of case was one arising out of a motor vehicle accident that involved more than two parties and produced more than one claim. These accounted for 38 per cent of the test cases. Next in order of frequency, with 18 per cent of the cases, were multiparty, multiclaim actions that arose from non-motor vehicle circumstances.[16]

The median length of time absorbed by the conferences was about thirty minutes,[17] but two conferences lasted less than fifteen minutes and two others over two hours.

Nearly all the cases that went to trial started out by demanding a jury[18] (94 per cent) and most ended up being tried by a jury (about 85 per cent).[19] The group of cases in which pretrial was optional was more prone to waive a jury than the one in which all cases experienced a mandatory pretrial conference.[20]

In all, 52 judges processed the test cases, 43 of them as both pretrial and trial judges, 6 as solely pretrial judges and 3 as solely trial judges.[21] One of the judges conducted 172 pretrial conferences; five conducted only 1 conference. Some judges conducted as many as 37 trials, whereas others conducted as few as 1 trial. The pretrial judge also presided over the trial in 18 per cent of the tried cases.

Attorneys who participated in the trials of the test cases were predominantly members of firms rather than individual practitioners. Defendants' counsel were more likely to be firm members than plaintiffs' counsel, and defendants' firms were more frequently large.[22]

Among plaintiffs' attorneys, the same attorney was more likely to be present at both trial and pretrial than was true of defense attorneys.[23]

Plaintiffs recovered some money in 92 per cent of the suits. As in New York and every other state where these facts have been researched, if the case proceeded to a trial, defendants avoided recoveries quite often—winning 39 per cent of the trial decisions.[24] However, it makes a difference whether the case is tried to a jury or the bench alone, for plaintiffs won only 56 per cent of the jury verdicts against 76 per cent of the bench awards.[25]

Recoveries by plaintiffs ranged from minuscule sums to $194,000. Most of the recoveries were small-to-modest, half of them less than $1,913 and 68 per cent less than $3,000.[26] Following the New York pattern, the median recovery in adjudicated cases was much higher than in settled cases—$3,350 against $1,790.[27]

A considerable number of cases reached trial—in all, 637—of which about two thirds (431) went to verdict or award. This means that of the whole group, 77 per cent settled before entering the trial courtroom and the remaining 23 per cent reached trial and 16 per cent completed trial. Only about 2 per cent of the pretried cases settled at the conference itself.[28] Full trials were typically under two days: about one third ran longer, whereas about one fifth (21 per cent) ended in one day of hearing.[29] In only 2 per cent of the tried cases was a new trial ordered; and mistrials occurred in but 1 case in 100. About 2 per cent of the tried cases were reversed or modified on appeal.

IV. WHAT PRETRIAL APPARENTLY DOES AND DOES NOT DO

AS WAS observed at the beginning of this report, it was traditional in the common law system of conducting civil litigation to give the parties and their attorneys free choice as to the use of pretrial procedures. The court was deemed not to have the authority, and certainly not the responsibility, to decide whether a claim or defense should be pleaded, or what tactical maneuvers the lawyers should employ as the lawsuit proceeded to trial. Indeed, so completely did the initiative rest with the litigants that the judge was thought of as a "referee"—a passive arbiter charged with seeing to it that the gladiators fought by the rules. If anything he had less initiative than his prize-fight counterpart, for he was not even supposed to shout, "Come on, boys, let's fight!"

Until the pretrial conference was invented in the second quarter of this century, the referee image of the judge persisted. The parties and their lawyers decided whether there would be a suit or not, and by their pleadings determined what issues would be raised between them. After the claims and defenses were stated, it was again up to the attorneys, not the court, to determine whether they would make motions to bring preliminary questions of law before the court for decision. In the case of pretrial discovery, which became broadly available to uncover evidence or leads to evidence, the lawyers once again had all the initiative. It can be assumed that they did and still do exercise their initiative and make their choices with regard to whether and how they conduct discovery, present motions, or solve pleading problems, by balancing potential gains and losses. In other words, for the advocates, procedural choices raise tactical problems and they solve them in tactical terms.

In New Jersey, too, the traditional pattern of lawyer autonomy prevails regarding discovery, motions, and pleadings. But in the pretrial conference procedure the arresting fact is that the lawyers have nothing to say about its use. Since 1948 the court alone initiates, insists upon, schedules, and manages the proceedings.

This discard of the advocates' usual prerogative probably underlies some of the opposition to pretrial. To the skeptical eye of a critic, the procedure emerges as an extra step that, whatever else it does, burdens even "routine" cases with unnecessary work and attention, uses up the limited energies of hard-pressed judges, and adds insult to injury by stripping the lawyer of his traditional advocate's right of choice. Especially for many of the lawyers who represent plaintiffs on contingent fees, which typically make no provision for added pay if there is added work, the pretrial is a burden they could cheerfully do without. Right or wrong, many lawyers and some judges think they perceive in pretrial certain negative features that impose on the whole concept a heavy burden of justification.

Without conceding all that, we can nonetheless admit that pretrial is not an end in itself and does not pretend to be; and that to be warranted and repay its costs, it must achieve an improved administration of justice sufficient to outweigh the time and trouble it involves. In the context of this study, those considerations pose the question of whether in the run of personal injury cases that pour into the New Jersey courts, pretrial yields more than it costs. The yield must be measured on two scales: improving the litigation process, and enhancing the efficiency with which the courts dispatch their workload.

It becomes necessary to devise special measures or tests to get at these matters. Of the two, the efficiency problem is relatively easy, because as we explain below, it involves straightforward supply-demand considerations.

But in what ways may the quality of the litigation process be improved? First and foremost, we believe, by improving the quality of the conduct of trials in any of the respects in which such an elusive quantum can be gauged. This problem will receive more attention later, but here it suffices to suggest that the elements to be considered are those whose presence or absence in various degrees might alter our confidence that a fair tribunal could reach a correct decision. Among them are the questions whether the lawyers advanced the decisive legal theories in a clear, complete, understandable way; and whether available evidence was brought forward in the same way, without confusion to the trier of the facts.

Second, litigation quality can be improved in an important sense by improving the process by which settlements are reached. Since most cases end in settlement rather than trial, any improvement here will have widespread effects. Many supporters of pretrial argue that one of its greatest virtues is that it tends to uncover each side's strong and weak points so that neither remains in the dark as to essentials of the case. In consequence, each side is supposed to be able to make informed evaluations of the risks of trial, and this in turn means that each time a case is settled short of a trial courtroom, the settlement will represent a more informed, hence a fairer, compromise. Judge Alfred P. Murrah has forcefully stated the argument that enlarged mutual knowledge of the case improves the litigation process:

we think it is in the interest of the administration of justice that each side of a lawsuit should have an opportunity to learn the adversary's contentions and prospective proof—his witnesses, lay and expert, and the law upon which he relies. It is only after learning of his adversary's case that a lawyer can fairly evaluate his own case in terms of money and properly advise his client as to settlement or other disposition. Pretrial procedure is designed to bring about a fair and expeditious resolution of every lawsuit. A fair resolution means an open resolution; it means dealing with open hands without surprise or deceit.[1]

On the face of it, there can be no quarrel with Judge Murrah's point that a lawsuit is settled more fairly if both sides are more fully aware of the issues and evidence. Our law has long since left behind the theory that justice should be awarded like chips in a poker game—according to luck, skill, and bluff. As the United States Supreme Court has said, "Mutual knowledge of all the relevant facts gathered by both parties is essential to proper litigation."[2]

This study did not make any direct measurement of the state of "mutual knowledge" in settled cases that had been pretried, compared with its state in settled cases that had not been pretried. The evidence available on the question is indirect, a product of analyzing the state of mutual knowledge *at trial* in one group of test cases compared with another group. Because the rules are written to discourage exchange of information between the pretrial and the trial and because there is no evidence that much disclosure in fact occurs in that interval, the state of the litigants' knowledge at the time of trial must reliably reflect the situation for most of the test cases that settled. To assume otherwise would not square with the logic of the situation, for a lawyer, when he bargains out a settlement after pretrial, is trying to forecast the probable trial result, adjusted for various uncertainties; and to make the forecast, he must consider all the evidence that he believes the trial will unfold.

At this point a few observations are necessary concerning the data and how they are to be used. The data upon which the study draws comprise the largest, most detailed aggregate of facts and figures ever assembled with respect to the functioning of pretrial. More important, the bulk of the information was obtained under controlled experimental conditions and therefore has unique weight as empirical evidence. Subject to the normal possibilities of error in investigations of this kind, the findings establish as definitely as one can realistically hope the results that pretrial conferences do or do not achieve under the conditions tested.

The test conditions set limits on what findings can be reported with the highest order of reliability according to accepted social research principles. In deference to those principles the report deliberately presents the strictly controlled test data apart from data of less rigorously scientific character. However, to avoid burying the meaning of the findings in a morass of methodological subtleties, we shall offer interpretations that go beyond the tight limits of the test design, making clear at each occasion that we are doing so.

Thus, under the strict limits of the test conditions, the findings speak authoritatively to this question: What difference did it make in New Jersey to administer a compulsory pretrial conference to each personal injury case on the docket[3] rather than only to those which one or both attorneys in the case chose for a pretrial? This requires analyzing how the A group cases (all pretried mandatorily) fared in comparison to the B+C group cases (about one half pretried at lawyers' choice). The comparison will be made according to the relevant measures and yardsticks devised for purposes of the investigation. The findings that emerge will express the differences, then, between a universal or all-cases-pretried regime and a nonuniversal, lawyers'-choice regime. They will not relate directly to the question: What differences does the pretrial conference bring about in the processing of personal injury cases in New Jersey? Nevertheless, being convinced, for reasons we shall give later, that the differences which emerge do actually reflect the influence of the presence or absence of pretrial, we shall not confine the report to stating merely the differences in results for the A group as against the B+C group, but will state what we believe to be the effect of the pretrial conference itself—that is, the difference between pretrial and no-pretrial.[4] We acknowledge that such statements may not command the same level of reliability as the controlled test data.

THE TEST FINDINGS IN ESSENCE

Three major findings emerged from the controlled experiment. They can be expressed as a gain, a loss, and a difference, all attributable to the impact of across-the-board pretrial compared with lawyers'-choice pretrial.

1. The *gain* was in improving the quality of the trial process in some pretried cases that reached the trial stage. The evidence of this is not of conclusive quality, but it is strong enough to credit. We believe it points to a distinct likelihood that in an appreciable fraction of the pretried cases the quality of the trial process was improved in the following respects: lawyer preparedness was promoted; a clear presentation of the opposed theories of the case was more common; improper gaps and repetition in the evidence were eliminated; and tactical surprise was curbed.

2. The *loss* was in absorbing appreciable quantities of judge time by the across-the-board pretrials with no compensating saving in the trial time demands the cases make. At the very least, it seems clear that the efficiency of the court was reduced rather than enhanced by requiring as a compulsory matter that each case go through a pretrial conference instead of leaving it to the lawyers to choose the cases to be pretried. On the basis of this study, there should be no hesitation in concluding that if New Jersey were to shift from a universal mandatory pretrial rule in personal injury cases to a lawyers'-

choice plan, there would not be any fall-off in the percentage of settled cases or any increase in the length of trials. Rather, there would be a saving of about one half the time the judges now devote to pretrial conferences—assuming the lawyers continued to choose a pretrial in about one half the cases, as they did during the test period.

3. The *difference* in outcome that appears on comparing the two groups of cases was a completely unexpected result. In both the A group and the B+C group, plaintiffs recovered *some* money in 92 per cent of the cases, so their frequency of recovery was not affected. But in the A group cases the average amount recovered was noticeably higher than in the B+C cases. The inference is that pretrials tend to produce a higher recovery in cases that are subjected to them. This has a flavor of irony, for as we have previously noted, it is not plaintiffs but defendants who showed the greater tendency to choose the pretrial conference.[5]

1. IMPACT ON "FAIRNESS" OR "QUALITY" OF THE LITIGATION PROCESS

New Jersey conducts pretrial conferences in civil cases primarily in order to improve the quality of the litigation process, as we have already seen.[6] This object is made quite specific for personal injury cases: as to them the 1959 *Manual of Pretrial Practice* indicates without ambiguity that the main aim of pretrial is better trials.[7] To determine whether pretrial conferences did or did not improve the trial process in the test cases requires at the start that one select the best yardsticks there are to tell whether a trial has been well conducted or not.[8]

A ready-made yardstick built into the system is the extent to which each group of cases produces erroneous trial judgments. To learn this it is necessary to inquire, How well did each trial determination stand up under formal attack by appeal or motion for a new trial? By the rules of the system, the first clue that all was not well in the trial court comes when one of the parties impugns the decision by asking for a new trial or appealing. Either form of attack provides an objective measure of at least one side's view that the trial process was defective. To be sure, the mere launching of an attack on a trial decision is equivocal, for the losing party may have exercised bad judgment in attacking or may have had collateral objectives in view, such as delay or attrition. On the other hand, *successful* motions for new trials and *successful* appeals are unequivocal evidence that the trial process was defective—that is, that an error was made that substantially influenced the decision. Although such "harmful" errors can be made in well-presented or well-prepared cases, it seems obvious that errors will be more frequent at poor trials. For that reason, the vulnerability of judgments because they were based on harmful errors, as reflected by the new-trial and appellate reversal rates, gives some indication of the quality of the trial. In a moment we shall examine the results of using that measure.

We also have attempted to use more sensitive measures of the "quality" of the trial, such as whether the attorneys were well prepared, whether the issues were advanced with clarity, whether the evidence was well presented, and whether "surprise" and maneuvering were avoided at the trial. Such facts as these do not register themselves and they are not entered in the course of any regular record-keeping process. To obtain them it was necessary to question judges and lawyers in a systematic way. The forms included in Appendix C were the means of doing this. The findings set out here begin with the gross statistics on appeals and retrials and then go on to consider the more refined questionnaire data.

The appeal and reversal rates permit no firm conclusions, for there were only twenty-seven appeals to analyze. It would not be prudent to lean heavily upon them because of the high risk that differences that appear might be the result merely of the luck of the lottery.[9] Also on account of the small number of appealed cases, intensive analysis of subclasses of them would not be rewarding. All that need be reported is that of the 27 appeals, 15 were from judgments in A group cases and 12 in B+C group cases; and whereas only 20 per cent of the A case judgments resulted in reversal or modification on appeal, 50 per cent of the B+C cases were upset.[10]

These skimpy data suggest that further investigation might show that the mandatorily pretried cases were more prone to appeal than the lawyers'-choice cases, but if appealed that they were less prone to reversal. With a sufficient number of cases, it could then be determined whether any differences in appeal and reversal rates were related to differences in the quality of the trial process.

Applications for retrial were more common than appeals, with nearly one in five of the cases that completed trial producing a motion for a new trial,[11] and with these motions proportionately distributed in the test groups. That the motions were made as frequently in one group as another does not end this line of inquiry, for it is the proportion that were *granted* that is significant. The reason is that the making of the motion for a new trial may be inspired by grounds other than real complaints about the quality of the trial process —for example, by error of the judge in instructing the jury, or merely by tactical delay. When the crucial factor of *success* of the motions was scored, the A group emerged with a rate of only 9 per cent granted against 19 per cent granted in the B+C group.[12]

A normal next step would have been a more refined analysis to take account of factors other than the presence or absence of pretrial, but there were too few cases for significant cross tabulations of that kind. Even the sizable difference in the percentage of successful B+C motions turns out to be more suggestive than probative because of the small numbers of cases involved.

The experimental data drawn from the 3,000 test cases produced the main body of evidence regarding the impact of pretrial upon the conduct of trials and inferentially on the litigation process. In the two test groups a total of 431 cases went through trial to judgment, 54 per cent from the A group and 46 per cent from the B+C group. An integral part of the experiment was to design measures to gauge the impact of pretrial as a factor influencing the "quality" of trials. If trials in the two test groups scored differently in the quality criteria so devised, the prima-facie explanation would be their disparate exposure to pretrial conferences. More refined analysis might then pinpoint the differences and identify more precisely the factors associated with particular findings.

In the questionnaires to judges and trial lawyers were twelve items that we believed were valid yardsticks for measuring the quality of the trial process in the test cases. The items related to four more or less separate aspects of the trial process: (1) how well the case was presented under general standards of legal disputation;[13] (2) incidence of gaps or excesses in the evidence;[14] (3) avoidance of testimony by unnecessary witnesses;[15] and (4) absence of maneuvering or "surprise."[16] We have assumed a priori that those are valid measures of trial quality.

As to the first, the essential controversies in a case must be well presented at trial if they are to be resolved fairly. Good presentation in turn requires that the attorneys have prepared carefully beforehand, that the claims and defenses be elaborated clearly, and that the central issues be crystallized sharply. In other words, the first yardstick assumes that cogent organization of ideas and arguments is a true test of a good trial and that organization depends on the lawyers being well prepared. Another factor is the skill with which the evidence is marshaled: Was all necessary proof brought forward and was extraneous or repetitious evidence, which could only confuse or bore the jury and court, kept out? A third and related factor is whether clarity was impaired by the testimony of unneeded witnesses. Finally, it was postulated that a good trial should avoid tactical surprise, an element universally conceded to be inimical to fair trial.

The instruments by which trial quality was registered asked the trial judges and lawyers both "yes-no" and unstructured open-end questions. For instance, in Form H the trial judge was asked to check *yes* or *no* to such question as: "Was evidence offered on extraneous or undisputed points?"; "Were the parties' theories of the case clearly brought out before the jury?"; and "Were any 'surprise' issues litigated?"[17] In addition, he was asked to specify his "major observations" regarding the usefulness of the pretrial conference in the trial just concluded, and blank spaces were left for his answer. Such unstructured questions seldom drew replies from either the judges or trial counsel, and when they did the substance of the replies only rarely went beyond the information elicited by the specific yes-no answers and yielded nothing worth recording in this report.

Analysis of the yes–no answers disclosed that in each of the major measures of trial quality, the all-pretried A group of cases had a higher proportion of good quality trials than the lawyers'-choice group. The first measure relates to how well the case was prepared and how clearly the theories and issues emerged.

Table 1. *Good Trial Presentation More Frequent in All-Pretried than in In-Part-Pretried Group**

	A	B+C
1. Both sides were well prepared	85%	84%
Number of judges' reports	129	98
2. Theories clearly brought out	94%	90%
Number of judges' reports	124	91
3. Issues emerged clearly	91%	88%
Concurring attorney's reports	107	84

*Significance levels: item 1, .95–.98; item 2, approximately .50; item 3, .70–.80.

Table 1 shows that the A group trials consistently surpassed the B+C cases in each criterion of good presentation. In our opinion the table offers important evidence that the across-the-board plan of pretrial in New Jersey produced more well-presented cases than the lawyers'-option plan under which only half the cases were pretried.[18] True, the margin of advantage for the A cases is not wide enough to rule out with conventionally desired confidence the risk of chance in the figures, but that, in courtroom parlance, "goes to their weight."[19] They are buttressed by other evidence of reassuringly similar effect.

Table 1 shows that more tried cases will be well presented in an all-pretrial system compared to an in-part-pretrial system, but does not say how *many* more will be well presented. The number will not be large because, so to speak, there is only limited room for improvement. This may be illustrated by reference to the figures on quality of trial presentation in the not-pretried B cases: it turns out that by the three criteria used in Table 1 more than 85 per cent of the B cases produced good quality trial presentations. The pertinent figures appear in Table 2, and although they are drawn from data outside the strict limits of the experimental design, provide evidence that is quite consistent with the test findings set out in Table 1.[20]

Table 2. *Good Trial Presentation Less Frequent in Not-Pretried Cases**

		A	B
1.	Both sides were well prepared	85%	85%
	Number of judges' reports	129	55
2.	Theories clearly brought out	94%	92%
	Number of judges' reports	124	50
3.	Issues emerged clearly	91%	88%
	Concurring attorneys' reports	107	50

*Significance levels: item 1, over .98; item 2, approximately .95; item 3, .80–.90.

The C group, on items 1, 2, and 3, scored 81%, 88% and 88% on responses in 43, 41, and 34 cases, respectively. For an explanation of the separate treatment afforded the C cases, see page 36 *infra*.

The first point to notice about the foregoing table is that "good" scores on all criteria were registered by at least 85 per cent of the tried cases regardless of whether or not they had been through a pretrial conference. With over 85 per cent of the not-pretried cases registering good trial presentation, the A cases could not be expected to surpass them by dramatic margins. Small differences may nonetheless be important, as an example from medical research makes clear. If only 2 per cent of the population suffers from disease X and a drug is found that is thought to reduce the incidence of the disease, we would not disparage its effect because a table of findings showed that the percentage of those free of disease had climbed "only" from 98 to 99 per cent. So in this test, only limited percentage differences can be expected.

The next point is the overall similarity in the patterns shown by the two tables. In Table 2, as in Table 1, the A cases had superior marks in respect to the frequency with which theories and issues emerged clearly at the trial (as scored, respectively, by the trial judges and both attorneys). As for the remaining item, the frequency with which both sides were well prepared, the A and B cases tied at 85 per cent. In short, Table 2 parallels Table 1 in evidencing that well-presented trials occurred with highest frequency in A cases.

The next line of analysis was to compare the group of tried cases in which the lawyers had opted for a pretrial conference—the C cases—with the other two groups. The results of the comparison with regard to the "good presentation" factor were similar to the results in each of the other tests of trial quality; that is, the C cases failed to perform consistently higher or consistently lower by the measurements we utilized. The results were scattered, with the C cases outscoring the A or B cases by narrow margins in some respects, and in other criteria, being outscored.

Neither cogitation nor detailed cross tabulation has provided any satisfactory explanation for the in-and-out performance of the optionally pretried cases with respect to trial quality.[21] The major findings on the trial quality of C cases are set out in footnotes at appropriate points. Had there been data on a larger number of C trials than the forty or fifty-odd available, detailed analysis might have clarified their vagrant performance. In all events, because of the clear direction of the data that the experiment produced on trial quality, we are confident that further information on the performance of the C cases would not disturb the inference that pretrial conferences tend to improve trial quality.

Moving to the second set of trial quality criteria, we find further evidence that the all-pretried A cases produced good trials more frequently than the B+C group. Table 3 shows that in a comparison of the incidence of offering unneeded evidence (because cumulative or extraneous) or omitting needed proof, A cases did better than the B+C cases.

Table 3. *Good Quality Evidence More Frequent in All-Pretried than in In-Part-Pretried Cases (Judges' Reports)**

	A	B+C
1. Evidence not offered on extraneous or undisputed issues	82%	77%
Number of cases	130	98
2. Cumulative evidence not offered	82%	79%
Number of cases	127	96
3. Evidence on essential issues not omitted	83%	73%
Number of cases	128	95

*Significance levels: item 1, .40; item 2, .70–.80; item 3, .10.

Again, in Table 3, the differences found were not large enough to be "significant" in the statistical idiom. However, they suggested that pretrial was indeed making a positive impact on the quality of trial evidence and that this impact might be detected by proper statistical methods. We tried to do so.

The first step was to identify and segregate in each of the two main groups in the test, the cases that scored well on *all three indicators* of good quality trial evidence.[22] This step produced a table comprised entirely of tried cases that had (1) developed all essential proof and (2) admitted no proof that was extraneous or (3) merely cumulative. In that compilation, constituting what might be called a "quality of evidence index," the A group produced a markedly higher percentage of good quality trials than the B+C group of cases.

Table 4. *Index of the Quality of Evidence at Trial**

	A	B+C
All three evidence factors reported favorably	62%	48%
	77	45

*Significance level: .05–.10.

Within the strict confines of the test design, Table 4 reports that the all-pretried A group produced a higher percentage of trials marked by good quality evidence. That is further indication that the pretrial conference tends to improve trial quality. Certainly such a finding is consistent with what might be expected in well-run pretrial conferences. When issues are stated, when the extraneous matters are weeded out, and when stipulations are entered into at pretrial, the evidence at a subsequent trial should contain fewer gaps and redundancies than if none of these events had occured.

Once again, when the all-pretried A group is compared with the not-pretried B group, the former scores better on the quality of evidence measure.

Table 5. *Good Quality Evidence Less Frequent in Not-Pretried Cases**

	A	B
1. Evidence not offered on extraneous or undisputed issues	82%	73%
Number of cases	130	55
2. Cumulative evidence not offered	82%	80%
Number of cases	127	54
3. Evidence on essential issues not omitted	83%	77%
Number of cases	128	53

*Significance level: item 1, approximately .20; item 2, .80–.90; item 3, .50–.60.
The C group, on items 1, 2, and 3, scored 81%, 79%, and 66% on responses in 43, 42, and 42 cases respectively.

Table 5 shows that the superiority of the A cases appears in every item and consistently indicates that the all-pretried cases that reached trial were more frequently free from gaps and redundancies in proof than the not-pretried cases that reached trial. This evidence thus continues the pattern and is a further indication that pretrial improves trial quality.

Another yardstick for measuring trial quality was avoidance of unnecessary witnesses, but it proved not to be useful and was discarded. Questions to trial counsel in the test cases on this factor produced a close division of opinion. Counsel for defendants reported that the all-pretried A cases were better at avoiding unneeded witnesses, whereas plaintiffs' attorneys reported that the in-part-pretried B+C cases scored higher on this measure.[23] Since this factor attempted to tap the same sort of information as the items in Table 3, which probed more deeply into quality of evidence, we view as without major significance the detected split in the attorneys' views.[24]

The inference that pretrial improves quality draws added support from a finding that tactical surprise was less common in the all-pretried A cases. Reducing surprise is important because an accepted mark of sound trial process is freedom from tactical ploys and fancy footwork by which one side gains a forensic advantage over the other.

Both trial attorneys (who were in a perfect position to know whether they themselves had been taken unawares by the course of the trial) reported being "surprised" much more frequently than the trial judges detected. The judges reported surprise in only 4 per cent of the cases, and virtually without distinction as to the kind of pretrial processing the cases had experienced.[25] Their responses have not been relied upon, because it seems apparent that the questionnaires asked the judges a question they were not well positioned to answer.

From the trial attorneys' replies it can be seen in Table 6 that the familiar pattern emerged, and again the A cases surpassed the B+C cases in a major measure of trial quality.

Table 6. *Absence of Trial "Surprise" More Common in All-Pretried Cases**

	A	B+C
1. No surprise	86%	79%
Number of plaintiffs' reports	140	112
2. No surprise	88%	84%
Number of defendants' reports	128	103

*Significance levels: item 1, .20–.30; item 2, .40–.50.

A reflection of that finding is seen when we compare directly the all-pretried and the not-pretried cases, as is done in Table 7.

Table 7. *Trial "Surprise" More Common in Not-Pretried Cases**

	A	B
1. No surprise	86%	81%
Number of plaintiffs' reports	140	58
2. No surprise	88%	79%
Number of defendants' reports	128	56

*Significance levels: item 1, approximately .30; item 2, .05–.10.

The C group, on items 1 and 2 scored 80% and 91% with responses in 54 and 47 cases, respectively.

Table 7 shows that in the third and last of the major measures, the all-pretried cases again emerge with a superior score.

Presenting data from Tables 4 and 6 in a rather free form and loose fashion, along with the other evidence on trial quality we would have a picture along the lines of Figure 1.

WHAT PRETRIAL DOES AND DOES NOT

Fig. 1. High Quality Trials Were More Common in the All-Pretried Group*

	All-pretried	In-part-pretried
 Both sides were well prepared	85%	84%
 Theories came out clearly	94%	90%
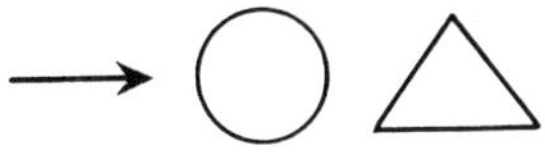 Issues emerged sharply	91%	88%
 Evidence was sufficient (without gaps or extras)	62%	48%
 At least one lawyer was not "surprised"	87%	82%

*Significance levels: good preparation .95–.98; clear theories, approximately .50; issues emerging, .70–.80; evidence sufficient, .05–.10; one lawyer not surprised, .10–.20.

COLLATERAL EVIDENCE OF PRETRIAL'S IMPACT UPON TRIAL QUALITY

Global opinions of the lawyers and judges in the test cases are strikingly like the more detailed data in suggesting that pretrial favorably affects trial quality in some cases. Answering on a case-by-case basis, the trial judges, trial attorneys, and pretrial judges were consistent in their views that in a fraction of the cases pretrial did have or would have had beneficial impact upon the trial process.[26]

First, the *trial judges* were asked in Form H the question: "Was the pretrial order, in your opinion, helpful in achieving a fair result?"[27] Affirmative replies were given by the judges in 24 per cent of the A cases and in 30 per cent of the C cases.[28] This implies that in roughly one out of four test case trials it was the opinion of the judge who presided at the trial that the pretrial conference (as embodied in the pretrial order) had served a constructive purpose for the trial's course. By implication, if there had not been a pretrial conference and order, the trial process would not have functioned as well to produce a fair result. This one-in-four positive effect does not mean the trial judges thought that pretrial had a negative effect in the remaining three fourths of the cases. We had not conceived of that as a serious possibility in devising the questions and neither did the judges in answering them, for none of their replies in any case suggest that harm to the trial process followed from the pretrial.

Another useful global evaluation of pretrial's effect—this time, potential rather than actual—came from the hindsight of test case *trial lawyers* who had declined a pretrial when offered the choice. These B case trial counsel were asked in Form I whether, given it to do over, they would elect a pretrial conference, and if so what difference it would make.[29] Of the plaintiffs' attorneys, 24 per cent replied in the affirmative to the "second thought" question; and of the defense counsel, 37 per cent checked *yes*, for an overall average of 30 per cent affirmative replies.[30] This was not just a "sour grapes" reaction, it seems, for when asked whether they believed a pretrial would "have made any substantial difference in the conduct or outcome" of the case, only 11 per cent of the plaintiffs' counsel and 20 per cent of the defense counsel checked *yes*. Thus, the opinions of the trial lawyers in the not-pretried cases and of the trial judges in the pretried ones coincided to the effect that pretrial could be beneficial in about one fourth of the trials.

Finally, the data report the forecast of the *pretrial judges* at the conclusion of each conference regarding "major results" it would have upon the trial. One subdivision of the question in Form F required a *yes* or *no* on whether the conference "will . . . probably . . . make for a fairer trial."[31] They replied in the affirmative in 24 per cent of the cases (*i.e.,* in 25 per cent of 1,058 A cases and in 22 per cent of 494 C cases). The same implications noted in the foregoing analysis of the trial judges' replies are in principle applicable here.

That the replies of all three groups of participants in test cases clustered around the 25 per cent figure in estimating the benefit of pretrial upon the trial process is probably only an interesting coincidence. What is important, however, is that all agreed so consistently that pretrial had benefited or would have benefited the trial process in an appreciable though minor fraction of the cases. That opinion of the participating judges and lawyers corresponds closely to the net conclusion toward which the more precise data point. While this correspondence may not be technically confirmatory, it is certainly reassuring.

QUALITY OF SETTLEMENTS

But what of the question raised at the beginning of this chapter regarding the impact of the pretrial conference upon cases that never reach trial because they are settled? Neither by means of the controlled test nor through any of the collateral studies did we attempt directly to determine the effect of the pretrial conference upon the "quality" of settlements. To measure the quality of a settlement is even harder than to measure the quality of a trial, and for fairly obvious reasons. Over the centuries the common-law trial process has developed certain formal attributes that have become embedded and widely accepted as essentials of due process. On the other hand, settlement negotiations have neither an agreed style nor agreed rules. Vagrant factors of all kinds influence the process by which a compromise is reached. Particularly is this so in personal injury cases, where the moral taint of "losing" is minimal and issues tend to reduce themselves to the question of "How much?" rather than "Who's right?"

As earlier indicated, a useful measurement of settlement quality rests on the principle that other things being equal a settlement will be properly arrived at if it is based on a mutual full exchange of information and evidence by the parties. It will not be of good quality if one side is in the dark about material matters the other side knows.[32] This desire for full mutual knowledge is the same basic value that underlies several of the yardsticks used to measure the quality of the trial process—preparedness, availability of needed proof, etc. In the absence of data drawn directly from the settled cases about the impact of pretrial upon the level of mutual knowledge, we believe that the trial data can be used as indirect evidence. Even though not all the items used to measure trial quality are relevant, some are, and all were of a kind in showing an advantage for the A group.

Since the all-pretried A cases produced a higher percentage of good quality trials according to our test criteria than the not-all-pretried B+C cases, we assume that the settled cases did likewise. We do not pretend to be able to measure the frequency or intensity of this effect and merely note the indications of its presence. Further investigation of the level of mutual knowledge in settled cases, with and without antecedent pretrial conference, would be a valuable research endeavor.

2. Impact on "Efficiency" of Court Processes

Pretrial is at the top of many lists of "remedies" for court delay, the most notable being the American Bar Association's "Ten Cures for Court Congestion."[33] That it belongs there has not been questioned seriously in the years since 1938, when the pretrial conference swept the country. State after state adopted it as a sure-fire antidote to overcrowded calendars and delayed trials. In New Jersey those problems were not critical after the 1947 court reorganization, so the state was not as smitten as others with the idea of using pretrial to get a stepped-up rate of cases disposed of per judge. Rather, as has been shown, pretrial was installed and maintained on a compulsory, universal basis for the support it was thought to give to the quality of justice.

But in recent years court efficiency has been a burning issue the country around, and so many leading judges and lawyers have spoken out for pretrial as a delay remedy that this facet of the problem commands high interest and deserves close attention. Even in New Jersey, trial delay has begun to loom, as the danger signs of lengthening dockets have appeared in several counties.[34]

It is helpful to see the problem of court delay as one of supply and demand.[35] Delay occurs when the demand made by a group of cases for courtroom processing exceeds the supply of court resources, namely, judge time available to process them. To deal efficiently with the problem, a remedy must restore equilibrium by favorably altering at least one side of the equation. The main force of the pretrial conference is supposed to be to cut down on the *demand* for judge time that the cases would make but for pretrial. This in turn will allow the judges to spread to other cases the time pretrial has saved, and quicker dispatch of court business will result. In theory pretrial can reduce demand for judge time in cases in two main ways: (1) increase their settlement rate and (2) shorten trial in cases that do not settle.

Both those effects take on more importance when it is understood that *trial activities* absorb roughly 60 per cent of the time outlays in civil cases by New Jersey judges of the law divisions, against 40 per cent for all their other activities, including the hearing of motions, administrative work, and pretrial itself.[36] Therefore, any "efficiency" device that appreciably reduces the percentage of cases reaching trial or the duration of trials hits the bull's-eye. That is what the pretrial conference is claimed to do, but does it in fact?

We have concluded that across-the-board compulsory pretrials in New Jersey accident cases did not in the 1960 test, and do not now, increase the frequency of settlements before trial.

That conclusion represents a rather free reading of the study data, but it is one to which many persuasive signs point. The first and most important of these is the clearest finding of all in the controlled test: To subject *every* case to pretrial as practiced in the test cases *did not save the judges' time by stepping up settlement frequency*. On the contrary, it consumed substantial time without any compensating gain in reducing the trial time demands of the cases.

Fig. 2. *The All-Pretried Group Did Not Produce More Frequent Settlements**

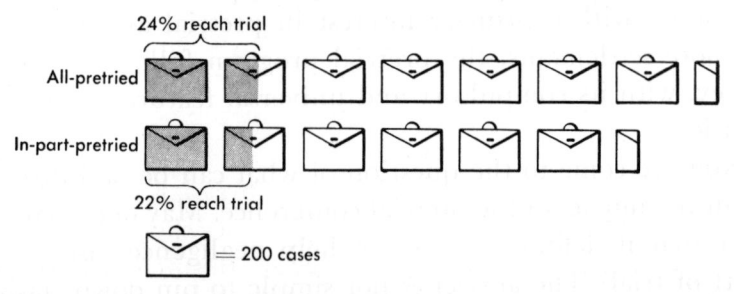

*Includes cases that settled during trials. Based on 1,418 A and 1,362 B+C cases. Significance level: .20-.30.

Figure 2 shows unmistakably that the system of pretrial for all personal injury cases in effect during the test period did not achieve a higher proportion of settlements than was attained at the same time, in the same counties, in the same type of cases, and before the same judges, by a lawyers'-choice program in which not quite half the cases experienced pretrials.

Whatever its achievements in other respects, on the settlement yardstick, the all-pretrial program lost judge time and efficiency compared to the experimental part-pretrial system. That observation is at odds with a vast array of claims, opinions, and hopes that have been accepted for years as dogma,[37] but it alone rests upon reliable research technique. "Only a scientifically controlled experiment," it has been said, can "permit us to learn exactly what was and what was not achieved" by a legal remedy designed to affect the administration of justice.[38] That is what was done here.

A very plain implication of Figure 2 is that if the Supreme Court of New Jersey were to shift tomorrow from the present compulsory, all-pretrial rule in negligence cases to lawyers' choice pretrial (and the lawyers' criteria for choosing remain about the same), there would not be a falling off in frequency of settlements or a step-up in cases seeking trial. If anything, there would be a slight tendency in the opposite direction—toward less frequent trials. A broader inference also emerges: For states with a primary interest in pretrial as a means to promote settlements, the pretrial program followed in New Jersey, with its compulsory and universal features, is not the solution.[39]

Now we come to the question of what can be said directly about the impact of the pretrial conference. May one correctly infer that it definitely does not help negligence cases settle short of trial? The answer is not simple to pin down statistically.

The effort to muster reliable evidence begins with an analysis of how frequently the not-pretried B cases settle compared to the two groups that were pretried.

Table 8. *Comparative Settlement Frequencies**

	B	A+C
Reached trial	22%	23%
Number of cases	701	2,079

*Significance level: approximately .70.

How close all three groups were in the vital statistic of settlement rate is clear when one recalls that 24 per cent of the A cases reached trial (Figure 2).[40] Then, since we see that the pretried and not-pretried groups settled with almost identical frequency, is that not proof that pretrial had no impact on settlement? That conclusion looks right, but it is superficial. The trouble is, the cases that were not compelled to go to pretrial but chose it anyway—the C group—might have been different in one or more material respects from the B cases they left behind in the not-pretried group. That possibility precludes inferences one might be tempted to make from just the blunt figures for reasons that are slightly involved, but necessary to explain.

It is as if in doing research on the connection between smoking and a disease linked to nervous tension the data showed that the disease occurred with the same frequency in persons who smoked through choice ("C" smokers) and persons who did not ("B" smokers). At first glance the inference would be that smoking had no effect on the incidence of the nervous tension disease. But the equal figures might mask real subsurface impact. For example, it may be that voluntary smokers were tense to start out with and had a high potential for the disease, which smoking *reduced* because it alleviated their tension. That they developed the disease in the same proportion as nonsmokers would veil the true picture. Many possibilities of masked effects of that type would exist, some of them running in opposite directions.

Analogous risks are present in the data showing similar settlement rates for voluntarily pretried and not-pretried cases. The C cases put on the trial list may or may not have had the same "durability"[41] or settlement potential as the B cases. If the "ideal" controlled experiment we proposed had been in effect, the test itself would have assured the "equality" of settlement potential between the two groups, and equal settlement percentages would then have meant that the pretrial conference was not effective in regard to settlement. But in the absence of the ideal research framework, it becomes necessary to try to discover by other means whether the B and C cases had similar settlement potentials.[42]

It is necessary to attempt to "control" artificially for the factors that are known or suspected to influence settlement potential. The only "known" factor is one that earlier Project research in New York has firmly established, namely, "size" of the case. That is defined as the approximate amount that an injury victim may reasonably be expected to recover assuming liability is found in his favor. After scaling the pretried cases for size with the aid of a special check item included in the research design, we inferred that the B and C cases had roughly the same recovery potential.[43] This ruled out size as a possible distorting factor.

Turning to the "suspected" factors (other potential determinants of durability), we compared the B and C cases for any such differences that might mask the effect of pretrial. This involved analyzing the C cases for special features that could both induce the lawyers to opt for pretrial and also affect durability. If such factors were discovered in different proportions in the B and C groups, we would have a "self-selection" distortion that might make more ambiguous the real impact pretrial was having on their settlement rates. A comparison of the two groups revealed that there were indeed differences in the frequency of certain factors that might be determinants of durability. It appeared that C cases were less likely to be simple motor vehicle actions and more likely to be complex— that is, of non-auto origin and to involve multiple parties or multiple claims.[44] However, when we controlled for those variables, we found that they had no correlation with durability. For example, motor vehicle and non-motor vehicle cases settled with nearly identical frequencies whether pretried or not; and so with multiple party or multiple claim cases.[45] It thus appears the two groups did not have different settlement potentials.

Moreover, although it is theoretically possible that pretrial did have a pro-settlement effect on some cases and an anti-settlement effect on others, and that those effects were equal and self-canceling, the hazard is too remote to be of serious concern. The evidence as a whole indicates that the three groups of test cases approached the pretrial list with similar settlement potentials and closed out at figures that were almost identical for each group.

We infer that the pretrial conference did not have a substantial overall effect to promote or retard settlement. Of interest in relation to that point is the fact that the pretrial judges, when asked to forecast the probable effect of the conference in promoting settlement ("will it probably eliminate the need for trial"?), checked *yes* only 10 per cent of the time.[46]

IMPACT ON TRIAL TIME

Theoretically, the second major way pretrial could enhance efficiency is by shortening trials in the cases that do not settle, but it seems not to do that all. Certainly it did not do so to any great extent. First, there is the evidence from the controlled test.

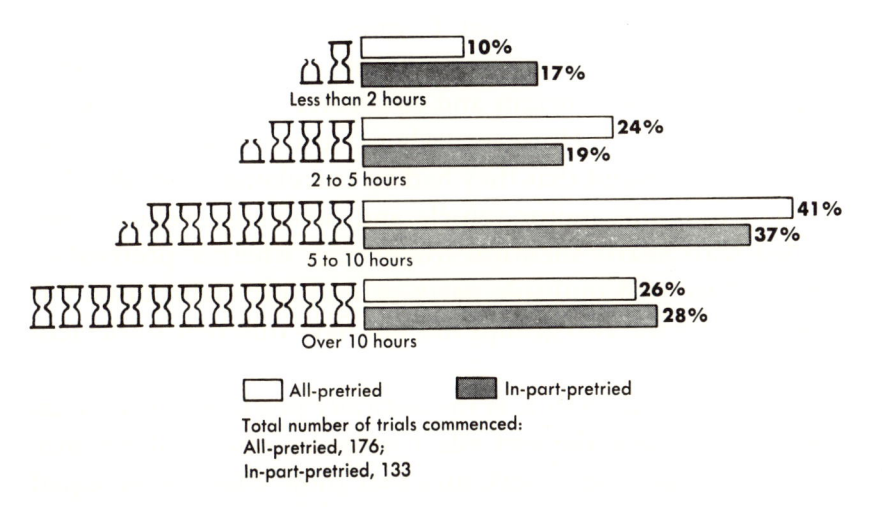

Fig. 3. *The All-Pretried Group Did Not Produce More Short Trials**

Less than 2 hours: 10% / 17%
2 to 5 hours: 24% / 19%
5 to 10 hours: 41% / 37%
Over 10 hours: 26% / 28%

☐ All-pretried   ■ In-part-pretried

Total number of trials commenced:
All-pretried, 176;
In-part-pretried, 133

*Significance levels: less than 2 hours, .05–.10; 2–5 hours, .30–.40; 5+–10 hours, .50–.60; over 10 hours, .70–.80.

If pretrials resulted in condensing trials, there should have been a down-the-line advantage for the all-pretried A cases. But Figure 3 shows no such results, and taken with the data on settlement frequency, gives clear indication that universal pretrial does not conserve total trial time in negligence cases. In fact, there is a hint in Figure 3 that giving a pretrial to all cases may even increase total trial courtroom time demands, for only 10 per cent of the A cases were disposed of with "quickie" trials of less than two hours, as against 17 per cent of the B+C cases.[47] Although it is curious that so many trials finish within two hours, the finding is in accord with official figures.[48]

Helping to account for the figures showing there was no substantial difference between the pretried cases and the others in trial duration is the interesting observation about the similar rates of trial completion in the three groups. Patently, cases that settle shortly after commencing trial will require far less time than if they persisted to verdict. A study by the New Jersey Administrative Office during two months of 1961 showed that among personal injury cases commencing jury trials, 33 per cent failed to go to verdict,[49] and this matches almost perfectly the figure of 32 per cent produced by the test data as the proportion of test cases not completing trial after beginning one.[50] The A, B, and C groups showed virtually identical percentages, each producing a trial-completion figure of 15–16 per cent.[51]

When the B+C group is broken into its subgroups and they are compared, further evidence appears that pretrial does not shorten trial time.

Table 9. *Not-Pretried Cases More Commonly Produced Short Trials**

Trial time (in hours)	B	A	C
1. 5 or less	43%	34%	28%
2. Over 5 to 10	35%	41%	39%
3. Over 10	22%	26%	33%
Number of cases	63	176	70

*Significance levels: B against A, item 1, .20–.30; item 2, .40–.50; item 3, approximately .70. B against C, item 1, .10–.20; item 2, approximately .80; item 3, .20–.30.

According to Table 9, the B group enjoyed the highest percentage of very short trials and the lowest percentage of very long trials. To be warranted, such a direct comparison between the B and C cases requires consideration of the distortion problem. It seemed logical to expect that the lawyers would have been more likely to opt for a pretrial conference in a complex rather than a simple case. It also seemed possible that the more complex cases might require longer trials. The data give color to the possibility of self-selection of that type, for 77 per cent of the C cases involved multiple parties as against 71 per cent of the B cases.[52] Also, C cases tended to include multiple claims more frequently than B cases.[53] The greatest difference of all was in the percentage of motor vehicle actions: they were much more prevalent in the B cases.[54]

Yet, the "better" performance of the B cases cannot satisfactorily be explained on the ground that they were less complex than others. When we controlled for the motor vehicle factor, the B cases continued to show shorter trials all down the line.[55]

The possibility is suggested by the evidence that pretrial makes the very short trials a bit longer. It may be that a pretrial conference gives attorneys in simple cases a bit more to do and to say at the trial than they otherwise would have had. Certain it is that whatever the underlying reasons, pretrial did not shorten trials with appreciable frequency, according to the statistical evidence. It is interesting to notice that this result squares with the case-by-case impression of the great majority of pretrial judges, who predicted in three fourths of the cases that the pretrial conference would not shorten the trial.[56]

FREQUENCY OF JURY WAIVER

An interesting piece of evidence that both lends support to and helps explain the finding that pretrial fails to result in shorter trials derives from an analysis of the figures on jury waiver in the test cases. The higher the proportion of jury trials in a particular group, the more likely is the group to show elevated trial time demands, because jury trials tend to take longer than judge-only trials.[57] To the extent that pretrial fails to discourage jury trials, it fails to achieve a potential saving of judical time in processing personal injury cases.

The evidence is that pretrial does not encourage the parties to waive the jury. At the beginning of their court careers nearly all the test cases had demanded a jury trial, knowing they could waive at a later point. For the A and C cases, the figure was 95 per cent and for the B cases 91 per cent.[58] Then came pretrial conferences for the A and C groups, but none, of course, for the B cases. After the conference, the litigants in the A cases relatively seldom exercised their privilege to waive the previously demanded jury, in contrast to the litigants in the B+C group. For the A cases, 10 per cent chose belated waiver, but in the B+C group 17 per cent did.[59] On the face of it, it is clear that obligatory universal pretrial resulted in a lower percentage of jury waivers than the lawyers'-choice pretrial.

Actually it was the B cases that waived most often, for in those the parties gave up a jury 18 per cent of the time after having initially asked for one.[60] Apparently, whatever reasons cause litigants to ask for a jury at the beginning of the case and to persist in wanting one afterward, those reasons are largely unaffected whether or not the case goes through a pretrial conference. Indeed, if there has been a pretrial, a slight tendency develops for the litigants (or at least one of them) to be confirmed in wanting the jury.[61]

AGE AT CLOSING

Claims are sometimes made that pretrial not only brings the parties together oftener but sooner. On the theory that the earlier a case closes the less chance it has to absorb judge time, we measured the elapsed time in the settled cases from the filing of the complaint to final disposition, to learn if pretrial accelerated the closing date in the test cases. The evidence is negative, as shown in Table 10.

Table 10. *All-Pretried Cases Did Not Settle Earlier than In-Part-Pretried Cases**

	A	B+C
Age at closing (in months)		
1. 12 or less	24%	24%
2. 13–18	34%	35%
3. 19–24	35%	35%
4. 25 and over	7%	6%
Number of cases	1,022	991

*Based on cases that settled before trial.
Significance levels: item 1, .80–.90; item 2, .50–.60; item 3, .80–.90; item 4, .30–40.

It is clear from the lack of down-the-line advantage for the A cases that universal pretrial does not bring quickened settlements in the mass of personal injury suits. From Table 11 there is, to the contrary, evidence that it has a slight tendency to inhibit earlier settlements.

Table 11. *Not-Pretried Cases Settled Early More Commonly than Pretried Cases**

	B	A	C
Age at closing (in months)			
1. 12 or less	26%	24%	22%
2. 13–18	39%	34%	32%
3. 19–24	32%	35%	38%
4. 25 and over	3%	7%	8%
Number of cases	511	1,022	480

*Based on cases that settled before trial.
Significance levels: B against A, item 1, approximately .30; item 2, .05–.10; item 3, .10–.20; item 4, .001–.01. B against C, item 1, .10–.20; item 2, .02–.05; item 3, .02–.05; item 4, less than .001.

Whether or not Table 11 can be read as strong proof that pretrial retards settlement, we think it safe to conclude that pretrial has no strong effect in the direction of speeding settlement.

THE "EFFICIENCY" SCORE IN SUMMARY

The foregoing series of findings and indications that pretrial does not produce more or quicker settlements, fewer or shorter complete trials, or fewer jury trials, signifies to us that the pretrial conference has for the mass of negligence cases no consistent tendency to decrease the judge time required to process them. On the contrary, since the conferences themselves take substantial judge time, the investment of effort with no compensating saving will entail loss of efficiency. How large is this loss in New Jersey? It is not possible to state its upper limit as confidently as its lower limit. The lower estimate we can compute with some assurance on the reasoning that pretrial unquestionably fails to save time in a minimum of 50 per cent of the cases. Those are the B cases, which had no pretrial and still settled 78 per cent of the time. They had counterparts in the all-pretried A group, which were given a pretrial without any betterment in their settlement rate. This direct investment of time spent in pretrial conferences could be eliminated with no adverse effect on the settlement rate.

Moreover, in a shift from universal pretrial to a lawyers'-choice plan there would not be any offsetting loss in efficiency by reason of trials tending to run longer. The test results show that obligatory universal pretrial does not shorten trials in the mass of cases or lead to a drop-off in the longer-running jury trials.

In short, if New Jersey were forthwith to abandon compulsory across-the-board pretrial of personal injury cases in favor of the lawyer-option plan which was in effect in 1960 during the controlled test, the Superior and County courts would be spared pretrial conferences in at least 52 per cent of the cases.[62] Assuming a persistent case load of about 19,000 negligence actions added to the calendar each year, we estimate a saving in judge time of approximately 3,200 hours annually.[63] To translate 3,200 hours accurately into judge years is an enormously complex task because no precise figures are available on the average hours a judge works yearly in the courts in question.[64] A further point is that the hours a judge spends in pretrial work are not convertible on a one-for-one basis into other court work, such as trial work. Unlike trials, which usually impose inflexible schedules, pretrial conferences can be used as fillers and fitted into odd corners of the day or week on short notice. If 3,200 hours of pretrial work were saved, the judges would not have even close to that many hours available for judical work requiring tighter scheduling, but we are unable to offer a precise conversion figure.

Without pretending it is any more than a round estimate, we would hazard that on the order of two judges a year[65] or about 5 per cent[66] of the available judge time in the Law Divisions would be conserved by shifting to a lawyers'-choice plan of pretrial. (See Figure 4.)

Fig. 4. Estimated Saving of Judge Time From Converting to Optional Program for Pretrial in Personal Injury Cases (based on certain assumptions)

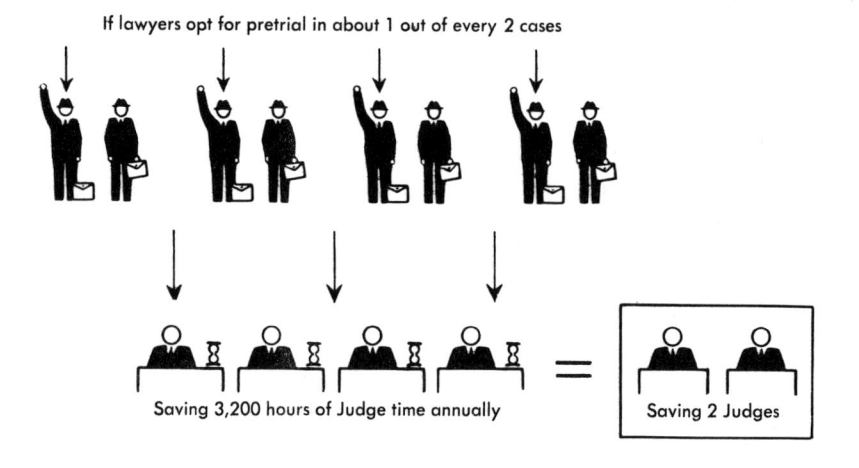

If lawyers opt for pretrial in about 1 out of every 2 cases

Saving 3,200 hours of Judge time annually = Saving 2 Judges

An efficiency gain of that order would not in our view be a sufficient ground to abolish a procedure that on the evidence contributes to improving the trial process in an appreciable number of cases and no doubt improves the quality of the settlement process in still others. Badly conducted trials can tarnish justice more surely than delayed trials. If there must be a choice, good trials later are preferable to bad ones now. It would be a grievous mistake in New Jersey or anywhere else to exalt the efficiency issue to decisive importance, choosing for or against pretrial solely on whether it helps courts stay abreast of their work load.

While delay in trials is not a trivial circumstance in administering justice, obsession with speed can risk injury to the quality of the whole process of justice. In a most perceptive passage, Judge Ralph Pharr of the Georgia Superior Court has made the point as we should like to:

> Into the furious frenzy of "speed" and alarm at "congestion" there appeared the magic words "pretrial conference." Not only those zealots of haste, but also conscientious, hard-working judges, weary from fighting the pressure of an ever-growing calendar and yearning to achieve a greater degree of justice by providing an earlier and better trial of cases, have seized upon pretrial with an eagerness similar to that with which the medical practitioner embraced penicillin and the other "miracle drugs" as the panacea for all ills. Pretrial was dreamed of by some as a magic spark, which, by bringing the lawyers and trial judges together, would with an atomic flash automatically dissolve all the mountainous masses of complicated cases. That it has not been a "cure-all" so anxiously sought has resulted in some disillusionment and disappointment. There has been engendered some measure of reluctance and resistance which tends to obscure the true purpose, scope and benefits of proper pretrial.[67]

3. Impact on Outcome of the Cases

It had never been claimed by either side in the debate that pretrial conferences in accident cases cause overall variations in who wins or how much. Certainly no one had hinted that pretrial influences the outcome of the cases in a particular direction, such as *for* liability, *against* liability, or the like. In New Jersey pretrial was adopted as a purely procedural rule, designed to improve the processing of civil cases. No doubt procedural rules often have side effects, operating in a way that at times stacks the cards for one class of litigants, at times for another. But there is nothing in the New Jersey pretrial rule or its history to suggest that the Supreme Court suspected it would have substantive impulses, such as assuring that plaintiffs would win more often, or that defendants would, or that verdicts would be larger or smaller.

Accordingly, when this study began, there was no forewarning from the New Jersey authorities that pretrial might alter the outcome of large numbers of cases in a consistent direction. Experience with other "purely procedural" innovations in Massachusetts and Pennsylvania indicated that possibility[68] and therefore the research design included items that would permit recording the outcome in each test case.

Later on, in reading the data to discover whether pretrial had an impact on outcome, we were concerned solely with whether exposure of cases to pretrial conferences seemed to make for *measurable* changes in the results. We were not concerned with trying to determine whether any such changes could be said to have made the results "more just" or "less just." This is not due to indifference but to inability, for only the courts themselves can meaningfully determine whether justice or injustice has been served in a particular case. Investigators have their hands full to observe and interpret the more measurable phenomena of the administration of justice.

When the results of the tests were tabulated, it quite unexpectedly appeared that pretrial evidently promotes larger recoveries; and that it does this without affecting who "wins" in the all-or-nothing sense, its whole impact being in the cases in which the plaintiff recovers something.

Table 12. *The All-Pretried and the In-Part-Pretried Cases Produced Recoveries with Equal Frequency**

	A	B+C
Percentage that recovered	92	92
Number of cases	1,330	1,306

*Significance level: .90–.95.

Table 12 shows that universal pretrial did not change the frequency with which plaintiffs "won" the contests in the all-or-nothing sense. In both the all-pretried and the in-part-pretried cases defendants paid out money in 92 per cent of the cases and avoided a recovery in the remaining 8 per cent. Those overall figures included both the settled and the tried cases, but there was a marked difference in the frequency with which defendants avoided payment in the tried cases. In trials that went to a verdict plaintiffs won the verdict in the A cases 62 per cent of the time and in the B+C group 61 per cent of the time.[69] Parenthetically, the nearly 40 per cent proportion of defendants' verdicts in negligence trials is a figure commonly encountered in other states.[70] The similarity in the frequency with which the two main test groups produced recoveries for plaintiffs showed that the lawyers'-choice system of pretrial did not alter the "victor" compared to the compulsory system.

When the not-pretried B cases were compared with the pretried groups, a similar picture appeared, as may be seen in Table 13.

Table 13. *Plaintiffs Recovered in Not-Pretried Cases with Same Frequency as in Pretried Cases**

	B	A	C
1. All cases	92%	92%	93%
Number of cases	684	1,330	622
2. Tried cases	60%	62%	61%
Number of cases	86	208	90

*Significance levels: Item 1, B against A, approximately .60; B against C, .20–.30. Item 2, B against A, .90–.95; B against C, over .95.

Once again, the data appear to say that the defendants paid and the plaintiffs recovered with unvarying frequency in all three groups, and it made no difference whether the cases had been pretried or not. This observation must, of course, be qualified to take care of the by now familiar point that direct comparison between the not-pretried and the pretried cases runs the risk of false appearances because of the masking of underlying differences in the groups. After testing for concealed differences by "control" devices like those discussed above, we satisfied ourselves that no substantial distortions had occurred.[71]

The next line of analysis was aimed at determining *how much* plaintiffs were paid in the 92 per cent of the cases in which they recovered, and whether the amounts varied from group to group. It was here that one of the most surprising findings of the study was uncovered: In the all-pretried A group, plaintiffs recovered appreciably more money than they did in the B+C cases. This differential held up whether the measure used was the average or the median amount recovered.

Table 14. *All-Pretried Cases Recovered More than In-Part-Pretried Cases**

	A	B+C
1. Average recovery	$4,133	$3,503
2. Median recovery	$2,043	$1,813
Number of cases	1,277	1,206

*Excluded from the calculations are a settlement for $194,000 and a verdict for $160,000, because they were considered atypical. The highest recoveries included are a settlement for $110,000 and a verdict of $95,000.

Table 14 shows a clear margin for the A cases, amounting to $630 on the "average" and $230 when the "median" is computed. Speaking in round terms, the all-pretried cases recovered on the order of 15 per cent more than the in-part-pretried cases. Such an impact from universal pretrial has not to our knowledge heretofore been either asserted or suspected. There is no danger of distortion by self-selection in the finding, for it rests on data assembled in strictest conformity with the controlled test design. It is not in any sense a statistical mirage; it shows up in the steady down-the-line pattern that emerges when the cases are distributed according to how many appear in each size bracket.[72]

The finding that A cases close out at larger sums cannot be explained in any other way, we believe, than that an unsuspected effect of the pretrial conference is to increase the overall amount plaintiff recovers in the cases that he does not lose outright. That interpretation is supported by aligning the not-pretried cases against all those that had a pretrial conference, whether compulsory or optional.

Table 15. *The Not-Pretried Cases Recovered Less Money*

	B	A	C
1. Average recovery	$3,118	$4,133	$3,927
2. Median recovery	$1,675	$2,043	$2,055
Number of cases	627	1,277	579

*The statements made in footnote to Table 14 apply here also.

As Table 15 shows, a head-on comparison of the B cases with the pretried cases reveals an even wider advantage for the latter. In percentage terms, the A and C cases produced average and median recoveries that, again speaking roughly, ran 20-30 per cent higher than the B cases. When distributed by size categories the same pattern emerged, with the pretried cases in both the A and C groups running to larger sums than the B cases.[73]

At this point it becomes vital to ask whether the figures can be taken at face value or whether there is too heavy a risk of distortion through self-selection. Logically a risk is present, for it is quite conceivable that the cases that made up the B group tended toward a lower recovery potential than the others. This could have come about if the lawyers in opting tended to pick the larger cases for pretrial and to leave the smaller ones not-pretried. A specific check was built into the test design to determine whether the groups of test cases had similar recovery potentials. The mechanism was a size-screening, performed as the A and C cases came on for pretrial conferences. The presiding judge in each case was asked to estimate the amount a court would award to the plaintiff, assuming the defendant to be liable. The judge had three choices, "Small," "Medium," and "Large," respectively defined as: less than $3,000, $3,000 to $7,500, and over $7,500. As Table 16 indicates, a remarkable correspondence appeared in the "size" of cases comprising the two groups.

Table 16. *Pretrial Judges' Estimates of Plaintiff's Recovery, Assuming Defendant Liable**

	A	C
Small	38%	38%
Medium	44%	43%
Large	18%	19%
Number of cases	1,143	538

*Significance levels for small, approximately .90; medium .70–.80; large .60–.70.

Having established that recovery potentials were distributed almost identically in various size categories of the A and C groups, we were able to infer that the distribution of potential recoveries in the B group was of a similar pattern. That is because according to the test design the A group of cases was composed of two subgroups, one of which was like the C group and the other of which perforce was like the B group, inasmuch as the sampling procedure used was such as to assure that the A group as a whole was like the B+C group as a whole.[74]

To sum up: In comparing the three groups, whether one looks at the percentage of cases in various size categories, at average recoveries or at median recoveries, the pretried cases realized larger sums than the not-pretried cases. Depending on which measuring technique is used, the superiority of pretried cases in recovery size is a figure on the order of magnitude of between 15 and 30 per cent.[75]

The data themselves do not tell why this should be true. Necessarily the line of explanation is that plaintiffs gained both a bargaining and an evidentiary benefit at the pretrial conference, for it paid off in both higher settlements and higher verdicts.[76] Since one of the indicated results of a pretrial conference is an increased exchange of information and evidence between the parties, it is quite possible to understand the basic dynamics by which plaintiffs might add strength to their position. Especially if the conference emphasizes plaintiffs' injuries, dwells upon medical witnesses and doctors' or hospitals' receipts and records, the result ought to be to magnify their value in the view of defense counsel. At least that sort of stress could in many cases impress the defendant to a greater degree than before with the serious prospect of a substantial damage award. This might lead the defendant to think in terms of larger offers, and by that psychological makeweight might inflate the recovery value of the case.

Another possible explanation is that plaintiffs' attorneys may normally be less experienced than defense counsel, who handle negligence cases in wholesale quantities. It would follow that plaintiffs' attorneys would benefit more from the judges' efforts to draw out the issues and evidence and from his amicable intervention at the pretrial conference, when those events occurred.

The rather paradoxical finding that pretrial tends to inflate recoveries without increasing their frequency may rest on the fact that there is little room for "improvement" in the frequency of recoveries, since in only 8 per cent of the cases does the plaintiff take nothing from his suit. At all events there is

WHAT PRETRIAL DOES AND DOES NOT

no doubt of the fact that pretried cases do recover considerably more than not-pretried cases; or, speaking most strictly, there is no doubt from the controlled test that in a mandatory universal pretrial setup, cases recover more by an appreciable percentage than in a lawyers'-choice pretrial program.

Support for the reliability of this finding comes indirectly from an interesting observation with respect to the extent judges agreed or disagreed with juries' verdicts in the test cases. Earlier studies by the Chicago Jury Project had found that in negligence trials the judge agreed about 80 per cent of the time with the jury's verdict on the *liability* issue but showed appreciable disagreement with the *size* of the jury's damage award.[77] Judges tended to find substantially smaller damages than juries. On the basis of those reports, we expected in this study to find that the presence or absence of a pretrial did not correlate with whether the judge agreed with the jury on liability (since there was no relation between which side won and whether there had been a pretrial). On the other hand, we did expect to find that agreement was less frequent between judges and juries on the size of awards in the pretried cases than in the not-pretried ones, since the pretried cases tended to produce *larger* awards whereas judges tend to give *smaller* awards. As the following tables indicate, both these expectations were borne out by the data.

Table 17. *Constant Frequency of Judges' Agreement with Juries' Liability Verdicts**

	B	A	C
Judge agreed with jury	81%	81%	80%
Number of cases	43	108	35

*Significance levels on all items: over .95.

Obviously, whether the all-pretried A cases are compared with the in-part-pretried B+C cases, or the not-pretried cases are arrayed head on against the others, Table 17 says clearly that judges agreed with juries in a relatively unchanging percentage of the cases. Thus, the indication is that pretrial made no difference for whether judges agreed with juries on liability.

Table 18. *In Not-Pretried Cases Judges More Frequently Agreed with Juries on Damage Verdicts**

	B	A	C
Judge agreed with jury	75%	62%	69%
Number of cases	28	79	26

*No effort was made to determine whether in fact the defendant-chosen C cases recovered more than the not-pretried cases with comparable potential. The data did not lend themselves to that sort of analysis.

Significance levels: A against B+C, .40–.50; B against A, .40–.50; B against C, .80–.90.

The differences in Table 18 are in the direction one would expect if pretrial conferences tended to increase the amount of damage awards. That is to say, the judges, who tend to award lower amounts than juries, could be expected to agree with the juries more often in the lower-verdict not-pretried B cases. Table 18 clearly shows more judge-jury agreement in the not-pretried group. While the forms did not ask the judges to disclose reasons that might have accounted for their higher frequency of agreement in the B cases, it seems a fair inference that the smaller size of B case verdicts was a weighty factor. Here, since the likelihood is remote that the judges chose to agree or disagree with juries' verdicts on any ground that could have been a factor in the lawyers' choice to put the case through pretrial (thus making it a C case) we have no hesitancy in comparing the B cases directly with the C cases, or with the A cases as well.

The finding that personal-injury-suit recoveries tended to be appreciably higher after the case went to a pretrial conference prompts two comments. The first is that plaintiffs' increased take-home in negligence actions was obviously an accidental by-product and not an intended result of the procedural rule mandating pretrial in every case. The other is that the findings reveal an ironical twist, beginning with the fact that it was the defendants who elected pretrial by two to one over plaintiffs in the lawyers'-choice situation and ending with the strong probability that in doing so the defendants helped inflate the amount of the plaintiffs' eventual recovery by a rather substantial percentage.[78]

SUMMING UP THE TEST FINDINGS

What if one were able to state the test findings categorically, as if they conclusively proved exactly what they seem to say and as if there were no need to qualify the observations to take account of possible statistical infirmities? In other words, what picture would appear if we deliberately darkened the filmy outlines suggested by the data and just assumed that further tests would confirm them? To see the resulting picture, we might imagine that a friend of the pretrial conference has taken the floor to enumerate all the good effects it allegedly produces. Then we can determine whether the test findings support or refute each claim.

Below we have set out typical claims in favor of the pretrial conference and have confronted them with our test findings. The results are mixed.

Does pretrial improve trial and the trial process?

(1) "Pretrial eliminates some appeals and reduces the chance of reversal in cases that are appealed."
   Not Supported: No correlation appeared between pretrial and the frequency of appeals, or between pretrial and the frequency of reversal in appealed cases.
(2) "Pretrial eliminates motions for new trials and reduces the chance that such motions will be granted if made."

Partly Supported: Pretrial did not affect the frequency with which new trials were sought, but reduced the likelihood of their success.

(3) "Pretrial increases the chance that the case will be well presented at trial."

Supported: In pretried cases that reached trial the attorneys were more frequently well prepared and the theories and issues more often emerged clearly.

(4) "In pretried cases the evidence is more frequently well presented."

Supported: Pretrial reduced the frequency with which trial evidence was offered on extraneous or undisputed issues and also reduced the frequency with which too much or too litle evidence was offered.

(5) "Pretrial eliminates unnecessary witnesses."

Not Supported: Pretrial did not have any effect on the frequency of calling unneeded witnesses.

(6) "Pretrial eliminates trial surprise."

Supported: In pretried cases trial lawyers agreed, whether they were for plaintiff or defendant, that they were less frequently surprised at trial than they were in not-pretried cases.

(7) "In the opinion of judges and lawyers, pretrial promotes fair trial."

Supported: Frequently pretrial judges forecast, and trial judges and trial counsel gave as their opinion that pretrial had favorable impact on trial quality.

(8) "Pretrial improves the settlement process."

Supported: The level of mutual knowledge of the litigants was more frequently high in pretried cases.

Does pretrial improve the efficiency of the court process?

(1) "Pretrial reduces the frequency with which cases require trial."

WHAT PRETRIAL DOES AND DOES NOT 69

Not Supported: Pretrial did not lead to fewer cases reaching trial.

(2) "Pretrial abbreviates the trial in cases that do not settle before trial."

Not Supported: Pretrial did not reduce the hours spent in the trial of cases that required trial.

(3) "Pretrial shortens trials by increasing the frequency of jury waivers."

Not Supported: Pretrial did not increase, but actually decreased, the frequency of jury waivers.

(4) "Pretrial shortens the time required to settle cases that do not reach trial."

Not Supported: Pretrial did not decrease the time lapse from filing to disposition for settled cases.

(5) "Pretrial judges believe that pretrial will frequently eliminate trials."

Not Supported: Pretrial judges infrequently predicated that the pretrial would eliminate the need for trial.

(6) "Pretrial judges believe that a pretrial conference will frequently reduce the length of trials."

Not Supported: Pretrial judges opined that a pretrial conference infrequently reduced the length of time required for trial.

(7) "Pretrial saves judge time overall by eliminating or shortening trials."

Not Supported: Pretrial consumed appreciable judge time without compensating saving.

Does pretrial have an impact on the outcome of the cases?

(1) "Pretrial does not affect the overall frequency with which plaintiffs recover."

Supported: Plaintiffs recovered something in all but a small fraction of the cases, whether or not there was a pretrial.

(2) "Pretrial does not alter the amount plaintiffs recover in cases in which defendant has to pay something."

Not Supported: Pretrial did alter the amount of plaintiffs' recoveries, appreciably increasing the average and median amount.

(3) "Pretrial increases the probability that the jury will find on the liability issue in the way the judge thinks it ought to."

Not Supported: The judge and jury agreed on the liability issue in not-pretried cases as often as in pretried cases.

(4) "Pretrial increases the probability that the jury will make a damage award with which the judge agrees."

Not Supported: The probability of the judge's agreeing with the jury went down in pretried cases.

The "Judge" Factor

To discover from the statistical evidence what a pretrial conference does or does not do is only a part of the task of evaluating the procedure for effectiveness. Conducting a pretrial conference is far from an assembly line operation and no one has ever supposed that each judge performs it like every other. Therefore, another part of the evaluation job is to determine what difference the judge himself makes in the effectiveness of pretrial.

The "judge" factor has several aspects: his personality; what he conceives the conference to be for and what he perceives his own function to be; and what he actually does when confronted with specific choices or problems at a conference.

The test data showed that some judges scored very differently from others on the performance chart for settlements.[79] That finding only underlined what was obvious in any event, namely, that the judge himself may be a crucial variable among the factors influencing the effectiveness of pretrial. It was therefore an integral part of the study to learn as much as possible about how the judges approached their work and discharged their functions in conducting pretrial conferences.

V. NEW JERSEY JUDGES SPEAK THEIR MINDS ABOUT PRETRIAL CONFERENCE IN PERSONAL INJURY CASES[1]

AN analysis has been made and is reported here of attitudes, impressions, and opinions of New Jersey judges on the functioning of the pretrial conference procedure in personal injury cases, as expressed in small-group seminars lasting half a day each. The information comes from the record of comments made at a Judicial Seminar on Pretrial Conferences held at Princeton, New Jersey, on September 5-7, 1962. Although the transcript does not lend itself to quantitative analysis in the same way as other Project data on the New Jersey pretrial conference, it does afford a highly relevant and informative judge's-eye view of the pretrial procedure, often couched in vigorous terms. Whenever the transcript shows a consensus on a given point, the text so indicates.

Probably the most noteworthy observation on the entire seminar is the firm conclusion that the judges hold widely disparate opinions about nearly every important aspect of the pretrial conference, including its very purpose and their role in it. A clear need emerges for authoritative guidance on basic policy matters.

The comments of the judges, often in their own words, have been marshaled under several headings in this report. Only in a few cases is the author of a comment identified.[2]

At the Princeton meeting, experts on pretrials attended each of the seminar sessions and summarized their overall observations at the conclusion of the conference. These summaries proved helpful in the preparation of this report. Also very helpful was an analysis of the judges' reactions to an actual pretrial conference demonstration, conducted "live" during a general session of the meeting.

The major conclusion that emerged from a study of the transcript of the seminars are these:

1. The judges have widely disparate aims and purposes at pretrial conferences. They have equally divergent—sometimes antithetical—ideas of what the conference is basically for and how actively and forcefully they should conduct themselves at a pretrial.

2. Wide differences of view exist among the judges as to the formality that should prevail during conferences. They also vary in their methods of reducing the order to writing.

3. Some judges do not adhere to the rules in conducting pretrial conferences; they either consciously disregard them or are unfamiliar with their provisions.

4. Many of the judges believe pretrial works well; but most judges believe the procedure has serious shortcomings in practice. Nearly all of them blame lawyers for these failings. They particularly object to the lawyers' casualness about the procedure, citing as evidence of this the attorneys' alleged overall unpreparedness and noncompliance with the plain terms of the rules.

5. Also widely criticized is the current practice of scheduling three conferences an hour, a pace many judges regard as unreasonably rapid.

6. The judges are not agreed on how to remedy the flaws in the pretrial procedures. Some believe that discovery rules should be amended. Some think conferences exclusively aimed at settlement should be held; others that the conference should be held nearer trial.

1. WHAT A PRETRIAL CONFERENCE IS FOR, ACCORDING TO THE JUDGES

   (a) HOW FAR SHOULD JUDGES GO IN ACHIEVING SETTLEMENTS?

The most persistent ambiguity about this subject in New Jersey is whether pretrial should deliberately aim to promote settlements short of trial. Though the text of the rules is somewhat muddy on this question, a fair reading is that the draftsmen viewed settlement as a desired by-product, not a full-fledged main objective, of a pretrial conference. Most judges hold a different view, expressed by one judge in these words:

The pretrial purpose is to the greatest extent . . . to get all lawyers prepared, get all orders prepared, *so we can go into settlement conference.* [Emphasis added.]

An interesting side light is thrown on the subject by the judges' responses to the live conference. Ninety-two questionnaires were turned in with comment of some sort, of which 37 mentioned as a "helpful result achieved" some variant of settlement. It was considered helpful by 21 of these judges because, among other reasons, the conference manifested a disposition by the attorneys to settle. Remarks were made that settlement was "enhanced"; "encouraged"; "closer"; "examined"; and "helped." The conference also "got the parties a step closer"; "produced suggestions for settlement conference"; "indicated advisability of prompt settlement discussion"; and "prepared case for settlement discussion." The extent to which the judges are preoccupied with settlement is indicated by the fact that the number of answers mentioning settlement was second only to responses that mentioned definition or clarification of issues. Concern with the settlement aspect of the conference is also evidenced by the fact that more than one third of the judges commented critically on the failure of the judge presiding at the demonstration to set the case down for a settlement conference or to explore settlement further in that conference.

Assuming that settlement discussions will occur at the pretrial conference, what should the judge's role be? This is a divisive subject. Some New Jersey judges take the view: "If they ask me, I will give them an idea of what I think the case is worth." Others need no invitation and spontaneously "suggest a number," taking the attitude that "the judge should lead the whole process and should put a figure in." The opposing view is based on the argument that to suggest a figure violates the judge's obligation of detached objectivity. Many judges, whether or not they take the initiative in suggesting figures, agree that the judge's job in fostering settlement is "to keep tossing the ball between the lawyers" or "to keep the ball in play."

Another aspect of this issue is whether the judge should speak directly to the litigants themselves about settlement, and if so, under what circumstances. Some judges express the view that direct discussions with clients are "fraught with a lot of danger" and that "under no circumstances" will they converse with them. Other judges state that they do speak to clients, usually upon request, but "perhaps on our own initiative." One judge sees no harm in asking attorneys whether they object to the judge's seeing the client. To do so requires exercising "discretion," for example, refusing when "the verdict is going to be a big one," or obtaining a "character sketch" of the client in advance. Views are also divided on whether the judge should urge settlement to an insurance company representative. Several judges, including a consultant judge from California, favor having a reporter present, in order to protect themselves against charges of improper pressure. The opposite opinion is based on the view that speaking to a client about settlement with a reporter taking down the conversation amounts to "coercion."

In summary, to meet the delicate problems raised by settlement discussions with clients, varied practices are adopted by the judges. These range from refusing to hold such sessions to taking the initiative in calling them. When they are held, the judges also diverge greatly in the handling of the matter of preserving a record of the discussions, some insisting on making a full stenographic transcript, others excluding the reporter completely, and others preparing a record in court after the in-chambers discussion is at an end.

There were lively differences of view on whether once the case has reached trial, the judge should call settlement conferences at all, and if so whether they should be held immediately before the opening of trial or during it. Some judges "always" call them, for the basic reason that "people don't get ready to settle until the horses are in the starting gate." The contrary view is based on concern for the harmful "psychological effect" on the waiting jurors or for the loss of "untold manhours of time" as jurors sit by idle during the discussions. Justice John J. Francis is of the view that cases settle "without the waste of time in chambers." An Essex County judge reports that once the "special settlement conference" has failed, any further attempt at settlement should "take place among the lawyers" and "not in the courtroom."

A further problem is whether the same judge should try the case when he has taken part in unsuccessful settlement discussions. The discussion produced no clear consensus, but one panel apparently believed that the judge who hears the case discussed at a settlement session "if at all possible should not be the one to try it," because, as one comment put it, the judge finds himself in "not a very pleasant position."

The impression obtained by a reporter, Professor Delmar Karlen, of New York University School of Law, is that none of the judges seriously challenge the conclusions of the Project's study that as many cases settle without the New Jersey type conference as with them. Nonetheless, the judges seem to agree that they can and should help to settle cases, and the reporter detected no defeatist or negative attitude, or indications that settlement discussions are considered a waste of time. Professor Karlen perceived a widespread belief that a "settlement conference," differing from the traditional New Jersey conference in timing, participants, mode of operation, and place of occurrence, produces results. Such conferences presently take place throughout the state, but differ from county to county in various aspects. General opinion is that such conferences should take place on the eve of trial, when the case is believed ripe for settlement.

Professor Karlen reported a prevalent view that the judge should be someone other than the one who will preside at trial and that attorneys in attendance should be trial counsel. If defendant's attorney does not have authority to settle where an insurance company is involved, some judges believe the presence of an adjuster is desirable. While some judges hold the client should never be present, most contend he should be available for conversation if the judge thinks that will be useful.

The decisive factors in achieving settlement are said to be more subtle than splitting the difference between demand and offer or use of formulae such as those based on the amount of "specials," and depend instead upon intangibles like demeanor and personalities.

(b) DIFFERENCES OVER THE TRIAL-SHAPING ASPECT OF THE CONFERENCE

Since the pretrial conference's main purpose, both historically and contemporaneously, has been and remains the preparation of the case for an efficient, orderly, mistake-free, and surprise-free trial, the judges might be expected to agree that the basic responsibility rests upon them to see that a good pretrial order is prepared. They are in fact virtually unanimous that this is the object, but many do not agree on how to accomplish it, chiefly because they are sensitive to improper intrusion upon the adversarial nature of the litigation process and to criticism from the bar. One judge reported finding himself in a "very embarrassing situation" for suggesting issues the lawyer had failed to raise.

Although Chief Justice Weintraub declares that "part of the judge's job [is] to smell out legal questions" and many others see the function of trying to "even up the scales" where the "attorney is incompetent" as "ideal" for the judge, or at least proper, differences of attitude and of practice obviously persist.

(It would appear that there is no excuse for such divergences on a point of basic principle. A clear and authoritative statement by the Supreme Court, by way of amendment to the rules, seems called for.)

The cleavage in basic attitudes, illustrated by the question of the judge's raising new issues spontaneously, erupts in many other forms:

(1) Shall the judge probe for details when factual allegations are set forth only generally? Wide differences in viewpoint exist. One judge is of the view that his main contribution to the pretrial order is "tightening up and stating more clearly and succinctly the factual contentions" and "smoking out" the case. Similarly, a colleague insists on being "inquisitive" and on knowing the "odds and ends," such as presence of a traffic light or specific physical conditions; but another favors a certain amount of surprise, taking the view that attorneys should not be "pinned down" on such matters as exact distance in automobile cases.

In general, the greatest gulf relates to whether the factual contentions underlying a claim of negligence by either side must be specifically elaborated. But a substantial split exists on the desirability of detailing the extent of injuries and damages. Whereas Chief Justice Weintraub voiced the opinion that specifics are "important," other judges see no aid to the trial judge in an order "loaded with details of the extent of injuries." A prevalent practice is to incorporate particulars about damages in the order by referring to "damages as set forth in interrogatories." Others refer also to "depositions" in this boiler plate statement, but there is widespread opposition to this practice.

Comments about the live conference reflected analogous differences of viewpoint. Some judges praised the "thoroughness of factual contentions" or the "full disclosure of all relevant facts" which resulted in "a clear presentation of factual details." Others asserted that the factual contentions were too "lengthy," or too time-consuming and that "discovery should have done" the job.

(2) What of the judge's role with regard to seeing that legal issues are spelled out? Here, too, the familiar split develops. For example, in contract cases one judge insists on knowing the nature of the breach, whether a warranty is claimed, and similar details—all to the end of narrowing down the issue. Taking the opposite position, another judge maintains that in "all contract cases" he merely states the legal issue as "contractual liability of the party," for the very reason that this "omnibus" formula will cover anything.

Some judges indicate that when a statute is involved, they insist that the section relied on be specified.

It is noteworthy that the most frequently asserted helpful result of the live conference was that issues were defined, clarified, or settled. The conference was praised because "full discussion of the legal issues" took place and thus they were "clearly pointed up." Frequently the point was made that the conference "set forth the legal questions that had to be briefed," for example, the content of the "foreign" law of New York, pertaining to the owner's responsibility for negligent operation of a tractor trailer.

Ernest C. Friesen, Jr., Staff Director of the Joint Committee for the Effective Administration of Justice, reporter for this aspect of the seminar, was of the view that as the seminars progressed, the judges shifted away from the attitude that they should accept passively pretrial memoranda presented to them without trying to narrow the issues further.

(3) Apart from the question of specificity, shall the judge decide the validity of the defenses and rule out any deemed insufficient? There is a reported consensus—with dissents, of course. Some opine that the judge has no power to strike defenses—even if the defense clearly appears to be sham. Justice Francis declares that a defense should not be included in the pretrial order unless the attorney gives "the specific facts to support his claim." This position is supported by Chief Justice Weintraub. But other judges doubt either the desirability or authority for that requirement. A tactic reported by one judge is to use "ridicule" to secure withdrawal of unsupported defenses asserted in the answer, while another reports obtaining withdrawals without difficulty. A number of judges believe an allegation of contributory negligence should be permitted to remain even absent factual support, but that the defense may be limited by order to solely the evidence produced on cross-examination of the plaintiff's witnesses. Some hold the view that the proper solution to the problem is to direct that a motion for summary judgment be made, while several opine that the pretrial conference should itself be treated as a hearing for motions. Whenever a specific motion is required, an unsupported defense is abandoned, according to the comment.

(4) Shall the judge actively enforce the rule requiring the pretrial order to list the pleaded issues which have been abandoned? Although Rev. Rule 4:29–1 (b), paragraph 8, apparently so provides, disagreement exists as to its meaning and force. One judge traces the genesis of this paragraph to a state

Supreme Court decision holding in effect that a pretrial order's silence on some of the legal issues raised in the pleadings does not introduce an inconsistency with the pleadings—hence, the pleadings are not superseded as to those issues and they remain triable. He believes some litigants "took advantage" of the decision on appeals before the Appellate Division to raise questions that had not been specifically abandoned although they "didn't make much of it in the pre-trial order." Paragraph 8 was therefore promulgated "in order to prevent any such thing."

Judges have developed a routine practice of entering a mere notation under paragraph 8 that "all [issues are] abandoned except as set forth in 7" (which lists disputed issues). This procedure is said to produce controversy that can be avoided by specifically spelling out any issues that have been abandoned.

(5) To what extent shall sanctions be imposed for a lawyer's unpreparedness or noncompliance with the rules? There is the usual diversity of views, and this is despite the fact that a large majority of the judges agree that an attorney's misconduct seriously impairs the conference. Some judges indicate they disapprove of sanctions almost as a matter of principle, one saying he "never had an occasion" to impose them and another stating that he is "absolutely opposed" to them. The reluctance to impose sanctions apparently stems from a feeling of comradeship for the practicing bar. There is strong sentiment against any step that would harm an attorney in the eyes of his clients, one judge suggesting, "it would destroy the Bar." Another would not approve any sanction that would affect a lawyer's livelihood or embarrass him.

Even those who approve of sanctions differ greatly in the severity of the penalties they would impose and on the question of whether imposition should be automatic. Among those who would impose sanctions, severity varies from outright dismissal to bluster. One judge said he finds dismissal effective, but in the instance in mind he reinstated the case after giving the attorney "a rough time." Apparently there are isolated cases in which dismissal of the complaint or suppression of defenses has been enforced as a sanction.

Some judges preclude introduction of evidence by appropriate ruling in the pretrial order, but are uncertain whether the trial judge enforces the ruling. It is also suggested that unprepared cases be taken off the calendar and subjected to a special fee as a condition of restoration. A variant of this suggestion is to put the case at the bottom of the list.

One proposed sanction is a "pronouncement" that the judge would not "do business" with an attorney who fails to prepare for the pretrial conference. Numerous judges suggest that sanctions take the form of fines or fees and that these be payable to someone other than the opposing attorney, to prevent waivers by the adversary. Justice Francis suggests that it be paid into a fund for support of indigent defendants.

As indicated earlier those approving of sanctions differ on whether or not they should be "automatic." The opinion of one judge is that "uniformity" requires automatic sanctions, but there is opposition to the suggestion. A perhaps revealing comment is the observation that only about "half a dozen lawyers" are "a nuisance and a headache" and "we cut them up with threats which we never go through with."

2. Views on Proper Deportment and Mood in Conducting a Pretrial Conference; How Best to Draft the Pretrial Order; and the Effect of the Order

Each judge follows his own inclinations as to the degree of formality he requires at the conference. In general, the sentiment is that there is no one best practice, that it depends on the personality of the judge, but there are some opinions holding that all judges should conduct pretrial the same way.

Present practice runs the gamut from first-name informality and coffee-drinking to strict courtroom decorum. One judge said, "I do everything except put [my] feet up on the table. If lawyers want to take their coats off, smoke, anything I let them." At the other extreme are statements to the effect that "you have to sit as if you were sitting on the trial of a case and be firm." Some judges routinely sit in the witness box; in chambers; at a table, robed, or unrobed; or on the bench, with a robe. Some do not allow smoking, while others do.

Techniques also vary with regard to the mechanics the judge utilizes in setting the pretrial order down on paper. Not all judges follow the sequence prescribed in Rev. Rule 4:29–1 (b), some pursuing a course they deem more practical. Most frequently, when there is a departure from the format described by the rule, it is to skip from paragraph 1 to paragraph 4, then proceed to 9, 2, and 3, in that sequence.[3]

As to when the pretrial order should be dictated, several judges favor doing so in the presence of the attorneys before the conference's end so they may correct any errors that may have occurred during dictation.

Professor A. Leo Levin, of the University of Pennsylvania Law School, found among the judges heavy sentiment to have the pretrial order supersede the pleadings completely. Fears were expressed that in light of the pressure under which orders are prepared serious errors might result if this were the rule. On the other hand, some suggested it might lead to better-prepared memoranda and more serious acceptance of pretrial conferences by attorneys.

3. SPECIFIC PROVISIONS OF THE RULES GOVERNING PRETRIAL CONFERENCES ARE DISREGARDED BY, OR UNKNOWN TO, SOME OF THE JUDGES

Some judges say the present pretrial conference rules "are adequate to fulfill the needs;" that the trouble lies not in the rules but in some of the judges, who disregard or are ignorant of them.

Apparently the mandates of the rules are intentionally disregarded by a number of judges. The most frequent departures are in refusal to cut off discovery. The rules say discovery "shall be completed within 100 days of the date of service of the complaint" (Rev. Rule 4:28), and that "leave . . . to make any further use of discovery proceedings . . . [after pretrial] is undesirable and should be granted only in the most exceptional cases." (Rev. Rule 4:29–1 (b) (10)). In the face of this clear directive, further discovery is nevertheless "granted rather liberally." Sometimes attorneys are given "three or four days to get it in," or it may be permitted without time limit "providing it doesn't delay the trial." In support of the practice it is said "justice requires" extensions, especially where the original attorney fails to prepare properly and thereby handicaps the trial attorney called in at a later time.

Another example is with regard to transfers. The rule declares that "at the pretrial conference it shall first be determined if the case is to be transferred to the county district court . . ." (Rev. Rule 4:29–1 (b)), but it is the practice in one county not to "bother" with the determination in a jury case even when the attorneys admit the case is proper for transfer.

Rev. Rule 4:29–4 declares that "Not more than 3 pretrial conferences of cases shall be noticed for pretrial within the same hour before the same judge" but the rule is officially ignored in one county, where four pretrials an hour are scheduled for each judge.

One judge, prefacing his remarks with the comment that the rules provide that only factual contentions shall be included in paragraphs 2 and 3 of the order, admits to "never" restricting himself in such manner, but rather, includes legal contentions as well. There is a certain judge who when the attorneys assert that the case will be settled, loses interest, "give (s) the memorandum to the stenographer and he will knock out the whole pretrial order." Reports have come to the attention of one judge about a colleague who completed eight pretrial orders in chambers while the attorneys were required to wait and sign them outside, in violation of the prescription in Rev. Rule 4:29–1 (a) that the parties shall appear "for a conference in open court." A similar violation is reported by another judge. In that instance attorneys' memoranda were sent to the court by mail, given to the stenographer for preparation of the order, and returned, also by mail, for signature.

In a few instances unfamiliarity with the rules, or ignorance of them, came to light. There was warm praise for some counties which have adopted a requirement that a separate sheet itemizing damages be submitted as part of the pretrial memoranda. When the members of one seminar were reminded that such procedure was already unmistakably required under Rev. Rule 4:29–3, which provides for "a detailed statement as to damages," one judge observed, "I don't think any of us knew about it." At another seminar the reminder drew the comment that the practice is "not observed too thoroughly."

Other misconceptions included: the belief that the pretrial order supersedes the pleadings in all respects; the view that Rev. Rule 4:29–3 (b) requires clients to be present at the conference in all instances and the idea that it is permissible to attach copies of attorneys' memoranda to the pretrial order, a practice specifically prohibited by Supreme Court order.

4. JUDGES USUALLY ATTRIBUTE THE FLAWS IN THE PRETRIAL CONFERENCE TO ATTORNEYS' UNPREPAREDNESS AND THEIR EXCESSIVELY CASUAL ATTITUDE TOWARD THE REQUIREMENTS OF THE PRETRIAL RULES

A recurrent theme throughout the seminars is that cases are reaching the pretrial stage without having been adequately prepared by the attorneys. The general complaint is summed up as follows:

> Judges are being criticized because most of our pretrials are perfunctory, not effective. In talking with some of you [judges], the reason given is that lawyers are not prepared. . . .

There is virtual unanimity of opinion that attorney unpreparedness is a problem, but estimates of its extent range from 20 to 99.99 per cent.[4] This condemnation reaches impartially the prominent attorneys, as well as the less prestigious. The attorneys do not go completely undefended. Some judges express the view that "basically the boys are complying," or are doing so "in substance."

In the eyes of the judges, the attorneys' derelictions assume many forms: failure to complete discovery, to confer among themselves, to review the files in advance, to file meaningful memoranda, and to send qualified advocates to the conferences. Of all the judges' grievances against attorneys' pretrial practices, incomplete discovery is said to be "the greatest obstacle to a good pretrial conference." In the view of several judges "complete" discovery, or no less than "substantial completion" is an "essential" of effective pretrials. Yet even at the demonstration conference, where the participants were presumably on their mettle, the attorneys blandly conceded that discovery had not been completed. Only 3 of the 92 judges who observed and commented on the demonstration thought the incomplete discovery worthy of mention.

Another complaint directed against counsel is their failure to confer among themselves in preparation for the pretrial conference. The consensus is epitomized in one judge's observation that both in law and in chancery "most of them [attorneys] . . . do not have anything you call a conference." The attorneys' idea of the preliminary meeting was defined as speaking about the case while "walking into the courtroom or [on] the steps of the courthouse." One person at the seminar, not a judge, but considered to be highly qualified in the field, believes that in a series of sixteen cases he observed in pretrial conferences, counsel had conferred only "while they were waiting for pretrial that day." Several judges are of the opinion that part of the blame lies with the failure of Rev. Rule 4:29–3 to spell out what attorneys must do in the course of "conferring."

Attorneys are reproached for often complicating the judge's job by failing to review their files beforehand. A common sentiment is that attorneys perform "a more competent and complete job" and help the judges "immeasurably" when they take the time to go through the files in the office. But the practice of some attorneys is to obtain the file only as they leave for conference, and "half the time" the files contain information unknown to them. One judge complains that when they arrive they still "haven't pinpointed the issues" nor do they know which theory of law "they are going on."

Further criticisms arise from the failure of attorneys to submit pretrial memoranda in advance of the pretrial conference in accordance with judges' requests. When obtained beforehand, it is only "with a considerable amount of effort." In two counties the judges complain that memoranda are late in "half" the cases. Even when on time, some memoranda are meaningless because prepared "by the girls in the office." One judge declares he has become expert enough to tell which secretary had prepared the memorandum.

There is severe condemnation of the practice of sending "flunkies," who come to the conference only "to bring the pretrial memorandum and sign the pretrial order." Frequent instances are cited of young attorneys arriving with numerous files which they have not seen before that morning. Such an attorney, one judge says, "does not even know the names of the files, let alone what is in them." Another basis for criticism is that junior attorneys, even when they have knowledge, lack necessary authority: "Even if you had an effective, trained junior he would not have the authority of the principal to enter an effective order." Such attorneys frequently appear with instructions "not to change a letter" of the memorandum. Estimates of the percentage of cases in which juniors or other ineffective attorneys appear runs from 15 to 90 per cent. When one appears he has a "killing effect" on settlement, elimination of issues, or tightening of factual contentions. But it is not the solution for these difficulties according to Chief Justice Weintraub, to insist that only the trial lawyers appear at pretrial conferences, for this would "tie up the trial time in other counties."

One of the chief contributing factors to the unpreparedness and delinquency of the attorneys complained of by the judges may be that counsel are aided and abetted in their behavior by the judges and the rules. The general attitude when attorneys fail to comply is summed up in one judge's view of the situation: "We don't ask them and care less and don't impose any sanctions if they don't." In addition to shying away from the use of sanctions and making generous grants of post-conference discovery, the judges also seem to defeat their own purpose by too lenient an attitude at the conference. One judge admits that when faced with an uninformed and unauthorized attorney, he and "several others . . . look at the young fellow and bail him out." Having a general idea of the case, they "add a little bit" and "try to get something out of it even though he is not prepared." Another judge has also resigned himself to the fact that "most cases are pretried by juniors who don't know anything about the case . . . and don't have any authority . . . you might as well go through the motions of completing the pretrial and get it moving from that point on." Some judges openly admit that "we pretry them because we have to pretry them to get a case . . . but they are perfunctory pretrials."

5. THE CURRENT SCHEDULING OF PRETRIALS REQUIRES TOO HURRIED A CONFERENCE TO ATTAIN BENEFICIAL RESULTS

Although one county thinks it possible to hold four pretrial conferences per hour, and so provides by rule, a frequent complaint expressed by the judges is that holding three conferences each hour, "the pace at which you are supposed to move these things along, doesn't give you the time that you would like to give." Even if one of the three is not ready, the available time is still insufficient "to get counsel in the proper frame of mind." There isn't sufficient time to "explain and analyze"; "a lot" of judges see "implications of facts, legal issues, but . . . they just simply don't have the time to do it." The normal difficulties experienced with such a schedule are very often compounded for a judge when he receives additional cases originally assigned to a judge who becomes unavailable. Therefore, "most of the time" judges have at least fifteen or sixteen cases a day, which is "too much." Inasmuch as the required pace cannot be maintained in the opinion of one judge, he advises his brethren to "forget that . . . fifteen or twenty lawyers are waiting" and take as long as necessary.

At the seminar the demonstration conference lasted for almost an hour. Many judges commented unfavorably on the length and detail with which the pretrial judge set out the factual contentions—perhaps implying that so much time was not required. However, 3 of the 92 judges who commented thought more time was needed.

6. THE JUDGES' SUGGESTIONS FOR IMPROVING PRESENT PRETRIAL PROCEDURES

In part, the judges' ideas for improving pretrial have appeared in the preceding pages of this report of their discussions at Princeton. The purpose of this section is to organize those ideas and to add a few that have not been mentioned previously.

(a) HOLD SEPARATE "SETTLEMENT CONFERENCES"

Supporters of conferences devoted solely to settlement attempts consider them important in reducing trial congestion. One judge spoke of "doing away" with pretrial conferences, substituting settlement conferences in their place. Several counties already have them as adjuncts to the regular conference. One judge reports that in a county where settlement conferences may be had if requested by counsel, "practically all [those cases] are settled." Another says that "for the most part" effectiveness is dependent upon the defendant's wanting the conference. Others urged that some sort of court-determined selectivity might be the key.

(b) HOLD THE CONFERENCE NEARER THE DAY TRIAL IS TO BEGIN

Some judges urge that the conference will be more effective if it is held closer to trial. Those who believe in the trial-shaping function of the conference say that only immediately before trial is the case "ready," or at least, that admissions and stipulations will then be easier to obtain. Those who seek settlements maintain that "litigants are conditioned to listen to settlement [only] when the sword of Damocles is about to drop." Proponents of change say that timing the conference to occur when trial is "imminent" will help reduce the number of cases in which discovery is incomplete at the conference, a cause of "unproductive and perfunctory" pretrials.

(c) REQUIRE FILING AND EXCHANGE OF THE ATTORNEYS' MEMORANDA SEVERAL DAYS IN ADVANCE OF THE CONFERENCE

Filing of the attorneys' memoranda a few days in advance of the conference, a practice already in effect by local rule in several counties, is thought useful by many judges. In the absence of that requirement, "nine times out of ten" only an "abstract complaint and an answer" are on file, providing "no information" to the judge. Then, at the conference he must "wade through it all . . . with the lawyers breathing down his neck," "losing about three to five minutes." A memorandum filed prior to the conference date, although "hastily prepared" and arriving by messenger, gives the judge something to read "the night before." There is general agreement that a rule requiring memoranda "at least three days" before would "benefit" the judge, while a five-day requirement in one county permits "half" the pretrial order to be prepared in advance by the stenographer. If, in addition, counsel are required to exchange memoranda at the same time, "even if the court doesn't do anything," each lawyer has an opportunity to telephone his adversary to comment, and if a junior appears at the pretrial he may have instructions on how much more to divulge.

(d) CLARIFY AND ENFORCE THE REQUIREMENT THAT ATTORNEYS "CONFER"

The judges are in general agreement that it is "desirable" in the interest of more effective pretrials for attorneys to confer beforehand. But they urge that compliance with this requirement could be enforced only if "confer" as used in Rev. Rule 4:29–3 is defined to state exactly what the attorneys are intended to do.

(e) REVISE DISCOVERY PROCEDURES

Unanswered interrogatories cause a "breakdown" in "intelligent pretrial," and place a burden on the court and court calendar because the high incidence of non-response results in motions which account for "probably 80 to 90 per cent of the whole [motion calendar]." Similarly, "canned interrogatories" used by some "active" insurance carriers prove burdensome and oppressive. There was agreement that interrogatories practice is much abused and that a remedy is urgent, but no consensus on the problem's cause or solution was attained. Some cast the blame on the time limits imposed by the rules for compliance. For Justice William J. Brennan, Jr., of the United States Supreme Court, a draftsman and leading exponent of the New Jersey pretrial rules, the answer lies with the judge to make the rules work. One proposal would lengthen the initial period in which to furnish answers, and provide that only an application to court can enlarge the time to answer. An alternate plan, supported by Justice John J. Francis, would formulate standard interrogatories which could be supplemented only by leave of court.

(f) COURT COMMUNICATION TO LAW FIRMS WHO SEND INEFFECTIVE ATTORNEYS TO PRETRIAL CONFERENCES

The impairment of the conferences by the presence of inept counsel from some law firms might be alleviated by "taking it up" with a senior member, telling such firms the "facts of life," or by notifying the firm that it is considered to be a "problem firm." One of the guest judges reports his experience in California to be that a "remarkable . . . change of attitude" occurs when he personally contacts some of the heads of firms to discuss the problem.

CONCLUSION

Except for the first suggestion listed above—to hold settlement conferences—the judges' ideas for improvements in pretrial procedures are directed at mechanics. No doubt mechanical improvements are welcome. Yet, if the summary of the teachings of the Princeton seminars set out at the beginning of this chapter is substantially correct, is not more needed than mechanical overhaul? If some of the judges on the pretrial bench are in doubt as to the very purpose of the conference and their proper function in it, should not this confusion be ended?

So it seems to us. We believe that the Supreme Court should resolve the questions of fundamental policy that are still wide open in several vital sectors of pretrial, and should lay down the clearest possible guidelines for the trial judges. If there are choices the Supreme Court believes are too narrow or difficult to make at this time, it should make known that these matters are discretionary with the trial judges. Surely it will not avail to tinker with the machinery of pretrial instead of coming to grips with basic issues.

VI. CLINICAL VIEWS OF THE NEW JERSEY PRETRIAL IN ACTION

AS A counterpoint to the judges' and attorneys' views on pretrial procedures drawn from the questionnaires and the judges' seminars at Princeton, the Project collected systematic impressions of disinterested observers who sat in on scores of "live" pretrial conferences. The primary concern in this facet of the study was to determine what picture an onlooker gets of the ordinary pretrial conference in New Jersey—what the judges do and how they do it.

Taken together, the impressions sketched by the observers' reports portray wide diversity, despite occasional threads of similarity. Objectives appeared to vary; the judges' actions differed from one court to another; and even a given judge changed his approach from conference to conference, or sometimes within a single conference. There was not any discernible correlation between what the judges did and how they did it in the observed cases and how well or poorly they scored in settlements in the test cases.

How the Observations Were Made

Serving as observers were staff attorneys and top law students who were familiar with the claims made for the pretrial conference but who were uncommitted as to its efficacy. It was thought that as outsiders they could approach the task with detachment, observing clinically and without preconceived attitudes the way various judges, some especially selected for observation, conducted pretrial. They monitored 105 conferences, which were conducted in normal fashion—save for whatever variations in judges' or attorneys' behavior may have resulted because of the observers' presence. In selecting the cases observed, no systematic sampling techniques were utilized, no case was chosen in preference over another, and observations were not even restricted to personal injury cases. Although the lack of statistical controls prohibited generalization from the cases observed, or even as to any particular class of cases, this method offered a valuable opportunity to gain some insight into attitudes and achievements in a wide variety of actions. Some of the conferences dealt with negligence claims (most of which were motor vehicle accidents). Many of the remaining cases were actions in contract, but also observed were pretrials in an action for malicious interference with the marital relationship and to declare a state statute unconstitutional.

All seven of the counties participating in the controlled test were observed. Eighteen judges presided—the one most frequently on fourteen occasions, two others at twelve conferences, and three at only one each. Some judges were deliberately picked for observation in an effort to learn whether their known settlement records would be reflected in the way they managed their pretrials. In the controlled test some of these judges had scored highest, some lowest, and others in the middle when the settlement percentages of their test cases were tabulated. These eighteen judges accounted for 67 per cent of all completed questionnaires received from the fifty-two judges who participated in the primary study.

The research design of this substudy called for two separate sets of observations, conducted two years apart and utilizing different techniques. It turned out that the findings derived from the sets of observations were very similar.

The first series of observation was conducted in March, April, and June of 1960 and not only furnished a flesh-and-blood picture of pretrial's operation in the forty-three cases viewed, but served as a pilot study, sharpening the research tools for use in the subsequent observations. Observer forms A and B (copies of which are included in Appendix C), were the forms used in the 1960 conferences. For each conference the observer completed one Form A. After each member of the Project staff had observed all his assigned conferences he completed one Form B, comparing the conferences, and where applicable, the judges.

In June and July, 1962, the balance of the cases—sixty-two in number—were observed. A single instrument (Observer Form C, a copy of which is included in Appendix C) replaced the two used earlier, and required the observers to look for and comment on specific aspects of the conference, instead of soliciting general impressions, as in 1960. As a check against individual bias two observers viewed each conference and submitted separate reports without consulting one another. Comparison of the reports showed a high degree of correlation.[1]

Common Aspects of the Judges' Performance

As we have seen, the New Jersey pretrial conference rule not only sets forth the subjects that may be considered at the conference but also requires that a pretrial order be made in every case that is not disposed of by transfer or settlement at the conference. The coverage of the order is specified in detail. In varying ways and with differing efforts the judges produced what the rules required: a pretrial order covering the prescribed subjects.

Moreover, it was uniformly reported that regardless of variations in approach or conduct of the conference, every judge remained in control of the proceeding. Even the judge who presided at what observers called "casual" conferences indicated his displeasure at the use of his first name by an attorney. Occasionally attorneys not participating in the case under consideration broke in to consult participating attorneys. Once, counsel for an improperly served defendant intruded in a conference that was in progress.

Uniform too was the reluctance with which the judges applied sanctions. Judges, perhaps out of camaraderie, were consistently lenient when discovery was not completed, when clients were not available by telephone, and even when attorneys did not appear.

Yet the judges' general adherence to the dictates of the rules, their uniform exercise of control and their typical disinclination to penalize errors and omissions by members of the bar, did not dim the strong sense that conducting a pretrial conference was very much an individual procedure.

Varying Objectives

The pretrial rules and the manual that describes their use are not unequivocal as to the objectives of the conference. And the observers reported that the judges were not uniform in the goals they tried to achieve at the conference. Some conferences were clearly oriented toward preparing the case for trial; some toward achieving settlements; and some were hybrid in their orientation, meaning that substantial effort was devoted both to disposing of the case before trial and also to preparing it for trial. A sense of the variations—as well as an impression of the nature of the proceedings—can be obtained from a few actual examples.

In example No. 1, a trial preparation conference, a lady sued for injuries allegedly sustained when she was struck by a bus from which she had just alighted. The twenty-minute conference began with the judge's reading of the pretrial memoranda. He then requested that counsel stipulate the exact location and time of the accident. Plaintiff's counsel gave his version of the facts, and defendant's attorney admitted operation and agency. Despite the judge's urging, plaintiff's attorney refused to admit that plaintiff was not technically a passenger; the judge requested briefs on the point. Then, over defense counsel's objection, the judge removed the issue of assumption of risk from the case. Finally, with occasional comments and clarifications from counsel, the judge dictated a pretrial order. Settlement was not discussed.

In example No. 2, a two-car collision suit, the conference was oriented toward settlement, with no attempt at obtaining stipulations, little discussion of the facts of the case, no disclosure of evidence, and no analysis of legal questions. The judge read the memoranda, asked the attorneys for the replies to interrogatories and for the doctor's bills. Then he calculated the "specials" and announced that the total was $555. He suggested that the case be settled, warning that failure to settle would result in transfer on the ground that it was unlikely the recovery would be more than $3,000.[2] Defendant's counsel offered $1,250, the judge asked plaintiff's counsel if he would take $1,500, and at this figure the case settled. No pretrial order was prepared.

Example No. 3, a "hybrid" conference, involved an action to recover for personal injuries sustained by a pedestrian struck by a motorcycle that had jumped the curb. This case had been previously pretried but required an additional conference because the defendant had completely changed his story. The judge seemed familiar with the case and merely asked the attorneys to state their legal theories. After discussing and explaining the relevant law, he prevailed on defendant's counsel to drop the defense of contributory negligence and his cross-claim. Routine stipulations were made. Then the judge requested legal memoranda on the disputed issue of agency and the potential problem of admissibility in evidence of testimony given in the Magistrates' Court. He next considered with counsel the prospects of settlement. The judge acknowledged there was a problem because the defendants were judgment proof, suggested recourse to the Unsatisfied Judgment Fund as a remedy, and apparently endorsed as satisfactory a figure proposed by the plaintiff's attorney. Counsel agreed to continue to explore settlement. A pretrial order was made.

Inconstancy

Observation of individual judges revealed that they were inconstant from case to case or even from step to step in a single conference. It often occurred that a judge was observed in one conference trying seriously to draw out the fact allegations, clarify the law, and foster agreement between the attorneys; while at another he was inert, and made no attempt to pierce the perfunctory statements tendered by counsel. Even in the same conference, the judge was reported as "active" in one aspect and "passive" in another.

Judge A illustrates how inconstant the judges often were from case to case. At one conference he was confronted with pretrial memoranda he thought were inadequate, yet he refused to listen as one of the attorneys tried to amplify. At another conference the judge patiently and painstakingly assisted plaintiff's counsel in spelling out specific factual contentions which underlay the claim.

Fluctuations of a judge within a particular conference demonstrate the difficulty of classifying the attitude of a particular judge. For example, a judge who was so determined to learn the facts that he snatched a client's letter out of counsel's hand, failed to seek any particulars of allegations that the parties were proceeding at "slow" or "excessive" speeds. In a conference in a dental malpractice case the same judge insisted that the attorney call his client to learn whether his asserted injury was to the upper or to the lower jaw but made no attempt to determine the number of expert witnesses to be

VIEWS OF PRETRIAL IN ACTION

called or to ascertain the substance of their testimony. Another judge, who presided at the conference in a two-car collision case, insisted plaintiff particularize his claim of negligence but made no effort to determine what defendant meant by the allegation that he was driving in a "reasonable and prudent manner."

Diversity

The most striking observation was how widely the judges differed among themselves in the methods and techniques they used, as well as in their aims at the conference. The diversities appear in such activities as how they administered their conferences, what they did in preparing the cases for trial, and in settling or transferring the cases.

1. administration of the conference

Preparation for the conference was not uniform. Some judges appeared to learn of the case only as the details unfolded during the conference; others appeared to have done "homework" in some but not all of their conferences. Variations abounded with regard to how formally they presided. Only one judge conducted his conferences in chambers. A number of judges held conferences around the counsel table, often in mufti instead of black robe; bantered with counsel; and permitted smoking. Other judges preserved courtroom decorum, including announcement of their arrival by the bailiff's "All rise!"

Furthermore, the mechanics involved in setting the order down on paper also varied according to the predilection of the judge presiding. Frequently an order was prepared by simply dictating the contents of the attorneys' memoranda to the court stenographer with, at most, insignificant changes. Other orders took form in the judge's own language after he had carefully read the memoranda and questioned counsel. Two judges handed the attorneys' memoranda to the stenographer, who then typed the order from them.

2. PREPARATION OF THE CASE FOR TRIAL

A pervasive problem was the need to get concrete assertions in place of the vague generalties in the pleadings. Judges differed in the degree to which they insisted on clear, accurate statements of the factual details to support the legal contentions.

In a personal injury motor vehicle case the judge carefully established that the injuries were sustained when plaintiff's hand was caught in a car door, obtained precise information as to the number of doors on the vehicle, the side from which plaintiff exited and the location of the car. In a pedestrian knockdown case he insisted that the defense of contributory negligence be spelled out, so that it became clear that defendant was claiming plaintiff had seen the car.

On the other hand, another judge seldom went beyond the attorneys' memoranda and halted any line of inquiry when the attorney was not responsive. In the case in which plaintiff was attacking the constitutionality of a statute, the judge did not adjourn the conference for unpreparedness of the attorneys but made an order that contained no sign of an attempt to reveal the grounds for the attack.

The problem of uncovering legal issues was twofold—to bring forth issues not raised by counsel and to eliminate extraneous or untenable theories. Judges varied as to how far they went in their efforts to make legal rulings, to advise attorneys on the merits, and to suggest legal theories.

One judge radically reshaped the whole legal issue from a claim for negligence to one in contract for declaratory relief, adding the issues of waiver and estoppel. Sometimes the judges ruled that legal theories be removed; at times they merely suggested it. One judge advised plaintiff to withdraw an allegation of "wilfulness" to forestall denial of coverage by an insurance company; another struck the defense of "assumption of risk"; another the defense of "unavoidable accident." One discussed the relevant law and persuaded defendant to withdraw his cross-claim. In other instances judges suggested additional issues and ruled against proposed amendments to claims.

On the other hand some judges appeared content to let legal issues remain as set forth in the pleadings. One judge included in the pretrial order the defense of contributory negligence despite his expressed opinion that under the circumstances of the case it had no meaning; and another, who commented that he didn't know of what the alleged "contributory negligence" consisted, allowed the defense to stand without attempting to discuss it.

Judges seemed to discourage the use of the conference as a forum for "poor man's discovery." One judge commented that not by pretrial but by interrogatories should a litigant learn witnesses' names. Another denied a request for information regarding policy limits of an insurance contract with a statement that discovery was the proper way to uncover that information. Rarely was the conference used as a place for encouraging counsel to disclose evidence, obtain documents, discuss witnesses, or obtain admissions and stipulations; but where these elements came to the fore they too showed diversity.

Few of numerous opportunities to mark documents were taken. One order stated, after a mild attempt by the judge to mark this essential document, that the lease "will be produced at trial." At the conference for a case in which plaintiff sought money for work, labor, and services the judge readily acquiesced in counsel's request that a pertinent release not be marked until trial. However some judges did mark contracts, promissory notes, and photographs of damaged vehicles.

Stipulations were infrequent, though one judge insisted that the location of a key stop sign be stipulated and waited for counsel to search their files to find a basis for agreement. Another judge obtained a stipulation that plaintiff was an invitee. But still another permitted a defendant to turn aside his request that counsel agree on plaintiff's status at the time of the accident.

Admissions pertaining to ownership and operation of the vehicle were rather common but efforts to go beyond these routine areas of agreement were less frequent and less successful.

3. DISPOSITION OF THE CASE

Techniques and approaches differed among those who sought to produce settlements and among those who determined that cases should be transferred.

Settlement, as we have noted, was often an important purpose of the conference and sometimes its sole objective. Some judges were militant in their efforts to bring the parties together, while others adopted a more casual air. One judge, who opined that the case under discussion did not belong at trial, insisted that counsel "talk settlement." Another threatened transfer to the district court unless the case was settled. At some conferences judges suggested specific figures for compromise, at some they conferred with counsel in chambers, and at others only made tentative inquiries about the possibility of settlement.

The criteria for determining the suitability of a case for removal to a lower court did not emerge clearly, in part because the order was often entered without discussion.[3] However, observers did report that transfer occurred when the special damages were only $125, when a medical report showed only contusions and abrasions, and when only $20 out of a $1,620 special damage claim was for medical expenses, the rest being for property damage. In contrast to these cases, where potential damages seemed to be the essential consideration, one judge ordered transfer after plaintiff's attorney, in response to the judge's question, stated he would accept $2,500 in settlement rather than his initial request of $3,000.

The Judges' Performance Evaluated

The test findings clearly showed that among the judges there was a differential capacity for settling cases—as high as 85 per cent of the cases pretried by one judge settled before trial, while as few as 64 per cent of the cases pretried by another judge settled before trial. To determine whether there were any readily identifiable correlates between success in achieving settlements and observable actions at pretrial, the reports of observers on the "high settlers" were scrutinized with special attention. No correlation was apparent between high settlement rates and pretrial conference practices. For example, Judge X had the highest percentage of settlements before trial of any judge in the test, but observers found that he conducted the pretrial conference in an unenthusiastic manner; dictated the order from the submitted memoranda with little or no discussion of salient points; and never pressed an attorney who was hesitant to reveal the evidence underlying legal contentions. By contrast, another "high settler" was portrayed as "active." He made dispositive legal rulings, probed to find out the specific facts of the claim, marked documents in evidence when appropriate, requested that briefs be filed on troublesome legal issues, asked attorneys for settlement figures, commented on them, and on occasion, took attorneys into chambers for additional settlement talks.

That a judge who actively participated in the pretrial conference scored no higher in settlement performance than a judge who made no apparent attempt to mold the course of trials or to dispose of the cases before they reached the courtroom tends to confirm the impression that the conduct of the conference is a highly personal procedure. It underlines the difficulty of trying to evolve prescriptions and categorical dos and don'ts for effective pretrial.

The statistical data showed that the pretrial conference does not affect the settlement potential of cases in gross. These nonstatistical observations demonstrate how elusive and difficult to isolate are the factors that tend in any degree to promote settlements in specific cases.

Impressions and Conclusions

Judges vary enormously in their performance. A judge running a particular conference may disclose an activist philosophy toward the function he serves in the proceeding or take a passive role with respect to some or all of the issues. He may vary from issue to issue, sometimes involving himself very forcefully, sometimes accepting whatever the attorneys have revealed or left undisclosed. It is difficult to classify a judge as consistently active or consistently passive on most aspects of his work because he changes from case to case and even from issue to issue.

Thus, it is difficult to find or construct a "typical" pretrial conference in New Jersey. At best it is possible to state only generally that as actually conducted conferences seem aimed at settlement, trial preparation, or both; are controlled and molded by the judge who handles details in his own style, but is like his brothers in being hesitant to impose sanctions and in predictably producing a pretrial order unless the case is actually disposed of at the conference. When settlement is a factor, a variety of techniques are used, and when trial preparation is a factor the same is true. The emphasis seems to be on reducing abstractions and molding the legal issues rather than on disclosure of evidence, discussion of witnesses, and the like. But the most accurate statement remains that guiding a pretrial conference is a personal procedure with the judge.

Judges vary not only in performance but also in the results they achieve. Yet the relationship between performance and result does not clearly register to an observer. A seemingly forceful judge and an apparently inactive one rate nearly equal in settlement and achievement, above all their colleagues. While it is clear that differing capacities exist, the elements of the difference are obscure and elusive.

In the end, the major lesson from observing scores of "live" pretrial conferences is to underline that conducting these proceedings calls for marked judicial artistry. Intangible factors, deep in the personalities, predilections, and philosophies of the judges and lawyers, combine with the special vagaries of the case to affect the course of the conference and of the entire litigation. To improve a judge's conduct of the conference, general exhortations to the judges to "be more effective" are not enough. Even specific check lists, cataloguing dos and don'ts, are of very limited use, since what works for one judge seems not to work for another.

The search for the elusive keys to better pretrial conferences must continue. If it turns out that the judge's personal characteristics are nearly the whole story, perhaps the answer will be to assign only the judges who are gifted in this type of work or to recruit judges or auxiliary judicial personnel thought to be especially well qualified by personality to conduct pretrial conferences. It may be that to some extent pretrial artistry can be learned or transmitted. Self-improvement may be aided also if the Supreme Court will lay down authoritative guidelines on the broad questions that require policy pronouncements; and if efforts by the judges at self-education in the conduct of pretrial conferences in the manner of the seminars at Princeton in September, 1962, continue on an earnest footing.

VII. TECHNIQUES AND "ARTISTRY" IN PRETRIAL

OF ALL the variables that bear on how a pretrial conference runs and what it achieves, the key factor is the judge himself—what he is, what he does, and how he does it. Since the judge's personal qualities are the least likely elements to yield to change, attention has focused instead upon improving his techniques. In scores of seminars for trial judges conducted across the country in the past three years, a prominent feature of the program regularly has been "judicial techniques" in pretrial conferences. Many experts on pretrial share the belief that certain techniques are especially effective to assure a successful conference, and that these should be diligently applied. For that reason it was a natural part of this research effort to attempt to isolate particular techniques and to determine how they work in New Jersey negligence cases, and in general.

This problem involved work in the library as well as in the field. A methodical combing of the mountainous literature on pretrial revealed that relatively few authorities have addressed themselves to the question of what the pretrial judge should do—*specifically*—to make the conference an effective one. One can only speculate on why the bookshelves are so short on the specifics of good pretrial and so long on generalities. The answer perhaps lies in the fact that the impetus for the pretrial movement came from a provision of utmost generality, Federal Rule 16. The draftsmen of that rule, Judge J. Skelly Wright has observed, spoke in general terms because they desired to preserve flexibility in how the conference was managed,

so that it could be made to conform to the personality if not the eccentricity, of the judge who is to use it. And a good judge will make the procedure conform to some extent at least to the personalities of the lawyers who participate.[1]

Whatever its origin, it is clear that the prevalent view today is that in pretrial "there are as many . . . different techniques . . . as there are judges or lawyers,"[2] and that only the broadest generalities evoke a consensus among the experts. For example, leading spokesmen normally assert that for run-of-the-mill cases: pretrial is the "best friend the trial judge will ever have";[3] its chief function is to prepare the case for trial;[4] settlement is often a by-product;[5] but should not be forced;[6] court and counsel should prepare in advance;[7] and the conference should be held close to the date for trial.[8]

Of the infrequent published efforts to specify in detail what the pretrial judge should do, one of the earliest was by United States District Court Judge Alexander Holtzoff, who in 1952 presented a series of detailed and explicit suggestions about how a judge ought to "actively" manage a pretrial conference, and urged that he take the initiative.[9] One of the most comprehensive was Judge William K. Thomas' in Ohio in 1956.[10] Conceding that "not every judge likes or is suited for pretrial,"[11] he urged that there be "fundamental uniformity in the essential elements"[12] of each conference regardless of variations among judges; and that there be a "planned order of discussion" in which the judge served as "an active though impartial interrogator" in order to develop the issues and encourage agreement on all possible points.[13] He set out concrete examples in particular types of cases and presented a series of check lists.[14]

Building on the earlier efforts, a volume entitled *California Pretrial and Settlement Procedures* appeared in 1963. It heavily accents the specific, setting out detailed check lists for both the pretrial judge and counsel.[15] While "flexibility" is the "cardinal principle,"[16] the authors insist that among the "musts" for the pretrial judge are that he "pierce counsel's verbalisms" to uncover details that frequently are hidden in them,[17] that he "pinpoint the exact factual contentions," eliminate "spurious" defenses asserted merely to put plaintiff to his proof,[18] and assume the "initiative."[19] A word-for-word illustration of a successful maneuver to overcome counsel's resistance to specificity is also included.[20]

In addition to the published literature, an important source of information on what the judges should do at pretrial came from the program of direct observation of "live" pretrial conferences reported in detail in Chapter VI and resketched only briefly at this point. As was explained there, the observers tried to identify the techniques actually in use among New Jersey judges and to correlate the judges' variations in performance with statistically developed differences in their effectiveness. They made a preliminary set of observations in the spring of 1960 while the test cases were in the controlled pretrial process, and a final series occurred in 1962. Staff attorneys and top-ranking law students did the observing, recording the results in accordance with check lists or questionnaires. In all, the observers monitored 105 conferences presided over by 18 judges. The cases they saw were run-of-the-calendar, with no effort to confine them to personal injury actions. It turned out that nearly two thirds were negligence suits and that the others were mainly contract actions.

It was earlier noted that while the observations were not derived by rigorously designed sampling procedures and do not qualify as scientific survey findings, they provide interesting glimpses of how selected New Jersey judges performed at pretrial conferences. Mainly they demonstrated how widely the pretrial judges vary in their approach to their roles and functions, and in their techniques of administering the conference, preparing the pretrial order or enforcing compliance with the rules.

The observers discovered neither a "typical" conference nor a "typical" judge. Variations ranged from mechanical matters (such as whether the judge sat on the bench in robes or mingled informally with the attorneys and whether he had read the suit papers and pretrial memoranda prior to the conference) to broad issues such as whether he took an active or passive role in obtaining stipulations of fact, reducing issues for trial, and formulating questions precisely; whether he insisted that attorneys obey the pretrial rules to the point of imposing sanctions; and whether he raised and pressed the subject of settlement. There was no discernible correlation between the judges' record of effectiveness in the test cases and the techniques reported by the on-the-spot observers in the cases they monitored. Judges with similar performance records not only did not act like one another; a given judge acted differently at successive conferences or even on successive issues in the same conference.

The Princeton seminars on pretrial for New Jersey judges on September 5-7, 1962, produced further evidence that the judges vary enormously in how they conduct a pretrial conference.[21] Some are vigorous and severe; some are laissez-faire and informal. Some will speak to the clients, others refuse to. All along the line, the judges make individual choices of action or inaction; and if they decide to act they choose a way of acting that accords with their basic philosophies about pretrial and also with their personal style, temperament, and mood.

All this evidence of inconsistency and subjectivity on the judges' part dims the prospect of finding pivotal factors in pretrial aside from the human equation. While conducting pretrial was known at the start to be far removed from mere mechanical exercises like writing entries in a docket book or making out a sales check in a shoe store, it turned out to be, even more than suspected, "a very personal procedure."[22] Pretrial emerges as a procedure only slightly amenable to fixed routine and prescribed agenda.

These observations were made carefully and systematically, yet they did not serve to identify any consistently effective technique. Their unproductive outcome suggests that it is unlikely that the pretrial techniques that spell successful results can be discerned by observers and correlated generally or predictively to performance. In turn, the lack of correlation between what judges do and how well they do it supports the view that an effective pretrial conference is a function of artistry more than routine, or at least that there are variables at work that we have not been able to isolate.

It is unrealistic to expect to find across-the-board solutions or sure-fire dos and don'ts in an area that abounds in so many intangible factors, human variables, and complex legal and psychological elements. But the fact that pretrial's effectiveness is so largely dependent on the judges' personal artistry does not lead to the conclusion that nothing else makes any difference, or that it is useless to try to help judges improve their pretrial techniques..

There appear to be two steps in a soundly conceived program to help the judges improve their conduct of pretrial conferences. The first step is to assure that the objectives and aims of pretrial are stated clearly and explicitly. To achieve this the rule-making authorities must resolve some of the major issues surrounding pretrial in negligence cases and must state their conclusions in such clear terms that the pretrial judges will have no doubt what is expected of them.

A directive that says no more than that a pretrial judge must strive at the conference to prepare the case to promote a "just result," "obtain a settlement," or insure a "fair trial"

TECHNIQUES, "ARTISTRY" IN PRETRIAL 111

obviously gives him little guidance. The first line of assistance to the trial judge is for the rule-makers to resolve the basic issues of policy that constantly arise in the conduct of pretrial conferences. Among these are:

(1) whether a deliberate purpose of the conference is to bring about settlement, or whether the pretrial judges are to confine themselves to preparing the case for a well-conducted trial;
(2) whether the judge is obliged to be an active principal, and if necessary, to initiate inquiries, raise questions, and require actions by the attorneys on subjects covered by the pretrial rules, or whether he is to function as a passive referee;
(3) whether in the absence of a party's formal application, given to the adversary on timely notice and with a chance to oppose, the judge is empowered to make orders striking claims or defenses as unfounded or unsupported;
(4) whether the judge is obliged to compel disclosure of theories and evidence and to place limits on the scope of proof at the trial under pain of sanctions provided for in the rules; and
(5) whether any sanctions are to apply automatically if prescribed conditions are satisfied, or whether all sanctions are to be discretionary.

If feasible, the rule-makers should offer illustrations of how the announced principles might work in specific situations. "A Statement of Pretrial Principles," which is in Chapter VIII, suggests how this might be done.

A second step in assisting the pretrial judge to a proper concept of his function is to provide a guide to commonly encountered issues and problems. Its aim would be to stimulate the judge to devise by creative thought the most apt techniques to deal with particular questions arising before him.

The guide might be called "The Judge at Pretrial" and its accent would be on inspiring his thoughtful involvement in the conference, not on automating him. For that reason it should not be presented as a check list of dos and don'ts, full of tedious details in no way relevant to the case at hand. The automatic check list has two failings, the first being to stifle the judge's creative interest in the case before him and the second being to give him a false sense of the effectiveness of merely covering and checking off items on a list.[23]

Proposed here is a guide that would not pretend to "guarantee" good results. It would be suggestive rather than imperative and would make clear to the judge that *his* contribution would be the crucial factor in whether the pretrial achieved anything. The guide, in short, would credit the judge with responsibility and ingenuity, and would not pretend to admonish what he should *always* do or *never* do in conducting a conference. Also set forth in Chapter VIII as a guide is a suggested version of "The Judge at Pretrial." It is based upon certain assumptions regarding the policies and purposes that pretrial ought to serve in personal injury suits. To the extent that a state has different objectives in view and reaches different conclusions about basic questions of policy, the issues requiring consideration will vary and so should the guide.

VIII. A PRETRIAL CONFERENCE PROGRAM FOR PERSONAL INJURY CASES

ANY procedure that saddles litigation with added costs in time, effort, and inevitably, money has the burden of showing that it yields more than it costs. The pretrial conference is no exception to that rule.[1] If soundness in theory could discharge the burden of proof, pretrial would easily make the showing, satisfying all its critics save those who are hypersensitive about damage to the adversary tradition. But ideal theory is not the only test, and the fact that pretrial indisputably looks good on paper does not mean that it assuredly works well in the courtroom. In this study the effort has been to learn how much of value pretrial actually yields in practice, and primarily how well it does in gaining either or both of its major objectives—to improve the quality of the trial process, and to enhance the efficiency of court operations.

It is an article of faith with pretrial's supporters that a pretrial conference achieves both goals at once. Implicit in that conviction is the assumption that if a conference has done all it should to prepare the case for a good trial it will *ipso facto* have cultivated the ground for settlement. The idea that a proper pretrial conference is a two-in-one exercise is a meretricious yet tenacious one. It loses its attractiveness when examined closely in the light of the actual steps that should logically be taken for each of the purposes in question.

If one were to give names to the steps designed to achieve each purpose, one might say that the activities at pretrial that are calculated to promote a good quality litigation process by mapping the course of the proceedings en route to the trial courtroom and inside it are "trial oriented."[2] Those mainly aimed at fostering efficiency by inducing compromise short of trial are "settlement oriented." It seems to us that each object calls for various sorts of actions by the judge and lawyers involved, that some of the actions are identical for both purposes but some are not, and that this means a single conference will not automatically do double duty. In large measure this is because there will be a change in what issues are relevant as the object of the conference changes. But even in dealing with the same issue or subject matter a judge might proceed by widely divergent paths depending on whether his object is to shape the case for trial or to ease its settlement. Let us look at the specifics of a personal injury pretrial.

In an accident case there are a half-dozen subjects that plainly ought to be treated whether the aim of the conference is to promote trial quality or to improve the chances for settlement. The nature of the action must be outlined. Factual contentions of each side as to how the accident happened should be explored for their bearing on issues of liability. The judge should try to draw from the attorneys any admissions and stipulations they will agree to. The plaintiff ought to make known what injuries and money damages he claims, and the defendant ought to make known his responses to the claims. Before the conference is over the lawyers should specify which, if any, law questions are still open for determination and state which have been abandoned.

Each of those items is important to understanding what the case is about and what is in dispute. Each seems indispensable, whatever the objective of the conference, and they can therefore be called "common" subjects or items.

Even so, wide variations are possible in the way in which the conference might endeavor to develop a common subject. For example, while in either event the judge ought to encourage a precise definition of the issues that are open, in a settlement conference it is not vital for the judge to make a decisive ruling that a particular question is an issue for trial; whereas he ought to do exactly that in a trial-oriented proceeding. Again, a settlement conference would be little concerned with having the attorneys prepare beforehand meticulous written statements as to their admissions, but a trial-oriented proceeding insists on it. In general, admissions, statements, and positions at a settlement conference can be tentative or hypothetical; but at a trial conference they must be exact and definitive. Thus, the end in view will shape the treatment of the subject matter.

Moreover, a trial-oriented conference when carefully conducted will include many steps that would have no place in a settlement conference. The court should insist that each side tender a precise formulation of its factual contentions, including the specific respect in which the plaintiff claims the defendant was negligent or in which the defendant claims the plaintiff was contributorily negligent. The pleadings should, if necessary, be formally amended to add, drop, or modify allegations to reflect the litigants' current posture. Legal issues remaining open should be formulated word-for-word, to leave no ambiguities as to the parties' positions, much as if the judge were devising instructions for the jury. The same care should feature the reduction of stipulations to writing. Exhibits should be marked in evidence when this can be done appropriately. Quite exact plans for trial should be made, including if possible setting a day, estimating its length, directing exchange of needed briefs, limiting the number of witnesses, and providing, in the case of experts, for advance exchange of summaries of their testimony. In a proper case, the judge should make dispositive rulings as, for instance, striking allegations unsupported by any suggestion of evidence, or granting partial summary judgment. Actions such as those listed are essential predicates to a pretrial order definitively shaping a case for trial, but not for a settlement.

Conversely, a judge takes many steps to promote settlements that would be out of place in mapping a comprehensive plan for the future course of the litigation. For example, to brighten chances of settlement he should review prior efforts by the litigants to reach a compromise and then discuss the dollar value of particular items of injury and analyze the dollar gap between the amount the plaintiff demanded and the defendant offered. Very likely he should outline the risks to each side of various elements of liability and damage. Perhaps he should disclose his own reaction to the factual and legal issues presented. No doubt he should explore the costs to be anticipated if the case were to be litigated to the finish.

From the foregoing sampling it can be seen that many lines a judge should follow at a settlement conference would be irrelevant to an orderly trial, and some might be actively prejudicial. In a one-judge county, for instance, there would be the problem of who should preside at the trial of a case in which the judge at pretrial had indicated his belief that the plaintiff's damage claims were much exaggerated or that a tendered defense was sham or dubious.

That sketch of some of the differences in content and emphasis in the two types of conferences is not an analysis that will be found in existing pretrial rules or manuals. Generally, they draw no distinctions because they are based on the two-in-one credo. The analysis is intended to suggest that if rationally performed, the steps at a pretrial conference will be responsive to previously stated ends.

In New Jersey, as we have seen, the stated end has in the main been trial improvement, ever since the original pretrial rule was adopted in 1948. The rules have sought to assure that in every negligence case the issues will be simplified, clarified, and narrowed, that admissions and amendments will be disposed of, that some of the mechanical problems of trial will be liquidated in advance, and that a pretrial order will emerge to steer the case on its course. We have already seen that in actual operation the typical pretrial conference in New Jersey is a mixed affair, in part concerned with shaping the case for trial, in part intended to promote a settlement.[3] Thus, the observers of 105 actual conferences reported that most judges conducted mixed or "hybrid" sessions. The judges were for the most part faithful to the rules, but at times ad libbed queries as to whether there was "any chance of settling this case" or whether the attorneys had "explored the possibility of settlement." Frequently a judge would give his estimate of a fair evaluation of the case and would point to the risk of a high verdict or to the large expense trial would entail. On occasion he would fortify this point by enumerating the witnesses who would be needed and the time their testifying would consume. Those matters all seem remote from a trial-oriented proceeding.

There is, to be sure, great appeal in the idea of killing two birds with one stone. The difficulty, in this case, if our analysis correctly states the situation, is that the stone will have to be a two-piece projectile in order to be sure the right missile is at hand for each bird. To further both pretrial purposes a judge must do first one series of acts and then the other, or mix them together as he proceeds. The sheer length of the conference then becomes a serious problem. Critics have already protested the burden of even shorter conferences for "routine" cases in which the lawyer receives no added compensation for added labor. Bearing in mind that over half the cases now recover less than $2,000,[4] and that in 75 per cent of the not-pretried New Jersey cases that settled the recovery was no more than $3,000,[5] we can see that an attenuated pretrial could price many of the cases out of the courts. It seems inevitable that in small cases serious economic hardship for lawyers will eventually result if it ever becomes standard to require them to make substantial preparations beforehand and then go through a two-stage conference.

Apart from burden upon the bar and the opposition this provokes, the two-stage conference can not possibly make sense unless its separate parts are sound. This in turn asks what type of pretrial conference program makes sense for negligence suits. A careful answer will require keeping in mind three questions: (1) What type of conference shall it be, trial-oriented or settlement-oriented? (2) How extensively shall the pretrial procedure be used—in *all* cases or in only *some?* If in some cases, are they to be designated by a compulsory rule; at the court's discretion; or at the lawyers' option? (3) Can any mechanisms be built into the program to help learn how it is performing as it goes along?

1. What Type of Pretrial Conference?

The least likely program to adopt is a broad-scale settlement procedure, for the very plain reason that unless the state has an extraordinarily low settlement rate to start with it will stand to gain little by trying to induce more litigants to compromise. That follows from the most dramatic finding of the New Jersey test, namely, that *without any* pretrial conference 78 per cent of the major court negligence cases settled. The 78 per cent rate for the not-pretried B cases was virtually identical with the rate in the lawyer-chosen C cases (77 per cent) the all-pretried A cases (76 per cent). We are satisfied from the evidence that the New Jersey pretrial procedure had no material impact on the overall settlement rates. While it is true that the New Jersey pretrial procedure was not expressly devised, and supposedly is not deliberately conducted, to promote settlements, in point of fact many judges did try very intensively to induce compromise.

Moreover, with nearly 80 per cent of the cases already settling short of trial, there is manifestly only limited room for improvement. It is unrealistic to expect a 100 per cent settlement rate, for some cases will go to adjudication however strenuously the court tries to bring about a compromise. A maximum realistic rate for a state to aim at is probably no higher than the 85 per cent figure approached by some courts in New York, where judges commonly roll back their sleeves and "bang lawyers' heads together" to obtain settlements. In other states for which figures are available, such as California and Colorado, settlement rates of about 80 per cent prevail from year to year, with moderate variations.[6]

Taking together the evidence that pretrial as conducted in the test cases did not favorably affect the settlement rate, and that there is but limited potential for improvement, a settlement conference as a regular procedure would appear a poor plan. To raise the settlement rate in New Jersey to 85 per cent, for an increase of only 7 per cent over the rate in the not-pretried cases, would require heroic efforts and offer bleak prospects. If all the B cases had been given the treatment, in every 100 cases it would have been "wasted" on 78, which settled without it. Of the remaining 22, it would at best work on 7 and would not touch the remaining 15. Thus, it would be necessary to expose those 15 and the 78 that settled anyway to futile settlement conferences in order to try to get 7 more settlements—an unattractively small efficiency ratio.

Substantial judge time would be lost in conducting the conferences, for the 15 to 22 cases that would require trial afterward ought, in addition, to receive a pretrial that would prepare them for the trial.

Finally, there might be very disagreeable side effects, such as those brought into relief by the comments of judges at the

Princeton seminars. Attorneys would know that vigorous settlement efforts would be made by the court and might use the prospect as a crutch, substituting it for careful preparation. Many of the judges for their part might find it unpalatable, or worse, to have to intrude actively in the bargaining process. They have forcefully argued that it demeans the court and reflects discredit on the administration of justice for a judge to take a strong part in settlement negotiations.

Although under special circumstances a settlement conference may serve a useful purpose,[7] the pretrial procedure that in our judgment makes sense is the trial-oriented conference. The test data show that such a conference can produce perceptible improvements in the quality of the trial process in an appreciable percentage of cases. Although we were not able to calibrate precisely the frequency of improvement, the evidence is persuasive that it occurred in enough cases to support the hope that a soundly conceived pretrial program can make gains in the vital "trial quality" sector of the administration of justice. To realize its potential, the procedure needs to be modified along lines discussed in Chapter VII and to be applied *selectively* to types of cases in which it has highest potential, instead of indiscriminately and across the board.

2. Selectively Applied Pretrial

In general, a sound program employing the pretrial conference to improve trial quality must find a device for picking cases for pretrial that does not miss many it should hit or hit many it should miss. At the same time it must avoid the waste in time and energy for judges and lawyers that results if it selects *all* cases on a compulsory basis, as the New Jersey rules presently do. The key problem then is to spot the "right" cases. After that it will be necessary to see to it that they are pretried by the "right" judges in the "right" manner.

The main feature of the selective program is that pretrial will normally be applied to certain classes of cases and normally not used in other types unless in a particular case exceptional circumstances exist. In effect, a general presumption will arise for or against pretrial, with a discretionary power in the judges to overturn it. The chief objective of the selection mechanism will be to identify cases most likely to reach trial, on the theory that they are the ones most likely to benefit from a trial preparatory conference and, conversely, that settlement-bound cases are least likely.[8]

In any effort to predict trial-bound or "durable" cases, the prime candidates are the "big" cases—those that are likely to recover more than $10,000 if liability is found. Extensive studies in New York, as well as findings in the present study, show that extra-large cases are much more likely to reach trial than small cases. This means that if one could determine early that a case was in the "large" category, one would have identified cases that would reach trial on the order of 35 per cent of the time instead of with half that frequency.[9] Furthermore, large cases are more amenable to pretrial than small ones because their stakes are high enough to warrant requiring attorneys to prepare for and attend the pretrial conference without unduly burdening them or their clients.

Courts could "find" the large cases by means of existing and proposed mechanical procedures that would be simple to install and administer. A brief post-card form, completed by the attorneys and filed with the clerk as he prepared to make up the pretrial calendar, would provide the basic data. Among the items of information would be the plaintiff's estimate as to the potential size of the recovery and both sides' reports of the approximate amount of time spent in conducting discovery. (The latter item is a strong clue according to recent evidence from the federal courts linking high durability with lengthy pretrial discovery.) Cases that consumed more than two days in discovery would be "scored" as likely to reach trial, compared with short-discovery cases. The attorneys would also report to the court their separate estimates as to how long the cases will require for trial, whether liability is seriously disputed, whether the case is likely to be settled, and whether it will benefit from a trial preparatory conference. Like size predictions, these estimates are designed to create a basis for assessing the likelihood that the case will reach trial. If the estimates are in agreement that the case will require two days or more for trial, that liability is disputed, settlement unlikely and benefit from a pretrial likely, the case will be a prima-facie candidate for pretrial. It will become eligible to be listed on the calendar of trial-preparatory conferences, along with the cases known to have a large size potential and those in which lengthy discovery was conducted.

Whenever, as a result of the screening procedure, a case is marked for pretrial conference, the court could retain residual discretion to remove it from the pretrial list for good cause. In any other case in which attorneys representing adverse parties agreed, the case might be ordered to a pretrial conference, subject to the court's discretion. The court might also send a case to pretrial on its own motion after affording counsel opportunity to be heard in opposition.

In addition to the obvious point that any mandatory, across-the-board rule or conflicting general rule would have to be repealed, minor procedural rule changes may be required by this proposal. Provision would have to be made for determining the potential recovery in a case before it reached trial. In New Jersey this could readily be done under proposed new Rev. Rule 29–2A, which will require in connection with pretrial a "statement of plaintiff's injury and damage claims and copies of the medical examination report or reports on which plaintiff and defendant rely."[10] Under the rule proposed here, the judge will use the information, not only to determine whether the case should be transferred to a lower court, but also whether it is a "large" case (likely to recover at least $10,000 if liability is found). Cases that are selected as "large" would then be ordered for a pretrial conference, unless the judge finds cause to the contrary.

An amendment to Rev. Rule 29–2A could readily require that counsel set out also: (1) number of days spent on discovery; (2) the estimated length of trial; (3) whether liability is seriously disputed; (4) likelihood of settlement; and (5) his opinion regarding the need for a trial-shaping conference.

3. MECHANISMS TO AUDIT THE PROGRAM'S IMPACT

An ideal pretrial conference program cannot yet be devised because not enough is known about the criteria for selecting appropriate cases or about the critical elements in determining the "right" kind of conference to hold or the "right" judge to conduct it. In setting up a pretrial program, the rule-making authority should incorporate means of obtaining needed knowledge through experience. Our plan would build upon the modest amount now known with regard to predicting which cases and which pretrial steps promise best results by introducing on a limited, temporary basis built-in procedures for testing and auditing the program in operation. One purpose would be to learn whether the predictive factors in use are sound and whether better ones are available.

It is not the purpose here to write a detailed research design, but in general it is recommended that a test check be run in two or three New Jersey counties along the following lines: If attorneys representing adverse parties in a case agree that there should be a pretrial conference, it should be held without opportunity for judicial veto, even in cases not denominated "large." The testing or audit period should last until disposition of all cases that received the suggested processing during one calendar year.

Evaluation of the program would take into account the success of the various plans for predicting durable cases by keeping track of the cases that reached trial, those that did not, and by measuring the quality of the trial process in those that persisted. Cases in which "wrong" predictions were made would be examined to determine whether negative factors could be isolated.

If the lawyer-option plan results in too many cases being scheduled for conferences, the antidote might be to introduce discretionary control by the judges, or to tighten their exercise of discretion. The main point is that experience would teach the court authorities which factors were working well and which were not.

A test plan might be introduced also for selective settlement conferences, based on a set of indicators that could be developed along lines parallel to those outlined above for trial-oriented conferences. The chief indicators would be an expression by lawyers representing adverse parties that a settlement conference would serve a useful purpose, in which case the conference would be scheduled. If only one attorney asked for a settlement conference and his adversary did not, the judge would have discretion to permit or refuse the request.

In sum, a sound pretrial program for personal injury cases would be oriented toward trial so far as purpose and type, would be selective in its application, and would provide built-in mechanisms for testing and auditing the program as it functioned. Experience would show what changes should be made in the interest of maximizing results. Coupled with other proposals in this report, this program might help the pretrial conference procedure realize its potential without the harmful side effects that have accompanied its indiscriminate use in personal injury cases in New Jersey. Perhaps the watchword should be: a pretrial conference program in which the procedure's use is not too broad, and its users not too bored.

A STATEMENT OF PRETRIAL PRINCIPLES

AUTHOR'S NOTE: The purpose of this Statement is to outline for the benefit of judges who conduct pretrial conferences in personal injury cases authoritative guidelines on basic issues that commonly arise at pretrial. Listed here are issues most often the subject of misunderstanding or disagreement, according to observations made in the Project's study of pretrial in negligence actions in New Jersey. These or similar principles can be integrated into a state's existing pretrial rules, either as a preamble or in another manner deemed appropriate by the rule-making authority. An important objective of the Statement will be to define the state's policy, whatever it is. It may be that some states will take stands opposite to those suggested here.

This Statement is designed to supplement rules prescribing *trial preparatory conferences* and not those providing for *settlement conferences,* which respond to entirely different considerations. As to certain of the issues posited, we express our ideas about the proper responses, on the basis of the research in New Jersey and our concepts of sound policy. As to other issues, we express no judgment regarding which stand is correct.

1. *Keynote*

Experience has shown that in the conduct of pretrial conferences in personal injury actions judges often hold divergent views with regard to basic issues that repeatedly arise. The principles stated here are designed to give broad guidance in an effort to promote harmonious responses to such questions, in the interest of achieving optimal results from the pretrial procedure.

2. *Purpose of the pretrial conference*

The objective of the conference is to produce a pretrial order that will heighten prospects for an orderly, informed disposition of the controversy and a well-conducted trial should one prove necessary. It shall *not* be a deliberate purpose of the conference to bring about settlement of the action or to open that subject for discussion.

3. *The judge's role*

These rules contemplate that the judge will have a creative and affirmative role in the conduct of the conference. Unless he sees specific reasons for a contrary course, he will actively direct each step of the proceeding, rather than assume that the attorneys are permitted to control its course and make the issues. Thus, it is appropriate for the judge on his own initiative to insist upon details spelling out any vaguely presented claims and also to raise issues not submitted by counsel. As a typical instance of the former, if a plaintiff has claimed "negligence" in the manufacturing of the harmful agent, the proper move for the judge may be to require that the plaintiff specify whether the alleged negligence is in the design, the materials, or the assembly of the product. With regard to raising issues, if only negligence has been alleged but the circumstances warrant a possible claim of breach of warranty, the judge is functioning properly when he raises that possibility.

4. *Striking unfounded claims or defenses*

Occasionally, at the pretrial conference a claim or defense is raised which, though lacking support in law or evidence, is tenaciously pressed by the party advancing it. The judge may make appropriate orders to strike such a claim or defense, notwithstanding the absence of a formal application, provided there has been timely notice and an opportunity to submit arguments in opposition. As an example: a defensive plea of "assumption of risk" may be struck if that plea is legally untenable under undisputed circumstances in the case. A factual claim or defense should not be permitted to stand "just in case" supporting evidence may develop for it at the trial.

5. *Compelling disclosure*

A related question that frequently comes up is whether a party may be compelled under pain of sanctions to disclose legal theories and to suggest what lines of proof he intends to adduce in support of his factual claims. If so, other issues are whether the judge should require the party to reveal the names of trial witnesses and the substance of their expected testimony; and what type of sanction—preclusion of proof or striking defenses, etc.—is appropriate.

6. *Imposing sanction*

When confronted with attorneys' lapses at pretrial, judges show understandable reluctance to penalize either the erring lawyer or his client's case. This unfortunately does nothing to discourage faulty preparation or failure to appear at the conference. To avoid unevenness in sanctions, the principle to be followed is that for an unwarranted failure to prepare or appear, costs payable to the court clerk in the amount of $...... shall be assessed against the defaulting attorney.

THE JUDGE AT PRETRIAL

This is a suggested guide to the judge conducting a pretrial conference in which the object is to prepare a personal injury case for trial. Its aim is to stimulate the judge to creative involvement in the conduct of the conference and not to supply a definitive check list of automatic dos and don'ts. Central to its use is that the points set out below are suggestions, not commands. The relevance or the utility of some of the suggestions depends on how the state has resolved many underlying issues of policy and principle relating to pretrial.

1. *Are there ways to increase the specificity of the factual elements of the case?*

Experienced pretrial judges assert that it is often useful in trying to pin down both the agreed facts and the disputed factual issues, not to rest on counsel's general statements, but to probe for specific details. Can the plaintiff be induced to specify the particular respects in which he claims the defendant was guilty of negligence in operating his car, maintaining the premises, or manufacturing the allegedly dangerous product?

2. *Is there a chance to eliminate sham issues from the case?*

If the defendant has pleaded contributory negligence, non-ownership of the vehicle, or lack of consent, is the defendant prepared to suggest lines of evidence in support of the plea? If the plaintiff claims permanent injuries, has he indicated the nature of the medical proof in support of his claim? If the appellate courts have ruled invalid a claim or defense, is there any proper way to rid the case of it even though no formal motion made prior to the pretrial conference?

3. *Are there issues of fact or law counsel have not tendered that are certain to arise?*

If at the end of the conference the case is to be ready for trial on the basis of the pretrial order, the judge must contribute more than a referee function. If the attorneys have made light of the pretrial proceeding because they hope the case will not reach trial or because they are unwilling to do the needed work of preparation, can the judge supply the omitted effort by drawing on his experience and ingenuity? For example, does he see an issue of breach of warranty in a case that as presented raises only an issue of negligence?

4. *Are there unique features in the case that call for special procedures?*

Can a partial judgment be awarded to dispose of some of the claims, defenses, or issues? Can provision be made for inspection of premises, sites, or "things" in order to promote further stipulations or admissions? Will it serve a useful purpose because of unusually complex problems of law, including admissibility of crucial evidence, to direct the filing of special briefs in advance of trial? Shall parties be ordered added or dropped in the interests of a complete and just resolution of the controversy?

5. *With regard to trial arrangements, are there opportunities for useful planning?*

Can any of the documents, such as hospital charts or medical reports, be marked in evidence by stipulation? Will it be useful to obtain from counsel the names of witnesses to be called at the trial [if this is permitted in the state]? Will it be right to obtain disclosure of the substance of trial witnesses' testimony?

NOTES

NOTES

INTRODUCTION

[1] "Pretrial" is at times used in this report as shorthand for "pretrial conference."

[2] Hans Zeisel, Professor of Law and Sociology at the University of Chicago, has been a vigorous champion of these efforts. See note III, 1 *infra*.

[3] The Project was created in 1956 to conduct systematic studies of the law in action by using social science as well as legal skills. Its earliest work focused on personal injury litigation as the key to the problem of excessive delay in civil litigation. See, for example, Franklin, Chanin, & Mark, *Accidents, Money, and the Law: A Study of the Economics of Personal Injury Litigation*, 61 COLUM. L. REV. 1 (1961); Rosenberg, *Comparative Negligence in Arkansas: A "Before and After" Survey*, 13 ARK. L. REV. 89 (1959); Rosenberg & Chanin, *Auditors in Massachusetts As Antidotes for Delayed Civil Courts*, 110 U. PA. L. REV. 27 (1961); Rosenberg & Schubin, *Trial by Lawyer: Compulsory Arbitration of Small Claims in Pennsylvania*, 74 HARV. L. REV. 448 (1961); Rosenberg & Sovern, *Delay and the Dynamics of Personal Injury Litigation*, 59 COLUM. L. REV. 1115 (1959).

CHAPTER I. THE PRETRIAL CONFERENCE IN PERSPECTIVE

[1] See Appendix E.

[2] Wright, *The Pretrial Conference, Seminar on Practice and Procedure*, 28 F.R.D. 37, 141, 157 (1960).

[3] Friesen, *The Minimum Requirements of a Pretrial Rule*, 33 ROCKY MT. L. REV. 523 (1961): "Pretrial is not the same thing to all people." A comprehensive definition must include as a pretrial conference "any discussion of an untried case, required by order or rule of court in which both sides are represented, having as its object the effective or efficient disposition of the case or its settlement." *Id.* at 524.

[4] New Jersey is not alone in this view. In Wyoming, a pretrial conference is "premature" until discovery is exhausted. Bentley, *How To Do Pre-Trial in State Courts,* 14 WYO. L.J. 1, 3–4 (1959). See also VAN ALSTYNE & GROSSMAN, CALIFORNIA PRETRIAL AND SETTLEMENT PROCEDURES 48 (1963) [hereinafter cited as VAN ALSTYNE & GROSSMAN] and Pickering, *The Pre-Trial Conference,* 9 HASTINGS L.J. 117, 125 (1958) for comments on the interrelationship between the pretrial conference and discovery. Occasionally, it has been suggested that a pretrial conference sould serve as "poor man's discovery." See p. 101, *supra.*

[5] The text of Rule 16 is set out in note 1, Appendix E.

[6] Actually, however, when efforts have been made to amend the pretrial order itself, the appellate courts have treated it as if it were no more than a pleading. See Appendix B, pp. 180–82.

[7] Thus, the New Jersey Revised Rules [hereinafter cited as Rev. Rules] provide in general that discovery proceedings shall be completed within 100 days after service of the complaint (Rev. Rule 4:28 (a)); that notice of the pretrial conference shall not be served until 100 days after service of the complaint (Rev. Rule 4:29–2); that cases shall be assigned for trial within two weeks after the pretrial conference (Rev. Rule 4:41–5). "Experience has shown that the pretrial conference is most effective if held shortly before the case is to be tried, preferably from three to five weeks in advance." VAN ALSTYNE & GROSSMAN 258. *But see* Bentley, *supra* note I, 4, at 3, and Pickering, *supra* note I, 4, at 122, opposing a rule fixing the time for the conference. It has been said that completed discovery is "essential" to an effective pretrial and that the latter "catalytically links" discovery with the trial. Murrah, *Pre-Trial Procedure,* 328 THE ANNALS 70, 72, 73 (1960); see also Wright, *Pre-Trial on Trial,* 14 LA. L. REV. 391 (1954).

[8] Brennan, *Pre-Trial Procedure in New Jersey—a Demonstration,* 28 N.Y.S.B. BULL. 442, 449 (1956).

[9] Murrah, *Pre-Trial Procedure—A Statement of Its Essentials,* 14 F.R.D. 417 (1954).

[10] Kincaid, *A Judge's Handbook of Pre-Trial Procedure,* 17 F.R.D. 437, 441 (1955).

[11] See Appendix E.

[12] Brennan, *supra* note I, 8. See also ABA, THE IMPROVEMENT OF THE ADMINISTRATION OF JUSTICE 60 (1961): "It should be kept in

Notes: I. PRETRIAL IN PERSPECTIVE

mind, however, that pre-trial is not properly a device to induce or promote settlements, but rather that they may be an incidental by-product of the conference procedure."

[13] Rev. Rule 4:29–1 (b), originally Rule 3:16 adopted in September, 1948.

[14] The *Manual* is prepared by the New Jersey Administrative Office of the Courts and does not have the authoritative force of a rule.

[15] This rule was put in its present form by an amendment effective September, 1961, and reads in full: "All pretrial conferences shall be conducted in open court, but the judge may conduct such conferences at counsel table. Settlement conferences may be held in chambers."

[16] See Appendix B, pp. 177–78.

[17] See pp. 114–17, *infra*.

[18] S.D.N.Y. & E.D.N.Y. Gen. R. 2. The English summons for directions serves a similar purpose. See Rules of the Eng. S. Ct., Order 30. For the origins of this ancient device, see MILLAR, CIVIL PROCEDURE OF THE TRIAL COURT IN HISTORICAL PERSPECTIVE 229 (1952). The role of pretrial in the reduction of unnecessary delay and expense in litigation of protracted cases is discussed in the Prettyman Committee Report to the U.S. Judicial Conference, *Procedure in Anti-Trust and Other Protracted Cases*, 13 F.R.D. 62 (1951). See also *Selected Bibliography, Trial of Protracted Litigation, Seminar on Protracted Cases*, 21 F.R.D. 395, 533 (1957); Kaufman, *Report on Study of the Protracted Case*, 21 F.R.D. 55, 58 (1957); Sunderland, *The Theory and Practice of Pre-Trial Procedure*, 36 MICH. L. REV. 215, 220-24 (1937); Wright, *supra* note I, 2, at 148-49.

[19] A common example occurs when the pretrial judge insists that a defendant who has set up "contributory negligence" specify precisely what he alleges the plaintiff did—failed to obey a traffic signal, changed lanes improperly, etc. The judge must "crash through" and clarify the "conscious ambiguity" of counsel to obtain the necessary detail. Friesen, "Techniques in Pretrial" 16 (unpublished monograph in Project for Effective Justice files). A comprehensive discussion of the "active" judge's techniques appears in VAN ALSTYNE & GROSSMAN 296–300.

[20] See Appendix B, p. 177.

[21] See Chapter V, pp. 78–79.

[22] See Chapter VI, p. 97.

[23] "It has been said [pretrial] does much to eliminate the skill, resourcefulness and ability of trial counsel as elements in winning lawsuits." Gourley, *Effective Pretrial Must Be the Beginning of Trial, Seminar on Practice and Procedure,* 28 F.R.D. 37, 165, 166 (1960); see also Nims, *Pre-Trial in the United States,* 25 CAN. B. REV. 697, 718 (1947); Vetter, *Pre-Trial in the Southern District of New York,* 19 THE RECORD 110 (1964); Comment, *California Pretrial in Action,* 49 CALIF. L. REV. 909, 914–15 (1961). The gladiatorial view of litigation is deeply ingrained, for "our native Common Law Procedure is in essence contentious; it is a combat between parties in which the Court is only umpire." POLLOCK, THE EXPANSION OF THE COMMON LAW 15 (1904). See note II, 24 *infra.*

[24] Lawyers, it has been said, "resent coercive settlement tactics which weaken their position as advocates." Note, *Pre-Trial Conferences in the District Court for Salt Lake County,* 6 UTAH L. REV. 259, 265–66 (1958).

[25] Probably the most famous statement is that of Justice Jackson concurring in Hickman v. Taylor, 329 U.S. 495, 516 (1947): "[A] common law trial is and always should be an adversary proceeding" and it is not intended that a learned profession "perform its functions either without wits or on wits borrowed from the adversary." Even a sturdy supporter of the pretrial conference has said that "a struggle—warfare, if you will—between vitally interested partisans, is most apt to expose the truth." Louisell, *Discovery and Pre-Trial Under the Minnesota Rules,* 6 MINN. L. REV. 633, 640 (1952). See also Vanderbilt, *Improving the Administration of Justice—Two Decades of Development,* 26 U. CINC. L. REV. 155, 181 (1957).

[26] Marshall, *Pretrial Conference: An Endorsement from the Bench,* 45 VA. L. REV. 141, 146 (1959) has observed: "It may sometimes occur that lazy or incompetent lawyers profit to the disadvantage of their skilled and diligent adversaries."

CHAPTER II. THE CONTROVERSY OVER THE EFFECTIVENESS OF THE PRETRIAL CONFERENCE

[1] See Appendix E.

[2] The pretrial conference had been mandatory in California, with minor exceptions, since the rules went into effect in 1957. Re-

portedly, prior to the 1963 amendments, conferences had become perfunctory in many cases and pretrial was widely criticized as a relatively useless formality. VAN ALSTYNE & GROSSMAN 63. Among the chief grounds for the opposition to pretrial which led to important revisions in 1963 were that: (1) pretrial was valueless in run-of-the-mill cases, like motor vehicle personal injury actions; (2) even if trial-preparatory benefits accrued, counsel often could have obtained the same results without a trip to court; (3) settlement discussions were delayed until the conference; and (4) trial delay was aggravated in some instances. *Id.* at 16. See also Comment, *California Pretrial in Action,* 49 CALIF. L. REV. 909 (1961). The 1963 amendments sought to meet the objections by enlarging the category of exempt cases and by providing for waiver of the conference. For a comprehensive treatment of the present rules and procedures, see VAN ALSTYNE & GROSSMAN.

[3] Kuykendall, *Pretrial Conference: A Dissent from the Bar,* 45 A. L. REV. 147, 148 (1959) levels a vehement attack upon the pretrial conference on the premise that it replaces the trial lawyer's functions with the judge's "personal views and predilections" in the administration of justice.

[4] One writer has said "many judges give little more than lip service and office space" to the pretrial conference. Probert, *A Survey of Ohio Pre-Trial Practices and Achievements,* 7 W. RES. L. REV. 428, 435 (1956). Pretrial has been condemned as a "meaningless formality" [Shumaker, *An Appraisal of Pre-Trial in Ohio,* 17 OHIO ST. L. J. 192, 198 (1956)] and a "mere formality" which is wasteful of time, as conducted by some judges [Pharr, *The Truth About Pretrial,* 47 A.B.A.J. 177, 178 (1961)]. See also Christenson, *When is a Pre-Trial Conference a "Pre-Trial Conference"?,* 23 F.R.D. 129, 130 (1958); *cf.* Ridge, *What Do Judges and Lawyers Want from the Mandatory Pre-Trial Conference Practice?,* 17 U. KAN. CITY L. REV. 83, 89 (1949).

[5] In brief, this contention is that the pretrial conference favorably affects a court's supply-demand balance by decreasing the demand that cases make for judge time in the trial courtroom. For a more complete definition of the concept see note IV, 35 *infra.* The literature abounds with reports and claims that pretrial makes for more efficiency: Bentley, *supra* note I, 4, at 7 describes a case in which a

week of trial time assertedly was saved when discovery provided for at the pretrial conference led to dismissal of a "big airplane case." Clark, *Objectives of Pre-Trial Procedure*, 17 OHIO ST. L.J. 163, 165 (1956) holds skillful practitioners can accomplish "literally wonders" in relieving congestion. Friesen, *supra* note I, 3, at 525 contends the conference can shorten a trial "by days." Jayne, *Forward [to Symposium]*, 17 OHIO ST. L.J. 160, 162 (1956) attributes to pretrial his court's ability to dispose of the legal problems of a population nearly twice its former size with no increase in the size of the bench.

[6] It has been contended that whatever the focus of the conference it forces the adversaries to review the case, to examine the strength and weaknesses of both sides, and to come to terms acceptable to all concerned. LEVIN & WOOLLEY, DISPATCH AND DELAY 65–66 (1961). After pretrial, "counsel for each side will know more about the case than either of them could probably have known before." Vanderbilt, *supra* note I, 25, at 180. See also Kincaid, *Pre-Trial Conference Procedure in California*, 4 U.C.L.A.L. REV. 377, 380 (1957).

[7] Marshall, *supra* note I, 26 at 143. Pretrial "makes for shorter and better trials . . . [and] it results in fewer appeals." Vanderbilt, *supra* note I, 25 at 181.

[8] See, *e.g.*, NIMS, PRE-TRIAL 62–68 (1959); Address by Judge Kaufman, Tenth Circuit Annual Judicial Conference, May 10, 1957; D.D.C. COMMITTEE ON DOCKET ACCELERATION REPORT TO THE CHIEF JUDGE AND THE COURT (1961); Bentley, *supra* note I, 4, at 7; Brennan, *Remarks on Pre-Trial*, 17 F.R.D. 479, 485 (1955); Caplan, *Pre-Trial System in the Municipal Court of Chicago*, CASE & COM. Feb. 1941, p. 17, 18–19; Clark, *Objectives of Pre-Trial Procedure*, *supra* note II, 5, at 163, 167; Murrah, *Some Bugaboos in Pre-Trial*, 7 VAND. L. REV. 603, 607 (1954); Nims, *supra* note I, 23, at 699; Rice, *Pre-Trials and the Improvement of the Administration of Justice*, 6 OKLA. L. REV. 249, 253 (1953); Shumaker, *supra* note II, 4, at 201; Vanderbilt, *supra* note I, 25, at 181. *But see* ZEISEL, KALVEN, & BUCHHOLZ, DELAY IN THE COURT 144–49 (1959) [hereinafter cited as DELAY IN THE COURT] urging after a study of delay in New York County's Supreme Court that unless pretrial actually steps up settlements by 25% "the court ought to stop pre-trials because it could dispose of more cases by having the pre-trial judge try cases instead."

[9] Kaufman, *op. cit. supra* note II, 8; Brennan, *The Continuing Education of the Judiciary in Improved Procedures*, Seminar on Prac-

tice and Procedure, 28 F.R.D. 37, 42, 50 (1960); Brennan, *supra* note II, 8.

[10] *Pretrial Comes to Cleveland,* 24 J. AM. JUD. SOC'Y 29, 31 (1940); see Cooper, *Pre-Trial Procedure in the Wayne County Circuit Court, Detroit, Michigan,* 6 MICH. JUD. COUNCIL 61, 74 (1936); see also Thomas, *The Story of Pre-Trial in the Common Pleas Court of Cuyahoga County,* 7 W. RES. L. REV. 368, 372 (1956), attributing to pretrial conferences a "larger number of jury waivers and reduced juries."

[11] These claims are usually made in general terms, without benefit of supporting facts, figures, or studies. For example, it is said: pretrial accomplishes "literally wonders" for calendar congestion by "shortening or eliminating the actual battle" (Clark, *supra* note II, 8, at 165); that "time will be saved and the case more intelligently and simply presented to the jury" (Marshall, *supra* note I, 26, at 143); and that pretrial "shortens the time of the actual trial" (Spangenberg & Ulrich, *Pre-Trial from the Viewpoints of Two Lawyers,* 7 W. RES. L. REV. 418, 427 (1956)). Some efforts at precise estimation of the alleged benefits conferred on litigation by the pretrial conference have been made. Illustrative of those who "pinpoint" their claims are two commentators on the Texas scene. Judge Rice, based on his experience, claims a saving in trial time of from 25% to 75% over not-pretried cases. Rice, *supra* note II, 8, at 253. Fifteen Texas judges in a survey estimated average savings in jury time of 27%, and ranged from 5% to 50%. Savings in judge time for "not settled" cases were estimated at 21% to 26%. Thode, *The Case for the Pre-Trial Conference in Texas,* 35 TEXAS L. REV. 372, 384 (1957). See also Kincaid, *Pre-Trial Procedure in California,* PHI DELTA DELTA, Dec. 1958, p. 15, 17; Olney, *An Analysis of Docket Congestion in the United States District Courts in the Light of the Enactment of the Omnibus Judgeship Bill, Seminar on Procedures,* 29 F.R.D. 191, 217, 221–23 (1961).

[12] Friesen, *supra* note I, 3, at 525; Murrah, *supra* note II, 8, at 606.

[13] Martz, *Pretrial Preparation, Seminar on Practice and Procedure,* 28 F.R.D. 37, 137, 140 (1960); Rice, *supra* note II, 8, at 253; Thomas, *supra* note II, 10, at 379. DELAY IN THE COURT 154 asserts it is "highly probable" pretrial conferences accelerate settlement.

[14] NIMS, *op. cit. supra* note II, 8, at 114, 137-38; Clark, *supra* note II, 8, at 168; Friesen, *supra* note I, 3 at 532.

[15] NIMS, *op. cit. supra* note II, 8, at 62; Brennan, *supra* note II, 8, at 484; Kincaid, *supra* note II, 6, at 380.

[16] McIlvaine, *The Value of an Effective Pretrial, Seminar on Practice and Procedure,* 28 F.R.D. 37, 158 (1960).

[17] Kincaid, *supra* note I, 10, at 443–44; Shumaker, *supra* note II, 4, at 202; Vanderbilt, *supra* note I, 25 at 181.

[18] NIMS, *op. cit. supra* note II, 8, at 114–18, 120–21; Kincaid, *supra* note I, 10, at 443; Laws, *A Trial Judge Looks at Pre-Trial Procedure,* 4 PRAC. LAW. Jan. 1958 P. 17, 19–20; Yankwich, *"Short Cuts" in Long Cases,* 13 F.R.D. 41, 47–48 (1951).

[19] "Counsel who regularly appear at pre-trial report that as soon as a case appears in the 'Active Pre-Trial List' they pull out the file and determine what has to be done to get ready for pre-trial. A deposition may be taken, a witness interviewed, a photograph taken, or a medical examination of the plaintiff secured." Thomas, *supra* note II, 10, at 387; *cf.* Friesen, *supra* note I, 3, at 530.

[20] Crary, *The Pre-trial in Action,* 37 IOWA L. REV. 341, 343 (1952); Shumaker, *supra* note, 4, at 204–5.

[21] Kuykendall, *supra* note II, 3, at 147–53; HOLBROOK, A SURVEY OF METROPOLITAN TRIAL COURTS—LOS ANGELES AREA 266 (1956).

[22] *Cf.* Ridge, *supra* note II, 4, at 85.

[23] Louisell, *supra* note I, 25, at 635.

[24] Bentley, *supra* note I, 4, at 6:

> [Some] counsel insist that we have gone too far . . . that to make counsel disclose witnesses and what they are going to say will ruin the art of advocacy—that it penalizes able counsel and aids the lazy counsel . . . I submit that we have changed the practice of law with these rules and that we have taken away some of the surprise and strategic advantages previously had by able and hardworking counsel, but that we have done so in the name of justice and we must stand by what we have done. As Courts, we are not interested in surprise or tactics as such, but are primarily interested in seeing that all of the proper and necessary evidence is presented for decision.

See also Marshall, *supra* note I, 26, at 146.

[25] Bentley, *supra* note I, 4, at 3. *Cf.* Clark, *supra* note II, 5, at 169; Vetter, *supra* note I, 23, at 111. For a vigorous statement to the contrary, see Brennan, *After Eight Years: New Jersey Judicial Reform,* 43 A.B.A.J. 499, 564 (1957); *cf.* Kincaid, *supra* note II, 6, at 379.

[26] The statistical evidence produced relates to whichever alleged objective of pretrial is under examination, and usually this means it deals with the "efficiency" question, and more particularly with settlement rates. At least a score of articles contain statistical data, mainly court figures on the number or percentage of cases tried or terminated

Notes: III. METHODS AND MATERIALS OF STUDY 141

without trial. Among the few reports that rest upon actual surveys (by questionnaires or interviews), the *California Law Review* study and Professor Thode's research in Texas contain the most systematically gathered data. See Comment, *California Pretrial in Action,* 49 CALIF. L. REV. 909 (1961); Thode, *supra* note II, 11. Smaller scale surveys were conducted in Ohio. See Probert, *supra* note II, 4; Shumaker, *supra* note II, 4. Neither those reports nor the many others that are based on court figures or informal inquiries afford a reliable basis for determining the impact of pretrial conferences upon settlement rates. Occasionally, the reports admit their deficiencies: "No definite claims can or should be made from these figures alone [for] there is no way to determine exactly what caused a law suit to settle . . ." Wright, *supra* note I, 7, at 399; "It is . . . not possible to apportion the contributions to the total result . . ." Olney, *supra* note II, 11, at 222.

Efforts to distill any conclusions from the reports' widely disparate findings on the effect of pretrial on settlements meet with the hopeless obstacle that the researchers used irreconcilable approaches. Some used the "before-and-after" approach, attributing a recent favorable upturn in settlement rates to the introduction of pretrial. Kincaid, *supra* note II, 11. Others used the "side-by-side" method, comparing settlement rates in a district where pretrial was used and favored with the rates in other districts. HOLBROOK, *op. cit. supra* note II, 21, at 261; Martz, *supra* note II, 13. Another found pretrial effective because the number of dispositions went up after it was introduced. McNaugher, *The Pre-Trial Court at Pittsburgh,* 6 U. PITT. L. REV. 5 (1939). However, the commonest approach was merely to compute the high percentage of cases settling and attribute the figure to the beneficial impact of the pretrial procedure in use, *e.g.,* Gourley, *supra* note I, 23, at 168; McIlvaine, *supra* note II, 16, at 160; Shumaker, *supra* note II, 4, at 201; Sunderland, *The Function of Pre-Trial Procedure,* 6 U. PITT. L. REV. 1, 4 (1939).

CHAPTER III. THE METHODS AND MATERIALS OF THE STUDY

[1] In 1959 DELAY IN THE COURT, expressing doubts regarding the settlement promoting advantage of pretrial based on a study of a New York court, specifically suggested that there be conducted "an official experiment under which the courts would pre-try some cases

and not others and would select the cases for each group by lot. A higher settlement ratio for the cases that went through pre-trial would give us the exact measure of its effectiveness." *Id.* at 143–44.

Professor Hans Zeisel, one of the book's authors, and a uniquely qualified commentator on problems of empirical research methods, had urged in 1956 the use of controlled experiments in answering troublesome questions of court administration. Zeisel, *The New York Expert Testimony Project: Some Reflections on Legal Experiments*, 8 STAN. L. REV. 730, 731 (1956). See also note III, 2.

For discussion of available research techniques, the difficulties involved, and the means used to overcome them, see Zeisel, *Social Research on the Law: The Ideal and the Practical*, in LAW AND SOCIOLOGY 124–43 (Evan ed. 1962). The New York County Supreme Court's experiment with impartial medical testimony provided, in Professor Zeisel's view, a classic example of the need for an imaginative research design at the outset. "[W]ith somewhat more vigor in the design of this experiment, data could have been provided which would prove (or disprove) these claims [of the report] to the satisfaction of the most critical observer." Zeisel, *The New York Expert Testimony Project*, *supra*. A study of the Massachusetts auditor system concluded "how astonishingly hard it is to tell whether a given delay 'remedy' has worked or failed in practice" because those who devise remedies "fail to provide in advance for the data that will be needed to answer that question." Rosenberg & Chanin, *Auditors in Massachusetts As Antidotes for Delayed Civil Courts*, 110 U. PA. L. REV. 27 (1961). A study of "comparative negligence" in Arkansas found that an analysis dependent upon satistical relationships to determine the effect of one factor on personal injury litigation immediately encounters the fact that "a whole constellation of variables affects the rate of movement of cases through the civil courts" and "isolating the effect of one factor is anything but simple." Rosenberg, *Comparative Negligence in Arkansas: A "Before and After" Survey*, 13 ARK. L. REV. 89, 95 (1959).

[2] "[W]hat was and what was not achieved" by a legal innovation can be evaluated only by "a scientifically controlled experiment." DELAY IN THE COURT 241. Professor Zeisel has stated that "short of a controlled experiment, all . . . evidence is imperfect" and in using substitute devices "only through a variety of converging approaches can one hope to reach safe ground." Zeisel & Callahan, *Split Trails and Time Saving: A Statistical Analysis*, 76 HARV. L. REV. 1606, 1624 (1963). External factors precluded implementation of the most desir-

able research design for this study which basically combined "before and after" and "control" techniques. *Id.* at 1608–9.

The combined techniques of a "before and after" survey and "side-by-side" comparisons were used in a study to determine the impact of substituting "comparative negligence" for "contributory negligence" in personal injury cases in Arkansas. Rosenberg, *supra* note III, 1. A devoted effort at a "before and after" survey of pretrial conferences in California was somewhat clouded by the fact that new discovery procedures went into effect along with pretrial and the investigators were led to the rueful opinion that their "respondents must have found it difficult to distinguish the effects of discovery from the effects of pretrial." Comment, *California Pretrial in Action,* 49 CALIF. L. REV. 909, 913 n. 41 (1961). See also Thode, *supra* note II, 11.

[3] A notice was published in the *New Jersey Law Journal* on December 4, 1959, describing the test program and explaining that in named counties, "Every other case will proceed through to a mandatory pretrial conference as presently required by the rules of the Supreme Court, whereas in the alternate cases counsel will be advised that the rule is being suspended and that no pretrial conference will be scheduled unless requested." 82 N.J.L.J. 593, 596 (1959).

[4] The Supreme Court may have considered that a system involving compulsory pretrial of some cases and compulsory exclusion of others from pretrial might raise constitutional problems of equal treatment under the law. *But see* DELAY IN THE COURT 242–50.

[5] See pp. 26–28 *infra.*

[6] For example, 45% of the cases added to the combined calendar of the Law Divisions of the Superior and County courts in these counties were auto negligence cases, compared with an overall proportion of 49% for such cases in the entire state. 1960–61 N.J. ADMINISTRATIVE DIRECTOR OF THE COURTS ANN. REP., Table G [hereinafter cited as 1960–61 REPORT]. Also, the counties included in the study reflected representative variations in population, urbanization, trial delay, and other features that might influence the impact of pretrial. For instance, the 1960 census showed test county Essex as the most populous county, with 923,545 residents, and Sussex as the second least populated, with 49,255 residents. 1961–62 N.J. ADMINISTRATIVE DIRECTOR OF THE COURTS ANN. REP., Supp. 1–2 [hereinafter cited as 1961–62 REPORT]. In a sample month, May, 1962, Hudson County tried 97 civil cases and Warren County tried 1. The average period from pretrial to trial was 7 months and 12 days in Morris County and but 2 months and 23 days in Hudson County. 1961–62 REPORT, Supp. 8–9.

144 *Notes:* III. METHODS AND MATERIALS OF STUDY

[7] During the 1960-61 court year, the Law Divisions of the Superior and County courts "removed from the calendar", *i.e.,* terminated by all means, a total of 19,688 cases, of which the 7 test counties accounted for 9,757, or 50%. Likewise, they contributed 48% of the 21,689 cases added to the calendar in all counties. *Ibid.*

[8] The Columbia University Bureau of Applied Social Research, an organization affiliated with the University's Department of Sociology, has for more than twenty-five years been developing information about the behavior and nature of groups in society.

[9] With immaterial exceptions, this study does not make any distinction between personal injury cases heard in the Superior Court and those heard in the County Court, since they have concurrent jurisdiction. Superior Court judges by law may sit in either court and County Court judges may sit in Superior Court on assignment by the Chief Justice of the Supreme Court. The interrelationship is described in Brennan, *New Jersey Tackles Court Congestion,* 40 J. AM. JUD. SOC'Y 45, 47 (1956).

[10] More than 20,000 separate letters, questionnaires, and forms were utilized to gather the data on the test cases. Allowing for multipaged forms, we estimate that more than 50,000 pages were filled in by the judges, attorneys, court clerks, and administrative staff, a remarkably generous effort. That great effort is without precedent, we believe, in the annals of research to improve judicial administration.

[11] Cases are "added to the calendar" when an answer is filed. Rev. Rule 4:41-4a. Personal injury cases comprise an estimated three fourths of the cases added to the calendar, according to the following calculations:

(1) Motor vehicle cases comprised 51% of the 25,230 cases added to the calendar from Sept. 1, 1962, to August 31, 1963. 1962-63 N.J. ADMINISTRATIVE DIRECTOR OF THE COURTS ANN. REP. Table C–2 [hereinafter cited as 1962-63 REPORT].

(2) Motor vehicle cases comprised 66% of the 3,000 personal injury cases of all kinds, which composed the study sample. Thus, the ratio of motor vehicle personal injury cases to personal injury cases of all kinds at the pretrial notification stage is 2 to 3.

(3) Assuming, for lack of reason to the contrary, that this 2-to-3 ratio remains constant between the time cases are added to the calendar and notice of the conference goes forward, the number of personal injury cases added to the calendar is therefore equal to 3/2 X 51% of

Notes: III. METHODS AND MATERIALS OF STUDY 145

the total (that is, 75% of 25,230) or 19,317, which we have rounded to 19,000.

[12] Appeals are not classified under a general heading of "personal injury," but they are to be found under the heading of either "auto negligence" or "negligence."

In the Supreme Court, of 102 civil decisions rendered during the 1961–62 court year, 14 "negligence" cases were decided and no "auto negligence" cases. Thus, at most, 13.7% of all Supreme Court appeals could be classified as personal injury negligence cases, 1961–62 REPORT, Table A-1.

In the Appellate Division, of a total of 540 civil appeals, 42 were "auto negligence," and 82 "negligence" cases. Assuming that all "auto negligence" appeals were personal injury cases and using the same assumptions and calculations heretofore used to project the number of personal injury cases from a known number of motor vehicle personal injury cases (see note III, 11 *supra*), we determined that a total of 63, or 11.6%, of the appeals were personal injury cases. Even if all "negligence" appeals were considered as involving personal injury, the percentage would rise to no more than 22.9%. *Id.* at Table B–1.

[13] Of the 188 cases discarded, 31 (most of which were on the military list) were still open as of March 31, 1962, the cutoff date for this phase of the field work in the test; 43 contained no claim for personal injury; and 114 were transferred to the district courts. Removal of these 188 cases from the test group did not bias the results.

(1) Ejection of nonpersonal injury cases merely eliminates 43 cases that did not belong in the group and there is no reason to believe that their accidental appearance in the sample affected its randomness in any material way.

(2) Removal of the 31 open cases could present a problem—obviously, it affected the figures on the average time required for cases to close—but for the fact that they constitute only about 1% of the sample. Also, the fact that most are on the military lists indicates that they were affected by a factor immaterial to the test program.

(3) At the commencement of the test it was agreed that if all parties requested, a case would be transferred to the district court, notwithstanding the moratorium during the period of the test on screening and transfer of small cases at pretrial conferences. The 114 test cases transferred presumably had potential recoveries of no more than $3,000, hence their removal could affect the data on small recovery

cases. But they appear to have been distributed randomly among the A, B, and C groups in the same general proportion as each group bore to the entire sample. Thus, 54%, 25%, and 22% of the transfers were in the A, B, and C groups respectively, which groups in turn accounted for 51%, 26%, and 24% of the test cases respectively. For a comprehensive treatment of the transfer process and the role of the district courts see Appendix F.

[14] Of 567 suits involving optional pretrials, plaintiff alone requested the conference in 162 cases, defendant alone in 344 cases, and both sides did so in 60 cases. See Appendix C, Form B, for the prescribed procedure followed by a litigant to obtain an optional pretrial. The test data did not include any information on why defendants had so marked a proclivity to opt for a pretrial conference. However, there appears to be some basis for believing that on economic grounds defense counsel may have been more willing than plaintiffs' attorneys to invest the time and effort needed for pretrial. A popular story in circulation may best articulate how the economics of the situation works out:

> There is in New Jersey representing insurance companies a law firm by name of Whitelip and Trembling. One day Waldo Whitelip inquired of his partner, "Evers, where is Junior today?" Evers replied, "W.W., he is up on a pretrial conference." Waldo responds, "What in blazes are they trying to do to us now? They are doing everything in the name of progress. Every time I want that boy he is at a pretrial conference. How many does he go to in a year?" Evers says, "W.W., I figure about 500 this year." Waldo cries, "Five hundred pretrial conferences! My heavens, they will put us out of business." Evers answers, "Well, you know we get $75 apiece for them." To which Waldo answers, "Seventy-five dollars apiece? Well, you can't stand in the way of progress."

"Automatic" opting was infrequent—only 18% (19 out of 104) of the firms (including single practitioners) who appeared in at least 3 non-mandatory cases invariably demanded a conference. However, this rate was not constant from county to county—in the two counties with the highest option rates, it was 29% and 26% respectively; in three other counties it ranged from 7-9%. The two highest rates of opting for attorneys were 95% (of 36 cases) and 87% (of 31 cases). A relatively small group of firms accounted for a large percentage of the optional pretrials: ten exercised 32% of the options, with defense requests again heavily predominant (187 of 203).

[15] Of 2,882 responses, 1,893 (65.7%) were motor vehicle cases; 702 (24.4%) involved owners and occupiers of land; 63 (2.2%) were based

Notes: III. METHODS AND MATERIALS OF STUDY 147

on products liability; and 224 (7.8%) were classified as "other" types of actions. For the three basic test groups the distribution was as shown in Table A, following.

Table A. Distribution of Type of Action by Test Groups

Type of Action	A	B	C	Total
Motor Vehicle	67%	69%	59%	66%
Owners and Occupiers of Land	23%	22%	29%	24%
Products Liability	2%	2%	3%	2%
Other	7%	7%	9%	8%
Number of cases	1,463	731	688	2,882

[16] *Table B. Type and Complexity of the Test Cases*

Motor vehicle, multiparty, multiclaim	38.0%
Non-motor vehicle, multiparty, multiclaim	18.0%
Motor vehicle, multiparty, single claim	14.0%
Motor vehicle, single party, single claim	13.0%
Non-motor vehicle, single party, single claim	9.0%
Non-motor vehicle, multiparty, single claim	7.0%
Motor vehicle, single party, multiclaim	1.0%
Non-motor vehicle, single party, multiclaim	0.2%
Number of cases	2,537

[17] From data compiled by the court clerks the duration of the pretrial conferences in 1,499 cases was tabulated as follows:

Table C. Duration of Pretrial Conference

Conference time (in hours)	A	C	Total
Less than ¼	0.2%	—	0.1%
¼–½	34.0%	28.0%	32.0%
½–¾	50.0%	47.0%	49.0%
¾–1	10.0%	14.0%	11.0%
1–1½	5.0%	9.0%	6.0%
1½–2	0.6%	2.0%	1.0%
Over 2	0.1%	0.2%	0.1%
Number of cases	1,030	469	1,499

By contrast, the Project's observers, who sat in on 105 actual conferences in 1960 and 1962, found that half of them ended within 20 minutes. A partial explanation is that transfers, which are often ordered very quickly, were permissible during the 1962 observation period, when 62 conferences were viewed. Some portion of the cases in the table above would have been transferred but for the moratorium on transfers during the test period. See note III, 13 *supra*.

[18] Jury demands were made in 95% of the A cases; 91% of the B cases; and 95% of the C cases. (These data are derived from responses in 398 cases that commenced trial.)

[19] A jury was actually empaneled in 88% of the A cases; 80% of the B cases; and in 82% of the C cases. (These data are derived from responses in 425 cases that commenced trial.)

[20] Original jury demands were waived by 10% of the A group and by 17% of the B+C group. In the B cases 18%, and in the C cases 15%, waived. (These data are derived from responses in 361 cases.)

[21] The 52 judges constituted 61% of the full-time judges (83) in the Superior and County courts during September 1, 1959–August 31, 1960. By September 1, 1961, the manpower of the two courts had been increased to a total of 101 (44 Superior Court, 57 County Court), and the 52 "test" judges comprised only 51% of the total. 1960–61 REPORT, app. p. 16.

[22] Among plaintiffs' counsel, 57% were members of a firm, compared to 66% of defendants' counsel. (Derived from responses of 258 plaintiffs' and 233 defendants' counsel.) Of firm members, 85% of the plaintiffs' counsel and 49% of defendants' counsel reported their firm comprised less than 5 partners or associates. (Derived from responses of 140 plaintiffs' and 137 defendants' lawyers.)

[23] For plaintiffs' side, in 75% of 202 cases the attorney completing the trial counsel report stated he attended the pretrial conference, compared with 55% of the 183 cases in which defendants' side responded. But 10% of the responding plaintiffs and 9% of the responding defendants indicated that they did not personally conduct the trial. Thus, plaintiffs' trial counsel may have been present at the pre-trial conference in no more than 65% of the cases and defendants' trial counsel in no more than 46%. For the source of this data see Appendix C: Form G, questions 1a, 1b, 1d.

[24] In New York City, defendants prevail in slightly less than 15% of the claims and suits that close before trial; in about 20% of the cases that close during trial; and in some 40% of the cases that go to verdict. Franklin, Chanin, & Mark, *Accidents, Money, and the Law: A Study of the Economics of Personal Injury Litigation,* 60 COLUM. L. REV. 1, 14 (1961). A survey in other metropolitan areas produced similar figures. *Id.* at 38.

[25] These figures are based on replies in 275 cases tried to completion to a jury and 33 tried before the bench. The lower percentage of defendants' awards in non-jury cases is entirely accounted for by the B group: of 11 cases, plaintiff won awards in 10.

[26] When plaintiff did recover something, the recoveries were distributed by size as set forth in Table D.

Notes: III. METHODS AND MATERIALS OF STUDY

Table D. Distribution of Cases That Recovered Something by Amount Recovered

Amount Recovered (dollars)	Number of Cases	Per Cent of All Recoveries
1–100	11	0.4%
101–300	80	3.0%
301–600	214	9.0%
601–1000	399	16.0%
1001–3000	945	39.0%
3001–6000	453	19.0%
6001–10,000	184	8.0%
10,001–25,000	109	4.0%
Over 25,000	41	2.0%
Total	2,436	100.4%

[27] See also note VIII, 4 *infra*. See Rosenberg & Sovern, *Delay and the Dynamics of Personal Injury Litigation*, 59 COLUM. L. REV. 1115, 1128–36 (1959).

[28] Of 1,754 pretried cases, 32 (1.8%) were reported to have settled during the conference. The A group had an at-conference settlement rate of 1.6% and the C group a 2.3% rate. By contrast, 200 (11.4%) of 1,754 of the A and C test cases had settled before the pretrial conference.

[29] For complete trials the breakdown was as follows:

Table E-1. Trial Duration of Cases That Went to Verdict

Trial time (in hours)	A	B	C	Total
less than 2	3%	12%	—	4%
2–5	17%	19%	14%	17%
5+–10	46%	44%	42%	45%
Over 10	34%	26%	44%	35%
Number of cases	129	43	50	222

When all cases that reached trial were tabulated—including those that ended before verdict—about ¼ required longer than two trial days, whereas ⅓ required no more than one trial day.

Table E-2. Trial Duration of Cases That Commenced Trial

Trial time (in hours)	A	B	C	Total
Less than 2	10%	22%	11%	13%
2–5	24%	21%	17%	22%
5+–10	41%	35%	39%	39%
Over 10	26%	22%	33%	26%
Number of cases	176	63	70	309

CHAPTER IV. WHAT PRETRIAL APPARENTLY DOES AND DOES NOT DO

[1] Murrah, *Pre-Trial Procedure,* 328 THE ANNALS 70, 74 (1960).

[2] Hickman v. Taylor, 329 U. S. 495, 507 (1947).

[3] That is, which remained on the docket 100 days after the complaint.

[4] The reason for believing that any differences between the A group and the B+C group reflect the impact of pretrial is very simple: no other factor is present to account for the differences. At the beginning of the test, as a result of the sampling mechanism, the A group and the B+C group were statistically matched insofar as material characteristics of the cases comprising each group. At completion of the first phase of the test (during which pretrials were conducted), two differences distinguished the A group from the B+C group, but we believe only one to be meaningful. The first, and vital, distinction is that all the roughly 1500 A cases had been put through pretrials, as against somewhat less than half of the B+C cases.

The second difference, we have concluded, played no part in the findings. This distinguishing feature is the product of the lawyers in the A cases having no choice but to pretry their cases, whereas in the C cases at least one side, and sometimes both, volunteered for an optional pretrial conference. This raised the problem of whether the "optionality" feature means that conferences in the C cases were different from those in the A cases. We decided they were not. Pretrials in the C cases were conducted by the same judges as in the A cases, without distinction of any kind. Conceivably, lawyers in C cases might have had a different attitude toward the pretrial conferences because they had asked for them. If so, the different attitude should have been reflected in some aspects or results of the C case pretrials. But nothing in the data derived by analysis and comparison of the C cases gives any basis for belief that "optionality" was an effective factor. They did not register any dramatic results from pretrial, such as might be expected of a psychologically susceptible group of cases. Moreover, the fact that defendants showed so high a preference for pretrial, and the suggested explanation for this (see note III, 14 *supra*) are further evidence that opting was a neutral factor so far as the test is concerned.

Thus, the surviving difference of potential importance between the A and B+C groups was the proportion of cases which were subjected

Notes: IV. WHAT PRETRIAL DOES AND DOES NOT

to a pretrial conference—in the former, all; in the latter, not quite half. Any differentiation between the groups in durability, trial quality, or outcome therefore inferentially can be taken to show the impact of pretrial.

[5] See note III, 14 *supra*.

[6] See pp. 6-9 *supra*.

[7] "The minimizing of opportunities for maneuver and surprise, the limitation of issues, particularly the factual issues, and the definition by the parties of their respective contentions upon such issues are just as vital in negligence causes as in other causes." N.J. ADMINISTRATIVE OFFICE OF THE COURTS, MANUAL OF PRETRIAL PRACTICE 2 (1959).

[8] See Pharr, *The Truth About Pretrial*, 47 A.B.A.J. 177 (1961) for an extraordinarily penetrating discussion of the whole subject of the pretrial conference. Judge Pharr states: "Thus far, there has been discovered no standard or accurate measure of the effectiveness of pretrial. There is no general yardstick to be applied." *Id.* at 178.

[9] Researchers in this field use the concept of "significant differences" to rule out the statistical risk that observed differences are merely a product of chance. Both sample size and percentage differences must be taken into account. A conventional test for reliability is "significance at the .05 level," a way of saying that the finding could occur by chance no more than 5 times out of 100. Here, to attain significance at the .05 level, considering the small numbers involved, approximately a 40% difference between the A and B+C cases would be necessary. See Appendix D.

In succeeding notes, whenever a decimal figure is used to report the "significance level" of the finding in question it should be read as expressing the number of times in 100 that the reported figure could come about by chance.

[10] The percentages reported are based on the number of appeals filed, even though 4 appeals from judgments in A cases and 3 appeals from judgments in B+C cases were discontinued. Based on the number of appeals surviving to decision, 27% of the A and 67% of the B+C cases were reversed or modified. Other oddities about the appeal rates are that the not-pretried cases produced only one half the rate of appeals produced by the pretried C cases—4% as compared with 8%, and that the solitary appeal that survived in the B group was modified while 63% of the surviving C cases were reversed.

152   *Notes:* IV. WHAT PRETRIAL DOES AND DOES NOT

Of course, too few cases are involved for the percentage differences here to be reliably indicative.

[11] The finding that motions for new trial were made in 1 of 5 tried-to-completion cases is based on estimate and projection. At the time the data were compiled, motions had been made in 67 cases. The time to move had expired in 228 cases but not in 40 others, and the amount of time elapsed was unknown in the remaining 90 cases. To determine the number of motions for new trial, it was necessary to allocate those for which answers were not available between "motions made" and "motions not made" categories.

Table F. Frequency of Motions for New Trial

(a) Actual Distribution

Motion	A	B+C	Total
Made	37	30	67
Not made—more than 10 days elapsed	130	98	228
Not made—less than 10 days elapsed	17	23	40
Not made—elapsed time not available	44	46	90
Number of cases	228	197	425

(b) Intermediate Projection

Motion	A	B+C	Total
Made	37	30	67
Not made—more than 10 days elapsed	169	135	305
Not made—less than 10 days elapsed	22	31	53
Number of cases	228	197	425

(c) Final Projection

Motion	A	B+C	Total
Made	41	36	77
Not made—more than 10 days elapsed	187	161	348
Number of cases	223	197	425

[12] Percentages are based on 61 motions. In the A group, 3 of 35 were granted; in the B+C group, 5 of 26. (Of 12 B group motions 3 were granted, and of 14 C group motions, 2 were granted.) Significance level: .70.

[13] See Appendix C: Form G, question 4c; Form H, questions 1a, 1b, 2a; Form I, question 2a.

[14] See Appendix C: Form H, questions 2b, 2c, 2d.

[15] See Appendix C: Form G, question 3d; Form H, question 2f; Form I, question 2c.

Notes: IV. WHAT PRETRIAL DOES AND DOES NOT

[16] See Appendix C: Form G, question 2b; Form I, question 2b.

[17] See Appendix C: Form H, questions 2b, 2a, 2f.

[18] The frequency with which trials improve following pretrial conferences does not vary with the type of case.

[19] See note IV, 10 *supra*. It has been pointed out that there are good theoretical and practical reasons for social science researchers to report and draw inferences about "statistical fringe data" that do not meet the statistician's customary standards of significance, because such data inspire creative theorizing. Zeisel, *The Significance of Insignificant Differences*, 19 PUBLIC OPINION Q. 319, 320 (1955).

[20] We believe that the B cases are substantially similar to both the A and the C cases in all respects that might influence the way in which they respond to pretrial. Careful analysis of the group failed to disclose any differences, except the following: the B cases had a higher percentage of motor vehicle cases, single party, and single claim cases than the other two groups. However, those differences appear not to be material, since when we controlled for "motor vehicle" and "complexity," neither turned out to be an effective factor. Hence, so far as we have been able to determine, the B cases had no distinctive features as against the A and C cases, and comparisons between their litigation careers and outcomes should indicate the impact of pretrial.

[21] Although the test forms contained twelve items on trial quality, two appeared to be of doubtful validity and were not used; and two items, we decided on reflecting, were more appropriately merged with two other items. That left eight indicators of trial quality and these were ultimately used to "score" the three case groups. The C cases were inferior to the A cases in seven of these and better than the A cases in one item. Compared with the C cases the B cases scored better in five items, tied once, and were inferior twice.

[22] There were 125 A cases and 93 B+C cases in which the judges responded on all three of the evidence items.

[23] Plaintiffs' counsel reported no unnecessary witnesses were called in 97% of the A cases and 99% of the B+C cases (significance level: .30–.40). Defense counsel reported no unnecessary witnesses in 96% of the A cases as against 94% of the B+C cases (significance level: .70–.80).

[24] See p. 37 *supra*.

[25] There were responses in 130 A cases and 97 B+C cases.

[26] Different "populations," of course, served as bases: pretrial judges reported on all cases in which a conference was held regardless of whether they reached trial; attorneys reported on tried cases in which no conference was held; and the trial judges were able to comment on only the small fraction of pretried cases that reached trial.

[27] See Appendix C: Form H, question 4b.

[28] Significance level: .50–.60. There were responses in 123 A cases and 43 C cases.

[29] See Appendix C: Form I, questions 3a, 3c.

[30] Plaintiffs' counsel responded in 62 cases and defendants' counsel in 57.

[31] See Appendix C: Form F, question 2e (iii).

[32] Murrah, *supra* note IV, 1.

[33] ABA SPECIAL COMMITTEE ON COURT CONGESTION, TEN CURES FOR COURT CONGESTION 11 (1959).

[34] In the period 1948-62, total cases pending on the law dockets of the New Jersey Superior and County courts increased from 10,495 to 23,693. 1961–62 REPORT, Supp. p. 5.

[35] See DELAY IN THE COURT 3; Rosenberg & Chanin, *Auditors in Massachusetts As Antidotes for Delayed Civil Courts*, 110 U. PA. L. REV. 27, 35–36 (1961). Compare with the text the analysis in Zeisel, *Delay by the Parties and Delay by the Courts,* 15 J. LEGAL ED. 27, 35 (1962):

[I]n the main, if one wants to study delay in a particular court system, the task is threefold: First, determine the demand end of our equation—how much court time would be required to remove the backlog? The second job is to determine the supply end—how much court-time is available? The third necessary step, how either to reduce the work-load or increase the available court-time, will seldom require basic local studies [because] the curative powers of certain specific remedies do not vary much from court to court.

Views vary regarding the proper beginning point to measure delay. Some say from time of filing, others from the date the case is ready for trial. See Olney, *An Analysis of Docket Congestion in the United States District Courts in the Light of the Enactment of the Omnibus Judgeship Bill, Seminar on Procedures,* 29 F.R.D. 191, 217, 219 (1961).

[36] This was determined by analysis of weekly time sheets submitted as a regular practice by New Jersey judges to the Administrative Office. The Project obtained time sheet data for 9 randomly selected weeks during the period April, 1961, to April, 1962, submitted to 23 judges. All were from the Superior or County courts in the 7 test counties.

Notes: IV. WHAT PRETRIAL DOES AND DOES NOT 155

In 145 weeks a total of 2,387 judge hours were devoted to civil law matters—60% to trials; 15% to pretrials; 9% to motions; 9% to settlement conferences; 3% to calendar calls; and 3% to miscellaneous work. See Brennan, *After Eight Years: New Jersey Judicial Reform,* 43 A.B.A.J. 499, 501-2 (1957), outlining the importance of weekly reports in New Jersey's judicial reform.

[37] In the vast published literature on the pretrial conference only a few dissent from the view that pretrial is bound to save court time by promoting settlements and eliminating trial work. For the usual view, see, *e.g.*, NIMS, PRE-TRIAL 64–65 (1950); Brennan, *New Jersey Tackles Court Congestion,* 40 J. AM. JUD. SOC'Y 45, 50–51 (1956); Murrah, *Pre-Trial Procedure—A Statement of Its Essentials,* 14 F.R.D. 417 (1954). ABA SPECIAL COMMITTEE ON COURT CONGESTION, TEN CURES FOR COURT CONGESTION 2 (1959) attributes "astounding" results to pretrial and makes it "Cure Number 1." *But see* McIlvaine, *The Value of an Effective Pretrial, Seminar on Practice and Procedure,* 28 F.R.D. 37, 158 (1960). Judge McIlvaine, an experienced and highly regarded federal judge, expressed "some doubts" that "pretrial procedures as we know them" have any effect on docket congestion. *Id.* at 158. See also Pharr, *supra* note IV, 8 at 177.

[38] DELAY IN THE COURT 241; and see, on the need for controlled experiments in law, the very helpful discussion at 241–50.

[39] See Chapter VIII, pp. 118–19, but *cf.* note VIII, 7, and text at page 120.

[40] Recent years' figures compiled by the New Jersey Administrative Office of the Courts on case dispositions in the Law Divisions of the Superior and County courts show that the settlement rate for all civil law cases consistently ranged from 22 to 24%, the identical percentage produced by the test cases (which were all personal injury actions). Since such actions account for most of the work of the major courts, the close correspondence between the Project and the court figures is reassuring. See 1959–60 REPORT, Table G; 1960–61 REPORT, Table G; 1961–62 REPORT, Table C-2; 1962–63 REPORT, Table C-2.

[41] The concept of "durability," its importance for the study of court delay, and an analysis of factors having consequence for durability, are set forth in Rosenberg & Sovern, *supra* note III, 27, at 1115, 1124–44. "[M]any sued cases have identifiable features that tend to differentiate them from the mass of cases settled without suit; and . . . these same features tend to distinguish cases reaching trial from those settled without trial." *Id.* at 1126.

[42] "[T]he tools [of social science research] can almost never be used in their pure form, because natural and social obstacles usually prevent the ideal research approach. Forced to operate against such odds, and limited to data that are never perfect, social science research requires at every turn ingenuity and prudence: ingenuity in overcoming the obstacles and prudence in judging how far the research design can be carried without breaking down—that is, in judging when half a loaf is better than none."—Zeisel, *Social Research on the Law: The Ideal and the Practical,* in LAW AND SOCIOLOGY 124, 126 (Evan ed. 1962).

[43] See pp. 62–64.

[44] At the outset the case composition of the B and C groups was as shown in the following table:

Table G. Type of Cases in the B and C Groups*

Type of Case	B	C
1. Motor vehicle	69%	59%
Number of cases	731	688
2. Multiparty	71%	77%
Number of cases	735	695
3. Multiclaim	54%	62%
Number of cases	727	684

*Significance levels: item 1, less than .001; item 2, .01–.02; item 3, .001–.01.

[45] Controlling for the type of case, as shown in the following table, we inferred that type of processing had no consequences for durability. Table H shows percentages of cases that settled before trial.

Table H. Type of Pretrial Processing Had No Consequences for Settlement*

	Per Cent Settled	
Type of Case	B	C
1. Motor vehicle	76%	79%
Number of cases	464	384
2. Non-motor vehicle	82%	78%
Number of cases	152	187
3. Multiparty	79%	78%
Number of cases	493	503
4. Single party	77%	79%
Number of cases	189	155
5. Multiclaim	78%	79%
Number of cases	364	397
6. Single claim	79%	78%
Number of cases	311	250

*Significance levels: item 1, .40–.50; item 2, .20–.30; item 3, approximately .95; item 4, .70–.80; item 5, approximately .70; item 6, .70–.80.

[46] See Appendix C: Form F, question 2e (i). The judges answered *Yes* in 9% of 1,102 A cases and in 11% of 517 C cases.
Significance level: .30–.40.

[47] The percentages given here relate to all cases that commence trial. The same relationship continues to hold for cases tried to judgment.

[48] Nearly 40% of all trials required less than 1 hour, and approximately 60% no more than 3 hours, according to the weekly official reports submitted for the 1962–63 court year by judges sitting in the Law Divisions of the Superior and County courts. 1962–63 REPORT, Tables C–1, F–1. Included in the classification "trials and appeals" are proceedings not classifiable as "trials" within the meaning of this report, but if those intruders are all assumed to require less than one hour and an adjustment is made accordingly the percentage of short-category trials (under 3 hours) would still be 37%, a figure consistent with the study findings. Table I is derived from Tables C–1 and F–1 of the 1962–63 Report:

Table I. Duration of Trials and Appeals

		Cumulative	
Trial Time	Number of Cases	Number	Percentage
1 hour or less	2,229	2,229	38%
1 hour+–3 hours	1,118	3,347	56%
3 hours+–1 day	654	4,001	67%
1 day+–3 days	1,582	5,583	94%
3 days+–5 days	267	5,850	99%
Over 5 days	78	5,928	100%

[49] 1960–61 REPORT, Supp. 18.

[50] See p. 22 *supra*.

[51] Of 1,418 A cases, 16% completed trial; and 15% of 701 B and 661 C cases.
Significance levels: B against A, .30–.40; B against C, over .98.

[52] These percentages are based on 735 B cases and 695 C cases. The pattern persisted in cases tried to completion.
Significance level: less than .05.

[53] Multiple claims were made in 62% of 684 C cases and in 54% of 727 B cases. The pattern persisted in tried-to-completion cases.
Significance level: .001–.01.

[54] Motor vehicles were involved in 59% of 688 C cases and 69% of 731 B cases. The pattern persisted in tried-to-completion cases. Significance level: less than .001.

[55] *Table J-1. Trial Duration of Motor Vehicle Cases Was More Commonly Short in Not-Pretried Cases**

Trial time (in hours)	B	A	C
1. 2 or less	26%	11%	10%
2. 2+–5	21%	24%	10%
3. 5+–10	33%	41%	46%
4. Over 10	21%	23%	33%
Number of cases	43	128	39

*Significance levels: B against A, item 1, .02–.05; item 2, approximately .80; item 3, approximately .40; and item 4, approximately .90. B against C, item 1, .10–.20; item 2, approximately .30; item 3, approximately .30; and item 4, .30–.40.

Non-motor vehicle cases also had shorter trials if they were not pretried, as shown in Table J–2.

*Table J-2. Trial Duration in Non-Motor Vehicle Cases Was More Commonly Short in Not-Pretried Cases**

Trial time (in hours)	B	A	C
1. 2 or less	19%	4%	13%
2. 2+–5	6%	24%	23%
3. 5+–10	50%	39%	30%
4. Over 10	25%	32%	33%
Number of cases	16	46	30

*Significance levels: B against A, item 1, .30–.40; item 2, .20–.30; item 3, .60–.70; item 4, approximately .80. B against C, item 1, .70–.80; item 2, .20–.30; item 3, .20–.30; item 4, .70–.80.

When read together, Tables J–1 and J–2 demonstrate that, regardless of processing, motor vehicle cases are of short duration more frequently than non-motor vehicle cases.

[56] See Appendix C: Form F, question 2e (ii). A negative answer was recorded to the question: "In your opinion will the conference probably [shorten the trial]" by 74% of the judges in 1,079 A cases and 77% in 501 C cases.
Significance level: .05–.50.

[57] Data from this study demonstrate that among all cases that commence trial, jury trials ran longer than non-jury, as shown in Table K:

Notes: IV. WHAT PRETRIAL DOES AND DOES NOT

Table K. *Jury Trials Took Longer than Non-Jury**

	Jury Trial	Non-Jury Trial
Trial time (in hours)		
1. Less than 2	5%	53%
2. 2–5	19%	31%
3. 5+–10	44%	17%
4. Over 10	31%	—
Number of trials commenced	258	36

*Significance levels: item 1, less than .001; item 2, .10–.20; item 3, .001–.01; item 4, less than .001.

The data for tried-to-completion cases revealed a similar pattern. As a final check, we controlled for all factors that we believed might have distorted the results but found the same profile in the sub-factors as emerged in the in-gross tabulations above.

In an analysis of comparative trial duration in the Supreme Court, New York County, it was concluded that a personal injury case tried before a jury requires on average 67% longer than if tried with a judge only. DELAY IN THE COURT 79.

[58] The 95% findings were based on 219 responses in the A cases and 94 in the C cases. The B+C rate, on 179 responses, was 93%.

Significance level: A against B+C, .40–.50; B against A, .20–.30; B against C, .40–.50.

[59] The waiver rate in the A group is based on 204 cases that originally demanded a jury. The waiver rate for B+C is based on 157 cases.

Significance level: .10–.20.

[60] There were 73 B cases in which a jury demand had been made. Significance level: B against A, .10–.20; B against C, .80–.90.

[61] If there are factors that have the twin effect of inducing lawyers to opt for a conference and at the same time resist waiving a jury, they have so far escaped our attention.

[62] The B group constituted 52% of the lawyer's-choice cases. The projection of this figure to future years assumes, of course, that factors which entered into the decision to opt for or against a conference during the test period remain roughly constant.

[63] For the steps and arithmetic to arrive at a figure of 19,000 as the number of personal injury cases added to the calendar annually, see note III, 11 *supra*. When those steps are taken with respect to the known number of pretrial conferences of all types held annually, they place at 11,000 the yearly number of personal injury pretrials.

160   *Notes:* IV. WHAT PRETRIAL DOES AND DOES NOT

Ibid.; see 1962–63 REPORT, Tables C–1, F–1; 1961–62 REPORT, Tables C–1, F–1.

Applying the study data on duration of conferences to 11,000 yields approximately 6,200 hours as the judge time devoted to personal injury pretrials yearly. [The computations are shown in Table L. Columns 1–5 show respectively: (1) time intervals used to measure duration of conferences; (2) percentage of A and C cases in each time interval; (3) how the 11,000 (*i.e.,* 10,989) conferences would be allocated to time intervals; (4) average length in minutes assigned to each interval; and (5) total number of hours consumed by the conferences in each time interval.]

Inasmuch as 52% of the cases having an option elected not to be pretried (see note IV, 62 *supra*) the time saving would be approximately (52% x 6200 =) 3,200 judge hours yearly, after rounding off.

Table L. Number of Judge Hours Annually Devoted to Pretrial Conferences in Personal Injury Cases

1 Pretrial Conference Time Interval (Hours)	2 Cases in Category (%)	3 Cases in Category (Number)	4 Average Time (Minutes)	5 Total Time (Hours)
Less than ¼	0.2	22	10	4
¼ +–½	34.0	3740	20	1247
½ +–¾	50.0	5500	35	3209
¾ +–1	10.0	1100	50	917
1 +–1½	5.0	550	75	688
Over 1½	0.7	77	105	134
Total	99.9	10,989		6,199

[64] In recent years the New Jersey courts have observed 210 working days, averaging an estimated 5½ hours on the bench or in settlement conferences. This computes at 1,155 judge hours per year. Letter from Mortimer G. Newman, Jr., Assistant Director of the New Jersey Administrative Office of the Courts, to Project, March 24, 1964. This does not include hours consumed outside the courtroom on various judicial functions. That total judge time is greater than "housekeeping" records would indicate is supported by an official federal time study. See 1960 U.S. ADMN. OFF. OF THE COURTS ANN. REP. 127. Total time at work per New Jersey judge in the courts involved would run to 1,700 hours per year assuming an 8-hour day for each of the 210 working days.

Notes: IV. WHAT PRETRIAL DOES AND DOES NOT 161

[65] The estimated savings of 3,200 hours (see note IV, 63 *supra*) divided by 1,700, the number of hours in a judge year (see note IV, 64 *supra*) equals 1.9 judge years.

[66] Judges in the New Jersey Superior and County courts devoted 47,714 hours on the bench and in settlement conference to all civil law matters during the 1963 calendar year. Letter from Mortimer G. Newman, Jr., Assistant Director of the New Jersey Administrative Office of the Courts, to Project, March 24, 1964. On the average, each judge spent 1,155 hours a year in such functions. *Ibid.* Hence, the equivalent of 41 full-time judges was necessary to dispose of civil law matters. A saving of 1.9 judge years by conversion to optional pretrial would be equivalent to 5% of the judge time expended in civil law matters.

[67] Pharr, *The Truth About Pretrial,* 47 A.B.A.J. 177 (1961).

[68] A Project study of the impact of adoption of compulsory arbitration of small claims in Pennsylvania concluded that there exists "the distinct possibility" that "almost one-third of the litigants may come out differently before arbitrators than they would have before a jury." Rosenberg & Schubin, *Trial by Lawyer: Compulsory Artibtration of Small Claims in Pennsylvania,* 74 HARV. L. REV. 448, 466 (1961). A study of Massachusetts' auditor system revealed "a marked rate of disagreement [between auditors and juries] in deciding . . . liability and damages." Rosenberg & Chanin, *supra* note IV, 35, at 49.

[69] There were responses in 208 A cases and 176 B+C cases. Significance level: .80–.90.

[70] See note III, 24 *supra*.

[71] Table M, following, controls for (a) type of case (motor vehicle, non-motor vehicle); (b) number of parties (single party, multiparty); and (c) number of claims (single claim, multiclaim) and demonstrates that differences in case composition did not change the finding that type of processing had no effect for whether plaintiff recovers anything, either in settlement or trial.

[72] Table N includes all recoveries, whether by settlement or trial.

[73] Table O shows all recoveries, whether by settlement or trial.

Table M. *Type of Processing Had No Effect on Whether Plaintiff Recovered Anything**

Subfactor	Per Cent in Which Plaintiff Recovered		
	A	B	C
1. Motor vehicle	94%	93%	95%
Number of cases	874	458	366
2. Non-motor vehicle	89%	89%	91%
Number of cases	438	211	248
3. Single party	88%	86%	93%
Number of cases	302	187	145
4. Multiparty	93%	94%	93%
Number of cases	1,018	485	475
5. Single claim	91%	89%	92%
Number of cases	579	308	237
6. Multiclaim	93%	94%	95%
Number of cases	723	357	372

*Significance levels: B against A, item 1, approximately .50; item 2, .90–.95; item 3, .40–.50; item 4, .80–.90; item 5, .40–.50; item 6, .90–.95.

B against C, item 1, .10–.20; item 2, .60–.70; item 3, .02–.05; item 4, approximately .90; item 5, .30–.40 item 6, .70–.80.

Table N. *All-Pretried Cases Recovered Less than In-Part-Pretried**

Amount recovered (dollars)	A	B+C
1. 1,000 or less	28%	30%
2. 1,001–3,000	39%	38%
3. 3,001–6,000	18%	19%
4. 6,001–10,000	8%	7%
5. 10,001 and over	7%	5%
Number of recoveries	1,228	1,208

*Significance levels: item 1, .10–.20; item 2, .60–.70; item 3, .20–.30; item 4, .10–.20; item 5, .05–.10.

Table O. *Not-Pretried Cases Recovered Less Than Pretried**

Amount Recovered (dollars)	B	A	C
1. 1,000 or less	33%	28%	27%
2. 1,001–3,000	40%	39%	37%
3. 3,001–6,000	17%	18%	22%
4. 6,001–10,000	5%	8%	8%
5. 10,001 and over	4%	7%	6%
Number of recoveries	627	1,228	581

*Significance levels: B against A, item 1, .01–.02; item 2, .80–.90; item 3, approximately .90; item 4, .01–.02; item 5, .02–.05.

B against C, item 1, .02–.05; item 2, approximately .30; item 3, .05–.10; item 4, almost .05, item 5, .10–.20.

Notes: IV. WHAT PRETRIAL DOES AND DOES NOT 163

[74] The assurance of similarity in "size" is not absolute because of possible sampling error. There were in fact differences in the A group as compared to the B+C group in such respects as the frequency of motor vehicle cases and complex cases. But there is no indication that these would lead to any overall "size" imbalance in the compared groups.

[75] See p. 62 *supra*.

[76] Table P shows the average recoveries for all cases in which there was a recovery in (1) settled cases and (2) adjudicated cases.

Table P. Not-Pretried Cases Recovered Less Money than Pretried

	B	A	C
1. Settled cases average	$2,853	$3,812	$3,632
Number of cases	575	1,099	526
2. Tried to completion cases average	$6,047	$6,837	$6,769
Number of cases	52	129	55

[77] Judges reported agreement with juries' findings on liability in 83% of personal injury cases, according to the findings of Chicago Jury Project. Broeder, *The University of Chicago Jury Project*, 38 NEB. L. REV. 744, 750 (1959). But the total amount judges reported they would have awarded had they sat without a jury totaled about 20% less than the total amount the juries did in fact award. DELAY IN THE COURT 73.

[78] See note III, 14 and pp. 62–64 *supra*.

[79] For 26 judges who pretried at least 25 cases during the test period, Table Q below shows the settlement rates.

Table Q. Pretried Cases Settled at Different Rates

Settlement Rates	Number of Judges	Settlement Rates	Number of Judges
85%	1	71%	2
83%	1	70%	3
81%	1	69%	1
80%	3	68%	1
79%	3	65%	1
77%	3	64%	1
76%	2	—	
75%	2	Total number of judges	26
72%	1		

164 *Notes:* V. NEW JERSEY JUDGES SPEAK THEIR MINDS

CHAPTER V. NEW JERSEY JUDGES SPEAK THEIR MINDS ABOUT PRETRIAL CONFERENCE IN PERSONAL INJURY CASES

[1] A synopsis of the Princeton Seminar.

[2] Statements made in this chapter are based upon the transcript of proceedings at the New Jersey Judicial Seminar on Pretrial Conferences, held September 5–7, 1962, and recorded in 16 mimeographed volumes. A set of these volumes and a footnoted copy of the text of this report, containing references to the transcript by volume and page, are on file with the Project. The volumes are titled as follows:

   I   Discussion of New Jersey pretrial study
   II Pretrial of a negligence case
   III Techniques of an effective pretrial conference
   IV Pretrial order and its effect
   V   Settlement techniques
   VI Preparation for a pretrial conference: use of sanctions
   VII Preparation for a pretrial conference: use of sanctions
   VIII Techniques of an effective pretrial conference
   IX Settlement techniques
   X   Pretrial order and its effect
   XI Evaluation of a negligence case for settlement purposes
   XII Settlement techniques
   XIII Pretrial order and its effect
   XIV Preparation for a pretrial conference: use of sanctions
   XV Techniques of an effective pretrial conference
   XVI Summary of group discussions.

[3] See Appendix A for text of Rev. Rule 4:29–1 (b).

[4] These impressions of attorney unpreparedness contrast sharply with the statistical data in the study, which report on a case-by-case basis that both sides are well prepared 84–85% of the time. Apparently global opinions held by the judges are less favorable than detailed reports on a case-by-case basis. *Cf.* pp. 34–36 *supra.*

CHAPTER VI. CLINICAL VIEWS OF THE NEW JERSEY PRETRIAL IN ACTION

[1] Statements made in this chapter are based upon the comments recorded in the observer forms—each having been assigned an identifying code number. These forms, as well as a footnoted copy of the text of this report, containing references to particular cases by their code numbers, are on file with the Project.

Notes: VII. TECHNIQUES, "ARTISTRY" IN PRETRIAL

[2] See Appendix F.

[3] The purpose and mechanics of "transfer" are detailed in Appendix F.

CHAPTER VII. TECHNIQUES AND "ARTISTRY" IN PRETRIAL

[1] Wright, *Pre-Trial on Trial*, 14 LA. L. REV. 391, 395 (1954).

[2] Comments by Judge Murrah, in *Proceedings of the Nebraska State Bar Association, October 1949,* 29 NEB. L. REV. 341, 342 (1950).

[3] Kincaid, *A Judge's Handbook of Pre-Trial Procedure,* 17 F.R.D. 437, 443 (1955).

[4] Murrah, *Pre-Trial Procedure—A Statement of Its Essentials,* 14 F.R.D. 417 (1953).

[5] Brennan, *Remarks on Pre-Trial,* 17 F.R.D. 479, 485 (1955).

[6] Clark, *Objectives of Pre-Trial Procedure,* 17 OHIO ST. L. J. 163, 167 (1956).

[7] Murrah, *supra* note VII, 4, at 422.

[8] Clark, *supra* Note VII, 6, at 165.

[9] The pretrial judge "must continually interrogate counsel," be "not satisfied" to rely on counsel's statement of the issues "without further analysis" and "draw on his own imagination" to suggest stipulations. Holtzoff, *Pretrial Procedure in the District of Columbia,* 3 CATHOLIC U.L. REV. 1, 3 (1952). Judge Holtzoff also amplifies his contentions that specifications of claims and defenses "should be called for and required" by illustrating several appropriate specifications that may be "exacted." *Id.* at 7. Judge Pharr has also offered specific guides to the pretrial judge. He advocates that the judge do his "homework" in advance of the conference; that he "carry the ball" by asking questions and "digging for simple, clear, and frank answers"; and that he "chart the trial." Pharr, *supra* note IV, 67, at 178. See also Holtzoff, *Federal Pretrial Procedure,* 11 AM. U.L. REV. 21 (1962); Murrah, *The Pretrial Conference: Conceptions and Misconceptions,* 44 A.B.A.J. 39, 40 (1958) citing to and concurring with Judge Holtzoff's views.

[10] Thomas, *The Story of Pre-Trial in the Common Pleas Court of Cuyahoga County,* 7 W. RES. L. REV. 368 (1956).

[11] *Id.* at 380.

[12] *Ibid.*

[13] *Id.* at 386.

166 *Notes:* VII. TECHNIQUES, "ARTISTRY" IN PRETRIAL

[14] *Id.* at 414–17.
[15] Van Alstyne & Grossman.
[16] *Id.* at 66.
[17] *Id.* at 296.
[18] *Id.* at 32–33.
[19] *Id.* at 298–99.
[20] *Id.* at 299.
[21] See Chapter V, p. 72 *supra.*
[22] English, *A Year of Pre-Trial Settlement Conferences,* 40 Chi. B. Record 343 (1959).
[23] *Cf.* Van Alstyne & Grossman. "There is no fixed or ideal way to conduct a pretrial conference. The scope of matters to be considered, techniques employed, and order of events all depend on the circumstances of each case. The pretrial judge's personal preferences and habits also play an important role, as do the capabilities and experience of participating counsel. The keynote is flexibility: the desired procedure is the one that produces results." *Id.* at 281.

CHAPTER VIII. A PRETRIAL CONFERENCE PROGRAM FOR PERSONAL INJURY CASES

[1] See p. 24 *supra.*
[2] See pp. 7–9 *supra.*
[3] See pp. 96–98, 102 *supra.*
[4] In 2,436 test cases in which there was a recovery, whether by settlement or by adjudication, the median was $1,913. See also note III, 26 *supra.*
[5] Of 575 B cases, which recovered something by settlement, 429 (74.6%) received no more than $3,000.
[6] See 18 Calif. Jud. Council Bienn. Rep. 1959–60; Martz, *Pretrial Preparation, Seminar on Practice and Procedure,* 28 F.R.D. 37, 137–38 (1960).
[7] A settlement conference may serve a useful purpose in a court suffering a particularly depressed rate of before-trial dispositions or in specific classes of cases which are found to be especially amenable to such exposure.
[8] Concededly, there will be a loss of potential improvement in the quality of the settlement process for some cases not bound for trial. See p. 25 *supra.*

Notes: VIII. PRETRIAL PROGRAM FOR INJURY CASES

[9] In the present study the test cases that recovered up to $6,000 reached trial 16% of the time; those that recovered over $10,000 reached trial 35% of the time. These findings paralleled related ones made by the Project in New York. But this time the experimental framework permitted scientific confirmation of the "size-durability hypothesis"—*i.e.*, the theory that the greater the amount of the recovery the plaintiff may realize (if the defendant is found liable) directly affects the likelihood that the case will reach trial instead of settling. See Rosenberg & Sovern, *Delay and the Dynamics of Personal Injury Litigation*, 59 COLUM. L. REV. 1115 (1959). The authors found that among cases of very large recoveries 40% or more reached trial. *Id.* at 1131. Basic economic reasons undoubtedly account for the tendency of smaller cases to settle compared with "heavier" cases. *Id.* at 1136. *Cf.* Levit, *Pretrial Procedures in the Los Angeles Superior Court*, 38 LOS ANGELES B. BULL. 433, 436 (1963).

The experimental framework of the study permitted confirmation of the size-durability concept, by establishing that it is possible to select in advance cases that will require trial, based on the judges' "size" estimates. The mechanics of the selection system were simple and are explained in detail in Appendix F, at page 219. Briefly, the pretrial judges made an estimate of the potential recovery in each case, assuming liability. The estimate was recorded as "Small" (under $3,000); "Medium" ($3,000–$7,500); or "Large" (over $7,500). When the results were later tabulated, it developed that cases selected as "Small" reached trial 21% of the time, and those said to be "Large" started a trial 31% of the time. Presumably, the New Jersey judges could achieve higher durability prediction "scores" by screening out the cases involving as much as, say, $20,000.

Table R. Cases Estimated by Judges to Have Large Potential Recoveries Were More Durable

	Small (Under $3,000)	Medium ($3,000–$7,500)	Large (Over $7,500)
Settled before trial	79%	74%	69%
Reached trial	21%	25%	31%
Number of cases	607	711	301

[10] See NEW JERSEY SUPREME COURT'S COMMITTEE ON PRETRIAL PROCEDURE DRAFT OF PROPOSED RULES TO IMPLEMENT REPORT, April 11, 1963, p. 12.

APPENDIX

APPENDICES

APPENDIX A. NEW JERSEY RULES OF CIVIL PRACTICE RELATING TO THE PRETRIAL CONFERENCE

THIS appendix contains the text of Rev. Rule 4:29 of the New Jersey Rules of Civil Practice, relating to the pretrial conference in effect on January 1, 1960, when the study began. Two amendments to the rules have been made since that date; however, neither has any substantive effect for purposes of this study. Rev. Rule 4:15-2 relating to the pretrial order is also set out.

TEXT OF THE RULES

RULE 4:29. THE PRETRIAL CONFERENCE PROCEDURE

4:29-1. PRETRIAL CONFERENCES

(a) In every contested action except an action for divorce, nullity of marriage and actions governed by Rule 4:94A and only as may be practicable in an action brought in a summary manner under Rule 4:85, the court shall direct the attorneys for the parties to appear before it for a conference in open court to:

(1) state and simplify the issues to be litigated and to amend the pleadings accordingly;

(2) obtain admissions of fact and of documents that will avoid unnecessary proof;

(3) limit by agreement the number of expert witnesses;

(4) specify all damage claims as of the date of the conference;

(5) consider such other matters as may aid in the disposition of the action.

(b) At the pretrial conference it shall first be determined if the case is to be transferred to the county district court as provided in Rule 4:3-4. If the case is to be so transferred an appropriate order of transfer shall be entered and it shall be discretionary with the court as to whether the conference is to be continued and a pretrial order entered. If the case is not to be transferred the pretrial conference shall continue and the court shall make a pretrial order reciting the action taken at the conference, which order shall recite specifically:

(1) A concise descriptive statement of the nature of the action. (For example: Pedestrian-automobile, intersection, negligence, personal injury action; pedestrian, personal injury, public sidewalk, negligence, nuisance action; action for breach of contract; action on a book account; action for possession of land; action under the Mechanics Lien Act; action for specific performance; etc.).

(2) The factual contention of the plaintiff as to the liability of the defendant.

(3) The factual contention of the defendant as to nonliability and affirmative defense.

(4) The admissions or stipulations of the parties with respect to the cause of action pleaded by plaintiff or defendant-counterclaimant.

(5) All claims as to damages and the extent of injury, and admissions or stipulations with respect thereto, and this shall limit the claims thereto at the trial. Where such claims have been disclosed in depositions or answers to interrogatories they may be incorporated by reference.

(6) Any amendments to the pleadings made at the conference or fixing the time within which amended pleadings shall be filed.

(7) A specification of the legal issues raised by the pleadings as amended or to be amended which are to be determined at the trial.

(8) A specification of the legal issues raised by the pleadings which are abandoned.

(9) A list of the exhibits marked in evidence by consent.

(10) If leave is granted to make any further use of discovery proceedings by way of additional interrogatories, depositions, or otherwise, such fact shall be stated as well as any time limit imposed for the completion thereof. Such leave at this stage is undesirable and should be granted only in the most exceptional cases. Any additional discovery must be completed prior to the scheduled trial date so that the disposition of the case will not be delayed.

(11) Any limitation on the number of expert witnesses.

(12) Any direction with respect to the filing of briefs.

(13) When a consolidated action, or an action which includes a third-party suit, a counterclaim, a cross-claim, or where there are several

plaintiffs or defendants separately represented by counsel, the order of opening and closing to the jury at the trial.

(14) Any other matters which have been agreed upon in order to expedite the disposition of the matter.

(15) The estimated length of the trial.

(16) When the case shall be placed on the weekly call.

Such order shall be signed by the court and attorneys for the parties and when entered, becomes part of the record, supersedes the pleadings where inconsistent therewith, and controls the subsequent course of action unless modified at or before the trial or pursuant to Rule 4:15–2 to prevent manifest injustice. The matter of settlement may be discussed at the side-bar, but it shall not be mentioned in the order.

(c) For failure to appear at a pretrial conference or to participate therein or to prepare therefor, the court in its discretion may make such order with respect to the imposition of costs and counsel fees and with respect to the continued prosecution of the cause, including dismissal, or of the defense thereof, as is just and proper.

(d) Illustrative forms of notice of pretrial hearing and of pretrial orders to be followed are set forth in Appendix C.

(e) Whenever trial briefs are ordered at a pretrial conference the order shall specify to which judge or other court official they shall be submitted and within what time. Where it appears that the trial will be presided over by a judge other than the pretrial conference judge, the latter shall file a copy of the pretrial order with the Assignment Judge or such other person as he may designate. It shall be the responsibility of the Assignment Judge in such cases to make appropriate arrangements so that it may be determined after the briefs are received whether the action is one which requires study in advance by the trial judge. If so, a day certain shall be fixed and the action assigned to a particular trial judge for disposition, such assignment to be at least 2 days in advance of the date so fixed.

[NOTE: Rule 4:29–1 was amended, effective July 1, 1960, to delete "and actions governed by Rule 4:94A."]

4:29–2. TIME FOR MAILING NOTICES

The county clerk shall give to all attorneys at least 2 weeks' notice by mail of the pretrial conference. The notice shall not be mailed until 100 days after the service of the complaint, except that upon application of a party with or without consent of the other party the court may direct the earlier mailing of the notice for good cause shown expressly stated in the order. Seventy days after the service of the complaint the county clerk shall mail to the parties or their attorneys a preliminary notice advising them that their case may be scheduled for pretrial shortly.

4:29–3. CONFERENCE OF ATTORNEYS; PRETRIAL MEMORANDA

(a) The attorneys shall confer before the date assigned for the pretrial conference to reach agreement upon as many matters as possible. Each attorney shall prepare and submit to the court at the pretrial conference a memorandum statement of the matters agreed upon and of the factual and legal contentions to be made on behalf of his client as respects the issues remaining in dispute, including specifically a detailed statement as to damages for the purposes of assisting the pretrial judge determining whether the action should be transferred to the county district court pursuant to Rule 4:3–4.

(b) Counsel for all of the parties should come to the pretrial conference prepared to discuss settlement and have their clients available in person or by telephone for this purpose.

4:29–4. SCHEDULING OF PRETRIAL CONFERENCES

(a) Not more than 3 pretrial conferences of cases shall be noticed for pretrial within the same hour before the same judge.

(b) The county clerk of each county is charged with the responsibility for preparing and mailing pretrial conference notices. He shall, before preparing and mailing the notices of cases to be pretried on a particular day, analyze the list, and to the extent possible notice all cases of the same attorney or firm before the same judge and consecutively. Where there is an integrated list, assignments shall be made to Superior and County Court judges without regard to the court in which the action was instituted.

(c) Each Assignment Judge and each judge of the Chancery Division shall schedule pretrial conferences for appropriate dates before the end of June of each year in such numbers as to produce adequate trial lists to meet the necessity for cases for trial in the early part of the succeeding September Stated Session.

(d) Pretrial conferences of cases pending in the Law Division of the Superior Court and County Court in the counties of Bergen, Essex and Hudson shall be scheduled in such manner that only one of said counties will hold pretrial conferences in any one week; pretrial conferences in the counties of Passaic and Union shall be held during the same week, which shall be a week other than the one in which pretrial conferences are scheduled in the counties of Bergen, Essex or Hudson. The Assignment Judges of said counties shall jointly prepare a schedule fixing the weeks from the effective date of this rule to the end of the court year, and annually thereafter, during which each of said counties will schedule pretrial conferences and shall cause such schedule to be published.

(e) In the week set aside in the counties of Bergen, Essex, Hudson, Passaic or Union for pretrial conferences, no actions shall be tried in the Law Divisions of the Superior Court or County Court of such county except that a trial begun and not completed prior to the pretrial week may be continued in such week.

(f) The provisions of this rule shall not preclude the Assignment Judge of any county from scheduling pretrial conferences at such times as may be necessary either to maintain a full trial calendar or to utilize fully the service of available judges.

4:29–5. PRETRIAL CONFERENCES IN OPEN COURT

All pretrial conferences shall be conducted in open court, and so far as convenient, in a regular courtroom.

[NOTE: Rule 4:29–5 was amended, effective September 11, 1961 to read as follows:

Rule 4:29–5. PRETRIAL CONFERENCES IN OPEN COURT; SETTLEMENT CONFERENCE IN CHAMBERS

All pretrial conferences shall be conducted in open court, but the judge may conduct such conferences at counsel table. Settlement conferences may be held in chambers.]

4:29–6. PRETRIAL CONFERENCE ORDER DICTATED IN OPEN COURT

The pretrial conference order shall be dictated in open court immediately upon the conclusion of the pretrial conference discussion, and it shall be signed by the judge and the attorneys forthwith.

4:29–7. PRETRIAL CONFERENCE AFTER GRANT OF NEW TRIAL

A pretrial conference shall be scheduled for every case in which a new trial is directed by the trial court or by mandate of an appellate court.

RULE 4:15. AMENDED AND SUPPLEMENTAL PLEADINGS

. . . .

4:15–2. AMENDMENTS TO CONFORM TO THE EVIDENCE

When issues not raised by the pleadings and pretrial order are tried by consent or without the objection of the parties, they shall be treated in all respects as if they had been raised in the pleadings and pretrial order. Such amendment of the pleadings and pretrial order as may be necessary to cause them to conform to the evidence and to raise these issues may be made upon motion of any party at any time, even after judgment; but failure so to amend shall not affect the result of the trial of these issues. If evidence is objected to at the trial on the ground that it is not within the issues made by the pleadings and pretrial order, the court may allow the pleadings and pretrial order to be amended and shall do so freely when the presentation of the merits of the action will be subserved thereby and the objecting party fails to satisfy the court that the admission of such evidence would prejudice him in maintaining his action or defense upon the merits. The court may grant a continuance to enable the objecting party to meet such evidence.

APPENDIX B. RECENT NEW JERSEY APPELLATE COURT DECISIONS REGARDING PRETRIAL

THIS appendix sets forth an analysis of state court decisions pertaining to pretrial conferences and pretrial orders written by the Supreme Court of New Jersey from 1949 through June, 1964, and by the Superior Court from 1959 through June, 1964. In all, 22 Supreme Court cases were found, and 21 Superior Court cases, 19 in the Appellate Division, and 2 at the trial level.

The purpose of this research was to determine the appellate courts' views on three aspects of the conduct and effect of pretrial conferences and orders:
(1) How active and forceful a part the pretrial judge should play in the conference;
(2) Utilization of the conference as a method of obtaining discovery;
(3) Impact of the pretrial order on the course of the trial process.

The decisions clearly demonstrate the desire on the part of the appellate courts for active, forceful participation by the pretrial judge in the conduct of the conference and the resultant shaping of the order. There is no doubt but that the mandate is for detailed and comprehensive pretrial orders, which set out all the disputed issues of fact and law, as well as complete statements of the factual contentions of each side.

No decision has been found that directly rules on the use of the conference as a means of obtaining discovery. However, one case indicates that the Apellate Division, at least, has a more liberal attitude toward discovery than is expressed in the rules.

The decisions reveal that the pretrial order controls the course of trial to no greater extent than would amended pleadings. Both the pleadings and the order are equally amendable. The courts demonstrate a liberal attitude in permitting amendments to the pretrial order and pleadings subsequent to the order. Formality is not required where the introduction of new issues is recognized and tried without objection.

(1) THE PRETRIAL JUDGE IS REQUIRED TO TAKE AN ACTIVE AND FORCEFUL PART IN THE CONFERENCE

In 1961, the Supreme Court, in *Mayfair Farms Holding Corp* v. *Kruvant Enterprises Co.*[1] declared that it is the duty of a judge at a pretrial conference "to compel the litigants to reveal fully their legal and factual positions so that they would know precisely what was involved before the case came to trial." The court added that "it is the role of the judge to see to it that the issues are fully understood" and observed that "anything less is a waste of time and money. . . ."[2]

In *Mayfair* the case came before the court on plaintiff's appeal from a judgment rendered for defendant in an action to recover the balance of the purchase price of lands. The case had been decided at the trial level upon a stipulation and exhibits, no oral evidence having been offered by either side. At the argument on appeal, it developed that counsel for both sides had privately prepared the pretrial order that the trial court signed without a conference. The parties, at the suggestion of the court, consented to a plenary retrial and a new pretrial was ordered.

Directions to the pretrial judge as to his function were also given by the Supreme Court in *Nusbaum* v. *Newark Morning Ledger Co.*[3] In the course of an opinion reversing a trial court's order directing a witness subpoenaed during discovery to answer certain questions, Justice Francis took note of the bulkiness of the pleadings. He stated that the pretrial judge should "require" the claims and issues to be so stated as to furnish a "specific guide" for the trial of the action.[4]

Implicitly, the appellate courts, by indicating their displeasure with orders that phrase the trial issues only in vague and general terms, have also instructed pretrial judges to take a forceful and active role in formulating issues at the conference. For example, in *Mason* v. *Niewinski*,[5] the court held that it was "meaningless" to phrase an issue as "duty under contract of taxi rental" and that such a "specification" could not be expected to be definitive for parties in adverse interest and to judges later dealing with the matter.[6]

From the foregoing decisions, it appears that the Supreme Court, in requiring judges to take an active part at the pretrial conference, has gone beyond the literal language of the pretrial rules in New Jersey.

The principal rule, 4:29-1, provides only that "the court shall direct the attorneys . . . to appear before it for a conference in open court" to state and simplify issues, obtain admissions, limit expert witnesses, specify damage claims, and consider all matters that may aid in disposition of the case. A pretrial order covering sixteen specified points is then to be prepared by the judge. Penalties "for failure to appear . . . or to participate therein or to prepare therefor" may be imposed by the court. While the terms used by the rules plainly contemplate that the judge shall insist that the lawyers prepare for the conference, attend it, and deal with the sixteen specified points, they do not tell him how far to press his insistence or what to do to compel an attorney who prepares and participates but does not reveal all the details the judge thinks he should, or does not yield to the judge's views in other respects. The question remains, when will the judge be considered too "activist"? No answer can be given because, although there have been appellate decisions indicating ways in which the judge must be *more* active, there have been none indicating when judicial activities have exceeded proper limits.

(2) No Reported Decision Has Indicated the Propriety of Using the Pretrial Conference as a Means of Discovery

Despite many instances in which the courts have issued directives that factual contentions should be fully set out in the pretrial order so that all issues may be recognized, apparently no appellate court has been required to decide to what extent, if any, pretrial can be utilized as an additional discovery mechanism. However, one Appellate Division decision has given a more liberal construction of the discovery provisions than is apparent from the language of the rules.

Rev. Rule 4:28 (a) provides that all discovery proceedings (with exceptions not pertinent here) "shall be completed within 100 days of the date of service of the complaint, unless for good cause shown the period is extended by order of the Court." This provision is supplemented in Rev. Rule 4:29-1 (b) (10) which pertains to the pretrial conference and states:

If leave is granted to make any further use of discovery proceedings by way of additional interrogatories, depositions or otherwise, such fact shall be stated as well as any time limit imposed for the completion thereof. Such leave at this stage is undesirable and should be granted only in the most exceptional cases.

Nonetheless, where the plaintiffs at pretrial had consented to an extension of time for the completion of discovery but thereafter attempted to limit it to depositions of the parties, the Appellate Division[7] refused to impose any restrictions upon defendant. The plaintiffs having given their consent without qualification at the conference, they could not thereafter complain. The court disregarded, first, plaintiffs' contention that at the conference they understood the request to pertain only to depositions of the parties; and second, the fact that defendant was aware of the identity and importance of the witness to be deposed, well in advance of the pretrial. Thus, the court ignored the opportunity presented to interpret rigorously the restrictive provisions of the rules; instead, it chose to enlarge the time in which discovery will be allowed.

(3) The Pretrial Order Does Not Control the Litigation Process Any More Firmly than the Pleadings

None of the decisions distinguishes in any way the effect of the pretrial order from that of the pleadings, insofar as control of the trial course is concerned. Every opinion tacitly assumes that the pleadings and order are to be read together and to be jointly amended where necessary; but the order imposes no greater limitations on the course of trial than would the pleadings alone.[8] The fungibility of the pleadings and pretrial order in the eyes of the appellate courts would appear to derive from the language of Rev. Rule 4:15–2 which provides:

When issues not raised by the pleadings and pretrial order are tried . . . they shall be treated . . . as if they had been raised in the pleadings and pretrial order.

The rule also provides that if previously unraised issues are tried by consent or without objection, amendment of the pleadings and pretrial order is not vital, but when objection is raised, leave to amend shall be freely given.

As early as 1953, the Supreme Court sustained a trial judge who permitted introduction of evidence on issues not raised in the answer or pretrial order, stating "the trial court undoubtedly had power to amend the pretrial order during the trial. . . ."[9] Also, in *Gaglio* v. *Yellow Cab Co.*,[10] the Appellate Division held the trial court's refusal to grant leave to amend the pretrial order an abuse of discretion, even though it was not requested until the end of trial. The appellate court broadly interpreted the rule permitting amendments and stated that "surprise is not enough" and that prejudice must appear before an objection to amendment can prevail.

In *Araujo v. New Jersey Natural Gas Co.*,[11] the Appellate Division went so far as to permit the pretrial order to be amended so that on a second trial a theory of law first raised on appeal could be litigated.

Numerous other decisions contain dicta indicating the appellate courts' acceptance of the view that pretrial orders are freely amendable.[12] A 1950 Supreme Court case[13] stated that the order controlled the course of the trial where not modified before or during the trial. In *Schlossberg v. Jersey City Sewerage Authority*,[14] the Supreme Court set aside an order to produce records because of irrelevancy, ruling that upon the failure of plaintiffs to amend the pretrial order to include issues of fraud, it became the duty of the trial judge "in the circumstances" to refuse the aid of the court.[15] The court's language clearly indicated, however, that had appropriate amendments been requested, the new issues could have been litigated, granting, of course, proper opportunity to defendant to prepare.

A 1960 Appellate Division decision[16] reversed a judgment and remanded for a new trial because the trial judge had permitted amended pleadings and an amended pretrial order, but had refused to grant one defendant an adjournment. The opinion stated "it was important and proper from the point of view of the paramount public right and interest to allow the amended answer,"[17] despite the fact that the original position of some defendants, which was reaffirmed in the pleadings, pretrial order, and during most of the trial, was completely reversed at a late stage of trial. During the course of trial new issues had been added by the judge on his own motion as well as by some of the defendants. In addition to the filing of amended answers the pretrial order was amended on the twenty-third day of trial to include two new issues. Upon remand, instructions were given that substituted pleadings be filed and that a new pretrial conference be held so that the exact position of the several parties would be manifest and their contentions clearly defined.

Even when it is addressed to functions exclusively reserved to the conference, the pretrial order has no binding effect on the course of trial. Thus, the Appellate Division approved the action of a trial judge in an equity case in disregarding a stipulation of fact made at a pretrial conference, with the result that an additional issue had to be litigated at the trial.[18]

When new issues are raised and litigated at trial by consent or without objection, failure to amend the pleadings and pretrial order is not a fatal defect. However, in the absence of a formal amendment of the pretrial order, the courts have stated that the new issues raised must be "squarely recognized"[19] as such by the parties or be "actually tried" and not merely overlooked.[20]

From the above decisions it must be concluded that so far as fixing the issues for trial New Jersey pretrial orders have no more binding effect on the course of the trial process than do pleadings themselves.

NOTES TO APPENDIX B

[1] 35 N.J. 558 (1961).
[2] *Id.* at 560.
[3] 33 N.J. 419 (1960).
[4] *Id.* at 427.
[5] 66 N.J. Super. 358 (1961).
[6] *Id.* at 367.
[7] DiDonna v. Zigarelli, 61 N.J. Super. 302 (1960).
[8] E.g., Colozzi v. Bevko, Inc., 17 N.J. 194 (1955).
[9] DeCaro v. DeCaro, 13 N.J. 36 (1953).
[10] 63 N.J. Super. 206 (1960).
[11] 62 N.J. Super. 88 (1960).
[12] E.g., Barr v. Francks, 70 N.J. Super. 565 (1961); Ross Systems v. Linden Dari-Delite, Inc., 62 N.J. Super. 439 (1960); Samuel Braen's Sons v. Fondo, 52 N.J. Super. 188 (1958); Proskurnja v. Elder, 73 N.J. Super. 466 (L.D. 1962).
[13] Mead v. Wiley Methodist Episcopal Church, 4 N.J. 200 (1950).
[14] 15 N.J. 360 (1954).
[15] *Id.* at 372.
[16] Band's Refuse Removal, Inc. v. Borough of Fair Lawn, 62 N.J. Super. 522 (1960).
[17] *Id.* at 557.
[18] Balazinski v. Lebid, 65 N.J. Super. 483 (1961).
[19] Mason v. Niewinski, 66 N.J. Super. 358, 368 (1961).
[20] Proskurnja v. Elder, 73 N.J. Super. 466, 472 (L.D. 1962).

APPENDIX C. FORMS USED IN THE NEW JERSEY STUDY

THIS appendix contains specimens of Pretrial Test Forms A through K, which were used to gather statistical data during the controlled test of the New Jersey pretrial conference procedure. Also included are specimens of Observer Forms A, B, and C used to record the impressions gained by viewers of "live" pretrial conferences.

FORM	EXPLANATION
Pretrial Test Form A	—Letter from Assignment Judge to attorneys in mandatorily pretried cases.
Pretrial Test Form B	—Letter from Assignment Judge to attorneys offering them optional pretrial conference.
Pretrial Test Form C	—Report by attorneys in cases that settled.
Pretrial Test Form D	—Roster of test cases by test group designation.
Pretrial Test Form E	—Record of court history of case.
Pretrial Test Form F	—Instruction form for pretrial judge; pretrial conference judge's report.
Pretrial Test Form G	—Trial counsel's report (in pretried cases completing trial).
Pretrial Test Form H	—Trial judge's report in case completing trial.
Pretrial Test Form I	—Trial counsel's report (not pretried case completing trial).
Pretrial Test Form J	—Letter from Assignment Judge to attorneys (case that settled prior to a mandatory pretrial conference).
Pretrial Test Form K	—Attorney's report (case that settled prior to a mandatory pretrial conference).
Observer Form A	—Form used by observers at pretrial conferences (1960).
Observer Form B	—Form used by observers at pretrial conferences (1960).
Observer Form C	—Form used by observers at pretrial conferences (1962).

FORMS USED IN THE NEW JERSEY STUDY

PRETRIAL TEST FORM A

SUPERIOR COURT OF NEW JERSEY

CHAMBERS OF
ALEXANDER P. WAUGH
ASSIGNMENT JUDGE

COURT HOUSE
NEWARK 2, NEW JERSEY

ESSEX COUNTY

RE: _____ v. _____

Docket _____ County File No. _____

Dear Sir:

      A test to evaluate the effectiveness of the pretrial conference is being conducted under direction of the Supreme Court. The above-entitled case will be pretried in accordance with the enclosed notice of pretrial. In conjunction with this experiment, a study is also being conducted as to the effectiveness of the procedure for the transfer of cases to the County District Court.

      Should this case be settled at any time (prior to trial, during trial or after trial), please fill out the enclosed confidential Pretrial Test Form C and send it to the chambers of the Assignment Judge within **ten days** after the settlement.

Sincerely yours,

Alexander P. Waugh

Assignment Judge

APPENDIX C

PRETRIAL TEST FORM B

SUPERIOR COURT OF NEW JERSEY

CHAMBERS OF
ALEXANDER P. WAUGH
ASSIGNMENT JUDGE

COURT HOUSE
NEWARK 2, NEW JERSEY

ESSEX COUNTY

RE: _____ v. _____

Docket _____ County File No. _____

Dear Sir:

  In order to evaluate the effectiveness of the mandatory pretrial conference procedure, in several counties a carefully worked out experiment is being conducted under the direction of the Supreme Court. For purposes of this experiment, in every second personal injury case added to the calendar, Rule 4:29 is being relaxed so as to make a pretrial conference optional rather than mandatory.

  The above-entitled case is one of those in which a pretrial conference will be optional. Accordingly, unless specifically requested by counsel, no pretrial conference will be scheduled in this case. If you (or your adversary) desire a pretrial conference in this case it is necessary for you so to notify the clerk in writing within seven (7) days of the date hereof. If neither you nor your adversary request a pretrial conference within the time specified, no pretrial conference will be had. Instead, in lieu of the notice of pretrial conference, a notice will be sent you, at about the same time that the pretrial conference would normally be held, advising you of the weekly call on which the case will be placed.

  In conjunction with this experiment, a study is also being conducted as to the effectiveness of the procedure for the transfer of cases to the County District Court.

  To assist the Supreme Court in this experiment it is earnestly requested that you determine, as objectively as possible, whether this is a case in which you would ordinarily request a pretrial conference if our regular rule made such conferences optional. The value and reliability of this study depend upon your sincere cooperation.

PRETRIAL TEST FORM B *(continued)*

      Should this case be settled at any time (prior to trial, during trial or after trial), please fill out the enclosed confidential Pretrial Test Form C and send it to the chambers of the Assignment Judge within <u>ten</u> days after the settlement.

                                    Sincerely yours,

                                      Alexander P. Waugh

                                      Assignment Judge

APPENDIX C

Confidential

PRETRIAL TEST FORM C

CONFIDENTIAL MEMORANDUM RE SETTLEMENT

(To be filled in by counsel in actions settled before trial, during trial or after trial and mailed to the Assignment Judge of the Court.)

_____ County

_____ v. _____

Docket _____ County File No. _____

1. Amount of Settlement: $_____

2. Time of Settlement: (Please circle one of the following symbols as appropriate)

If case was scheduled for mandatory pretrial	If optional pretrial was requested	If pretrial was not scheduled
A1 Between notice of pretrial and pretrial conference	C1 Before pretrial conference	B1 Before weekly call
A2 During pretrial conference	C2 During pretrial conference	B2 Between weekly call and selection of jury
A3 Between pretrial conference and selection of jury	C3 Between pretrial conference and selection of jury	B3 During trial
A4 During trial	C4 During trial	B4 After trial (*e.g.,* pending appeal or new trial)
A5 After trial (*e.g.,* pending appeal or new trial)	C5 After trial (*e.g.,* pending appeal or new trial)	

Attorney for

Date: _____

FORMS USED IN THE NEW JERSEY STUDY

PRETRIAL TEST FORM D

SUPERIOR AND COUNTY COURT PERSONAL INJURY CASES

Court Year 1959–1960

_____County

GROUP A — Cases Scheduled for Mandatory Pretrial Conference		GROUP B — Cases Not Scheduled for Mandatory Pretrial Conference		GROUP C — Optional Pretrial Requested
Name of Case	Docket No. & Cty. File No.	Name of Case	Docket No. & Cty. File No.	

APPENDIX C

PRETRIAL TEST FORM E

CASE HISTORY

(To accompany file)

_____ County

_____ v. _____

Docket _____ County File No. _____

1. If case was pretried, at end of conference, court clerk will please enter the following information:

   a. Name of pretrial judge _____

   b. Date of pretrial conference _____

   c. Amount of judge's time required for conference _____
   (in hrs. & ¼ hrs.)

2. Continuances granted (to be filled in by clerk once case is placed on weekly call)

Date	Requested by	Reason

3. If case went to trial, court clerk will please enter the following information:

   a. Name of trial judge _____

   b. Date of trial _____

   c. Case was terminated

   During trial (*i.e.*, after opening) [ ]
   or
   After trial concluded [ ]

   —Judgment NOV   YES [ ]   NO [ ]

   d. Duration of trial _____
   (in hrs. & ¼ hrs.)

4. If case went to trial, court clerk will please check the following:

   a. Was a jury demanded originally?   YES [ ]   NO [ ]

   b. Was case actually tried before a jury?   YES [ ]   NO [ ]

December 1959

PRETRIAL TEST FORM F

INSTRUCTIONS FOR GUIDANCE OF PRETRIAL JUDGES

1. When a personal injury case is before you for pretrial conference, make an evaluation of the case in accordance with paragraph 2 below. However, during the period of the test regardless of the evaluated amount of the case, no cases will be transferred at pretrial to the District Court.

2. In each personal injury case, at the beginning of the conference, please make a confidential estimate of the amount a trial court would actually award, starting with the following assumptions:

(a) that the case were to be tried without a jury and

(b) that defendant's liability were conceded. Please do not disclose this estimate to the attorneys in the case.

If the award is estimated at below $3000, check "Small" on Form F, item 1 (a); if between $3000 and $7500, check "Medium"; if over $7500, check "Large".

3. If a test case is one that would have been transferred by reason of under $3000 potential except for the test, check YES on Form F, item 1 (b).

Since the transfer determination is made on the basis of "reasonable probability that ultimate recovery will not exceed $3000," it is possible that some cases regarded as untransferable by you will nevertheless be estimated as "Small" (under $3000) cases.

4. At the conclusion of the pretrial conference please complete the remaining items in Form F.

APPENDIX C

Confidential

PRETRIAL TEST FORM F

RESULTS OF PRETRIAL CONFERENCE
(To be filled in by Pretrial Judge)

_____ County

_____ v. _____

Docket _____ County File No. _____

1. *Value of Case*

    a. What is your estimate of the amount a court would actually award in this case, assuming defendant's liability were conceded:

Small (under $3000)	[ ]
Medium (between $3000 & $7500)	[ ]
Large (over $7500)	[ ]

    b. If it were not for this experiment, would you have transferred this case to the District Court? YES [ ] NO [ ]

2. *Preparation for and Results of Conference*

    a. Had attorneys conferred before conference? YES [ ] NO [ ]

    b. Were attorneys well prepared for conference? YES [ ] NO [ ]

    c. Was a memorandum under Rule 4:29-3 submitted

        by plaintiff (s) ? YES [ ] NO [ ]
        by defendant (s) ? YES [ ] NO [ ]

    d. Was a settlement agreed upon during the course of the conference? YES [ ] NO [ ]

    If NO, please answer the remaining questions on this form.

    e. In your opinion will the conference *probably*

        i) Eliminate the need of trial? YES [ ] NO [ ]
        ii) Shorten the trial? YES [ ] NO [ ]
        iii) Make for a fairer trial? YES [ ] NO [ ]

3. *Witnesses*

    a. Was the number of non-expert witnesses limited or discussed? YES [ ] NO [ ]

FORMS USED IN THE NEW JERSEY STUDY

PRETRIAL TEST FORM F *(continued)*

4. *Facts*

   a. At the conference did either side obtain evidence or leads that were apparently new? YES [ ] NO [ ]

   b. If YES, were all the new matters probably obtainable by normal discovery procedures? YES [ ] NO [ ]

   c. Were stipulations made that will probably reduce trial time if trial is necessary? YES [ ] NO [ ]

5. *Clarifying Issues*

   a. Did the conference tend to clarify any essential issues that were unclear? YES [ ] NO [ ]

   b. Did the conference eliminate any unnecessary issues theretofore included? YES [ ] NO [ ]

6. *Results of the Conference*

   a. Please specify, in order of importance the major results, if any, of this conference:

      i)

      ii)

      iii)

   b. If this was an optional pretrial conference,

      i) Was counsel warranted in requesting the conference? YES [ ] NO [ ]

      ii) Why?

Date: _____

PRETRIAL TEST FORM G

RESULTS OF TRIAL IN PRETRIED CASES
(To be filled in by Trial Counsel)

(NOTE: If trial counsel was not personally present at pretrial conference, he will please consult with associate who attended conference.)

_____ County

_____ v. _____

Docket _____ County File No. _____

1. *General*

    a. Were you counsel for plaintiff?   YES [ ]   NO [ ]
                               defendant?   YES [ ]   NO [ ]
                               other? (Please specify) _____
    b. Were you present at the pretrial conference?   YES [ ]   NO [ ]
    c. Did opposing counsel confer prior to the pretrial conference?   YES [ ]   NO [ ]
    d. Did you personally conduct the trial?   YES [ ]   NO [ ]
    e. Are you a member of a firm?   YES [ ]   NO [ ]
    f. If YES, how many partners and associates do you have? _____
       How many of these do upper court trial work? _____

2. *Witnesses*

    a. Did you obtain the names of any theretofore unknown witnesses at the pretrial conference?   YES [ ]   NO [ ]
    b. Were any unnecessary witnesses called at trial?   YES [ ]   NO [ ]

3. *Facts*

    a. Did the conference produce evidence or leads that were apparently new?   YES [ ]   NO [ ]
    b. If YES, were the new matters probably obtainable by normal discovery procedures?   YES [ ]   NO [ ]
    c. Did any facts or evidentiary matters produced at pretrial result in shortening the trial?   YES [ ]   NO [ ]
                              lengthening the trial?   YES [ ]   NO [ ]
    d. Were you taken by surprise by any developments at the trial?   YES [ ]   NO [ ]

FORMS USED IN THE NEW JERSEY STUDY

PRETRIAL TEST FORM G *(continued)*

4. *Clarifying Issues*

    a. Did the conference result in any modification of the essential issues?   YES [   ]   NO [   ]
    b. If YES, specify whether there was:
        i) Abandonment of 1 or more issues   YES [   ]   NO [   ]
        ii) Addition of 1 or more issues   YES [   ]   NO [   ]
        iii) Clarification of existing issues   YES [   ]   NO [   ]
    c. Did the essential issues emerge clearly at the trial?   YES [   ]   NO [   ]

5. *Jury Waiver*

    a. Was a jury demanded originally?   YES [   ]   NO [   ]
    b. If YES, was the jury waived?   YES [   ]   NO [   ]
    c. If YES, was the jury waived before pretrial conference?   [   ]
                          at pretrial conference?   [   ]
                          after pretrial conference?   [   ]

6. *Results of the Conference*

    a. Please specify, in order of importance, the major results, if any, of this conference with respect to the trial:
        i)
        ii)
        iii)
    b. Compared with other pretrial conferences, was this one
                       more useful?   [   ]
                       less useful?   [   ]
                       about the same?   [   ]
    c. If this case is one in which a pretrial conference was requested
        i) Which party requested it?
                           Plaintiff   [   ]
                           Defendant   [   ]
                           Both   [   ]
        ii) If your side requested it, please state the reason:

        _____

        _____

        iii) In relation to this reason was the conference useful?   YES [   ]   NO [   ]

                                           _____
                                           Trial Counsel

Date: _____

APPENDIX C

Confidential

PRETRIAL TEST FORM H

RESULTS OF TRIAL

(To be filled in by Trial Judge)

_____ County

_____ v. _____

Docket _____   County File No. _____

1. *General*

    a. Was plaintiff's counsel well prepared? YES [ ] NO [ ]
    b. Was defendant's counsel well prepared? YES [ ] NO [ ]
    c. Did you agree with the jury's verdict
        as to liability? YES [ ] NO [ ]
        as to damages? YES [ ] NO [ ]

2. *Issues and Evidence*

    a. Were the parties' theories of the case clearly brought out before the jury? YES [ ] NO [ ]
    b. Was evidence offered on extraneous or undisputed points? YES [ ] NO [ ]
    c. Was merely cumulative evidence offered? YES [ ] NO [ ]
    d. Was evidence on any essential issue omitted? YES [ ] NO [ ]
    e. Were any claims abandoned during the trial? YES [ ] NO [ ]
    f. Were any "surprise" issues litigated? YES [ ] NO [ ]

3. *Quality of the Trial*   *(Answer regardless of whether or not case was pretried)*

    a. Please specify your major observations relative to this trial, so far as concerns the usefulness of pretrial conference.
        i)
        ii)
        iii)

4. *Impact of Pretrial*   *(Answer only if case was pretried)*

    a. Was the pretrial order, in your opinion, helpful in shortening the trial? YES [ ] NO [ ]
    b. Was the pretrial order, in your opinion, helpful in achieving a fair result? YES [ ] NO [ ]
    c. Did you make any substantial change in the pretrial order? YES [ ] NO [ ]

Date: _____

FORMS USED IN THE NEW JERSEY STUDY

Confidential

PRETRIAL TEST FORM I

RESULTS OF TRIAL IN NON-PRETRIED CASES
(To be filled in by Trial Counsel)

_____ County

_____ v. _____

Docket _____ County File No. _____

1. *General*

   a. Were you counsel for plaintiff? [ ]
      defendant? [ ]
      other? (please specify) _____
   b. Did you confer with opposing counsel prior to trial for the purpose of limiting the issues or stipulating facts or agreeing upon issues? YES [ ] NO [ ]
   c. Are you a member of a firm? YES [ ] NO [ ]
   d. If YES, how many partners and associates do you have? _____ How many of these do upper court trial work? _____

2. *The Trial*

   a. Did the essential issues emerge clearly at the trial? YES [ ] NO [ ]
   b. Were unnecessary witnesses called? YES [ ] NO [ ]
   c. Were you taken by surprise by any developments at the trial? YES [ ] NO [ ]

3. *Absence of Pretrial*

   a. If you were starting this case anew, would you exercise your option to ask for a pretrial conference? YES [ ] NO [ ]
   b. In your opinion, if there had been a pretrial conference would the trial have been longer? [ ]
      shorter? [ ]
      same? [ ]
   c. Would a pretrial conference have made any substantial difference in the conduct or outcome? YES [ ] NO [ ]
      i) If YES, please specify:

Date: _____

_____
Trial Counsel

PRETRIAL TEST FORM J

SUPERIOR COURT OF NEW JERSEY

Date:

_____ County

_____ v. _____

Docket _____   County File No. _____

Dear Sir:

    I have been informed that the above-entitled case was terminated or settled prior to the pretrial conference scheduled therein. In connection with the pretrial test being conducted under the direction of the Supreme Court, will you kindly fill out the enclosed Form K and return it to me within *ten* days. A return envelope is enclosed for your convenience.

Sincerely yours,

Assignment Judge

Encl.

FORMS USED IN THE NEW JERSEY STUDY

PRETRIAL TEST FORM K

SETTLEMENT OF CASES SCHEDULED FOR PRETRIAL BUT SETTLED BEFOREHAND

(To be mailed to counsel in Group A cases settled between notice of pretrial conference and scheduled date therefor)

_____ v. _____

Docket _____   County File No. _____

1. If a pretrial conference had not loomed as a standard procedure, is it more likely that this case would have gone to trial?   YES [ ]   NO [ ]   DO NOT KNOW [ ]

   Why? _____

2. Was the actual scheduling of a date for pretrial conference a factor in the settlement of this case?   YES [ ]   NO [ ]

   If YES, specify in what respect(s):

   _____
   _____
   _____

   _____
   Attorney for

Date: _____

APPENDIX C

PRETRIAL OBSERVER FORM A

COUNTY _____ OBSERVER _____

_____ v. _____

JUDGE _____ DATE _____

I. *General Information*

1. Nature of action *(i.e.,* personal injury, contract, etc.) and brief statement of facts on which complaint is based.

2. Length of Conference _____ minutes

3. Number of (other than nominal) plaintiffs _____ defendants _____

4. Persons present (other than judge and lawyers) _____

5. Were lawyers identified as "trial counsel"? YES _____ NO _____

II. *Preparation for Conference*

1. Had attorneys conferred beforehand (Rule 4:29–3)?

   YES _____ NO _____ DON'T KNOW _____

2. Had all discovery been completed? YES _____ NO _____ DON'T KNOW _____

3. Were pretrial memoranda submitted by plaintiff? _____ by defendant? _____

4. Were attorneys well prepared for the conference?

   YES _____ MODERATELY SO _____ NO _____

III. *Attitudes of Participants*

1. Were the attorneys cooperative? YES _____ MODERATELY SO _____ NO _____

2. Did the judge appear to expect useful results or was he merely going through the motions?

3. What appeared to be the judge's chief purposes, if any?

   Settlement _____ Issue Formulating _____ Stipulation-getting _____

   Other _____ Unascertainable _____

FORMS USED IN THE NEW JERSEY STUDY

PRETRIAL OBSERVER FORM A *(continued)*

IV. *Content of the Conference*

    A. *Trial Preparation*

        1. Were admissions or stipulation made with respect to matters which would otherwise have to be proved at trial? YES _____ NO _____ If YES, specify admissions.

        2. Were any issues clarified for trial? YES _____ NO _____

        3. Were any issues abandoned or added? YES _____ NO _____ If YES, specify issues.

        4. Were pleadings amended in any major respects? YES _____ NO _____ If YES, state amendments.

        5. Was leave granted to make further use of discovery proceedings? YES _____ NO _____ If YES, state nature of further discovery.

        6. Was number of expert witnesses discussed? YES _____ NO _____

                limited? YES _____ NO _____

        7. Were exhibits marked in evidence? YES _____ NO _____

        8. Did the judge order the filing of any memoranda of law or trial briefs? YES _____ NO _____

        9. Other matters discussed?

    B. *Settlement*

        1. Was settlement discussed? YES _____ NO _____

        2. If so, who initiated discussion? _____

        3. Did the judge give his estimate of the value of the case? YES _____ NO _____

        4. Approximately what proportion of conference was devoted to settlement discussion?

        5. Was the case settled in the course of conference? YES _____ NO _____

           If YES, what was the amount of the settlement? _____

PRETRIAL OBSERVER FORM A *(continued)*

6. If case was not settled, what was plaintiff's last demand? _____

   defendant's last offer? _____

   judge's estimate? _____
   (if any)

   In your judgment, what was the chief obstacle to settlement?

   Liability _____ Damages _____ Both _____

   Lack of authority to settle _____ Other _____ Couldn't tell _____

C. *Other Disposition*

   Transferred to District Court _____

   Set for weekly call   _____

   Marked off calendar   _____

   Other disposition (specify)   _____

IV. *Personal Observations*

   What do you think this conference accomplished, if anything? Would you classify it as merely perfunctory _____

   conducive to settlement _____

   helpful in trial-shaping _____

   other benefits _____

FORMS USED IN THE NEW JERSEY STUDY

PRETRIAL OBSERVER FORM B

COUNTY _____ OBSERVER _____

DATE(S) OF OBSERVATIONS _____

NO. OF CONFERENCES ATTENDED _____

NO. OF CASES SETTLED BEFORE CONFERENCE _____
        (*i.e.*, at call of Pretrial Calendar)

---

1. What differences, if any, did you note between the conduct of pretrial conferences by Judge X and Judge Y?

2. What differences did you observe, if any, between pretrial conferences in personal injury and other types of cases?

3. In about 50 words, summarize your conclusions as to the efficacy, or otherwise, of the pretrial conferences you observed.

4. Please report here your suggestions for improving the pretrial test forms, including those used by judges, lawyers and clerks, as well as by you as observer.

APPENDIX C

PRETRIAL OBSERVER FORM C

CUPEJ – NJPTX
June, 1962

PRETRIAL OBSERVER FORM

COUNTY _____ OBSERVER _____

CASE _____ v. _____

COUNTY FILE NUMBER _____

JUDGE _____ DATE _____

General Information

1. Nature of action (*i.e.*, personal injury, contract, etc.):
   _____

2. Length of Conference: _____ minutes

3. Disposition:

   Settled _____

   Transferred to District Court _____

   Set for weekly call _____

   Marked off calendar _____

   Other (please specify) _____

1. Formality with which conference was conducted
   (e.g., was conference held in open court?; was judge in robes?; did a reporter record the conference?; was smoking permitted?; etc.)

   Formal   Informal

   |____|____|____|____|____|
    1   2   3   4   5

PRETRIAL OBSERVER FORM C *(continued)*

2. Advance preparation for the conference

   A. By the judge

   (e.g., was he familiar with the issues in the case?; had he examined the pleadings and exhibits?; etc.)

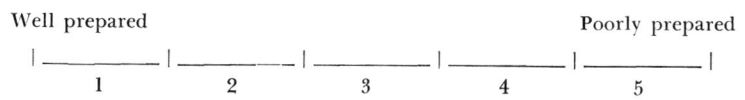

   Well prepared   Poorly prepared

   | _____ | _____ | _____ | _____ | _____ |
      1   2   3   4   5

   B. By the attorneys

   (e.g., had they conferred beforehand?; was discovery completed?; did they submit pretrial memoranda?; etc.)

   Well prepared   Poorly prepared

   | _____ | _____ | _____ | _____ | _____ |
      1   2   3   4   5

3. Judge's efforts to have lawyers state their positions in specific terms—to "reduce the level of legal abstraction"

   (e.g., did he ask each side to tell its story in simple, non-legal terms?; did he request specific details?; etc.)

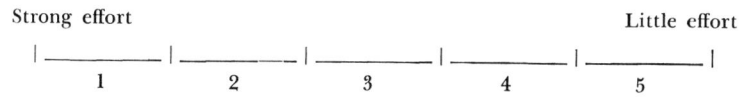

   Strong effort   Little effort

   | _____ | _____ | _____ | _____ | _____ |
      1   2   3   4   5

4. Judge's attitude toward the disclosure of evidence at the pretrial conference

   (e.g., did he request disclosure of impeachment evidence?; of the names of expert and non-expert trial witnesses?; did he require exchange of exhibits?; etc.)

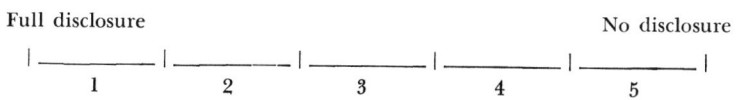

   Full disclosure   No disclosure

   | _____ | _____ | _____ | _____ | _____ |
      1   2   3   4   5

5. Judge's efforts to obtain stipulations and admissions

   (e.g., did he suggest stipulations?; did he attempt to narrow down requests little by little until the attorneys acceded?; did he simply record the stipulations that counsel were willing to agree to without pressure?; etc.)

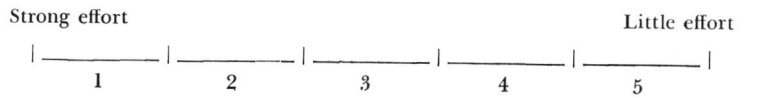

   Strong effort   Little effort

   | _____ | _____ | _____ | _____ | _____ |
      1   2   3   4   5

PRETRIAL OBSERVER FORM C *(continued)*

6. Judge's efforts to rule on legal questions

    (e.g., did he require legal questions to be defined by counsel in advance of pretrial?; did he require memoranda of law or briefs to be filed?; etc.)

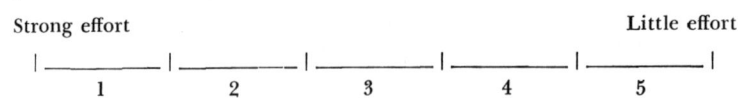

    Strong effort   Little effort

    |————|————|————|————|————|
      1   2   3   4   5

7. Judge's efforts toward settlement

    (e.g., did he talk to each side separately to determine the actual gap?; did he attempt to close the gap by pointing out the costs of trial, the adverse publicity and the like?; did he suggest reduction of attorneys' fees?; did he attempt to persuade client to accept figure agreed to by counsel?; did he suggest a settlement figure?; etc.)

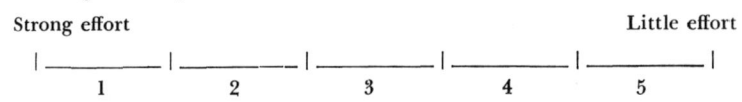

    Strong effort   Little effort

    |————|————|————|————|————|
      1   2   3   4   5

8. Judge's efforts toward shortening trial by having documents admitted into evidence

    (e.g., did he order documents numbered?; did he rule on objections to documents?; did he order that all documents found after the pretrial conference be displayed to opposing counsel and numbered within a fixed period before trial?; did he order them marked in evidence?; etc.)

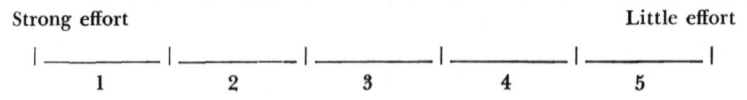

    Strong effort   Little effort

    |————|————|————|————|————|
      1   2   3   4   5

9. Judge's preparation of the pretrial order

    (e.g., did he simply dictate order from the pretrial memoranda of counsel?; did he attempt to specify the issues of law and fact that were in dispute?; etc.)

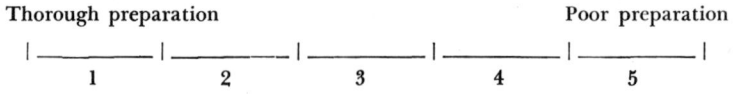

    Thorough preparation   Poor preparation

    |————|————|————|————|————|
      1   2   3   4   5

10. Judge's control of the conference

    (based on your overall reaction to the conference)

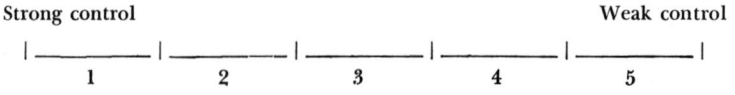

    Strong control   Weak control

    |————|————|————|————|————|
      1   2   3   4   5

FORMS USED IN THE NEW JERSEY STUDY

PRETRIAL OBSERVER FORM C *(continued)*

11. Sanctions used by the judge

   A. For lack of advance preparation
      (e.g., did he adjourn conference to give defaulting party time to prepare and set next conference at convenience of prepared party?; did he impose costs on unprepared party?; did he impose a financial penalty directly upon the unprepared attorney?; etc.)

   B. For failure to cooperate at the conference
      (e.g., did he dismiss or default the uncooperative party?; did he preclude evidence on particular points?; did he allow or threaten to allow other party time for additional discovery?; did he use summary judgment or threaten to use it to force out details?; etc.)

12. Miscellaneous techniques used by the judge
    (e.g., did he sever liability and damage issues for trial?; did he invoke the impartial medical expert procedure?; did he resolve discovery disputes and attempt to supervise future discovery?; etc.)

13. Evaluate the efficacy of the techniques observed based upon your impressions of what worked well and what did not work well. Please be as specific as possible.

APPENDIX D. CREDIBILITY OF THE FINDINGS

THE function of this Appendix is to draw together briefly in one listing the main problems of statistical method encountered in the study. These are, for brevity, called "self-selection," "optionality," "significance," and "compliance" or "nonresponse." All except compliance are treated in the main body of the report or in the Notes and will not be mentioned further here beyond defining them and designating the places at which they are discussed.

Self-selection is the problem raised by the departure from the "ideal" test design to permit lawyers to opt for a pretrial conference in cases that were not assigned by chance for mandatory pretrial. The possibility arose in the course of the test that cases picked for optional pretrial were different in ways that counted from the cases that were by choice not pretried. See pages 48–50.

Optionality relates to the question of whether the pretrial conference itself was affected by the fact that it was held in the C group cases because one or both attorneys requested it, rather than as a result of the luck of the draw. It is discussed at note IV–4, page 150.

Significance relates to the question whether observed differences in one group of cases against another were of sufficient magnitude, given the number of cases involved, to rule out the risk that the differences could too readily result from chance. See note IV–9, page 151. Whenever appropriate, the significance level for each finding is given in the note accompanying the presentation of the finding.

Compliance is the problem raised by the failure of some judges, attorneys, or clerks to submit completed test forms in some cases, or to respond to all the questions in a proper manner to permit coding and scoring the responses. As to some topics the compliance rate was 92–95 per cent (e.g., whether the case reached trial or settled beforehand); as to others, it was as low as 56, 52, or in one case, 42 per cent

CREDIBILITY OF THE FINDINGS

(clarity of issues at trial). The bare fact that less than 100 per cent of the replies were returned in respect to any given item is not as serious a problem as may at first appear. Only if the unsubmitted answers were "biased," and if recorded would have altered the direction of an observed relationship, would a substantive problem arise.

Following standard methods of statistical analysis, various assumptions as to the contents of the nonresponses were made and tested against the data actually received. Without recapitulating the precise figures (the details are on file with the Columbia University Project for Effective Justice), it can be said that the results satisfied us that distortions from nonresponse did not contaminate the findings. Only if nonresponses from the compared groups were both (1) non-random, and (2) on a given item ran in one direction in one group and in an opposite direction in the other, would our findings be awry. There was no evidence that this had occurred.

We are satisfied that the risks theoretically present in the findings are within acceptable limits and that the findings may be considered credible evidence, to the extent indicated.

APPENDIX E. PRETRIAL OF CIVIL CASES IN THE STATES

SINCE the promulgation of Rule 16 of the Federal Rules of Civil Procedure,[1] forty-four states have adopted some state-wide provisions for a pretrial conference procedure.[2] Despite absence of a formal state-wide provision in the remaining six states[3] some form of pretrial conference exists as well. This Appendix presents a roundup of the states' views as expressed in statutes or court rules of state-wide application. To attempt more than a survey of the scene would necessitate a large-scale study beyond the scope of the present effort, which is designed to reveal some of the wide diversity with regard to purposes, application, and administration of pretrial.

HOW IT CAME ABOUT

The enabling authority for the pretrial conference device varies. In thirty-three states it has been authorized or adopted by court rule.[4] Ten states have provided for the mechanism by direct legislative action,[5] while one state has adopted pretrial conferences under rules promulgated by the Judicial Council.[6]

FACTORS DETERMINATIVE OF A CONFERENCE BEING CONDUCTED

The states differ in making the conferences mandatory or optional. Only four states, including New Jersey, have some form of mandatory pretrial.[7] However, in two, California and Oklahoma, the conference can be avoided at the request of the parties with the approval of the judge. Oklahoma, diluting the mandatory nature of its rule further, authorizes the judge on his own motion to dispense with the conference. A conference becomes mandatory upon the application of a party in six states,[8] but in eight states it still remains within the court's discretion whether to hold a conference after request by a party.[9] In

PRETRIAL IN OTHER STATES

Kentucky the conference is discretionary with the court except in the circuit court, where it is mandatory upon motion of a party. In the balance of the states the rules authorizing the pretrial conference, like Federal Rule 16, are permissive, not obligatory.

Pretrial conferences are often restricted to certain courts. Alabama limits them to its courts of equity; Massachusetts adopts an opposite policy and restricts them to civil cases at law. A few states provide explicitly that conferences shall be conducted in the district courts,[10] or state more generally that they are to be conducted in the superior courts.[11] In Arkansas, they are limited to the circuit and chancery courts.

Only New Jersey excepts some types of cases (primarily domestic relations) from those that may be pretried.

All but nine (including New Jersey) are silent as to the stage in the litigation when the conference may take place. Of these nine, five authorize conferences after issue is joined[12] and the sixth, after all issues are "settled."[13] Connecticut instructs that upon the closing of the pleadings and claim for jury trial a case will be placed on the pretrial list (although pretrial conferences are not mandatory). California provides the time for the conference is after filing of a memorandum to set. New Jersey provides in effect that the conference may not be held earlier than 114 days after service of the complaint, for notice of pretrial may not be mailed for 100 days and must give the parties at least two weeks' warning.

North Carolina expressly excludes uncontested divorce cases and proceedings after judgment by default from the general rule. California's 1963 revision of the rules exempts four classes of action from pretrial: cases that will require no more than one day to try; cases previously tried; retrials on appeal from inferior courts; and cases that would fall within the jurisdiction of a municipal court.

WHO MUST ATTEND?

Most states require the attorneys for the parties to attend the conference. Two states, Arkansas and Vermont, do not specify any particular persons. Illinois specifies the attorneys with or without their clients as the court directs. Massachusetts requires the parties or their attorneys, while Texas calls for the attorneys and the parties, or their duly authorized agent. Connecticut provides that parties and their attorneys shall attend. Idaho is the sole state to refer to the required presence of any party appearing without an attorney.

PRE-CONFERENCE MEMORANDA AND POST-CONFERENCE ORDERS

Rarely is there any provision that the attorney must submit memoranda before or at the pretrial for use at the conference. In addition to New Jersey, Alaska and California are exceptions to the general rule. But only Alaska requires that the memoranda be submitted prior to the conference (3 days).

Pretrial orders are required in most states. Vermont is the only state that makes no provision for a pretrial order in any form. Maryland and Pennsylvania provide for orders at the discretion of the court, while Oklahoma requires the making of such record of the conference as the court directs. Connecticut judges must prepare a pretrial memorandum and may make an order that will control the case. Michigan provides for a summary of the results of the conference, and this controls the trial. North Carolina provides for entry of an order reciting the stipulations made and any action taken. In Alaska, the attorneys submit a proposed order for signature after the conference.

SUBJECTS TO BE DISCUSSED

Matters to be covered at the conference generally are the same as those set out in Federal Rule 16.[14] Aside from Oklahoma, all the states must mention as items for discussion: (a) simplification of the issues; (b) the necessity or desirability of amending the pleadings; and (c) the possibility of obtaining admissions of fact and of documents that will avoid unnecessary proof. All but five states mention the possibility of placing a limitation on expert witnesses.[15] Discussion of the advisability of a preliminary reference of issues is omitted in thirteen states[16] and the language is modified in some substantial respect from that used in Federal Rule 16 in ten other states.[17] Again, aside from Oklahoma, all the states explicitly provide for discussion of any other matter that may aid in the disposition of the case.

Many statutes and rules provide for coverage of matters not referred to in Federal Rule 16. Settlement is specifically mentioned by eight states.[18] Nonexpert witnesses are referred to by four. Iowa and California provide that parties shall not be required to identify witnesses. Oklahoma, on the other hand, holds counsel responsible for revealing the identity, addresses, and substance of the testimony of their wit-

PRETRIAL IN OTHER STATES

nesses. Idaho provides for disclosure of the identity of those persons who may be witnesses. Like New Jersey, California and Michigan provide for orders relating to further pretrial discovery.

Other items spelled out in the provisions of one or more states include: "Exceptions to the pleadings for impertinence or the answer for insufficiency where it is filed to a sworn bill for discovery and relief";[19] inspection of hospital records and X-rays;[20] mortality tables and proof thereof;[21] questions relating to *voir dire* examination and selection of alternate jurors;[22] facts of which the court will be asked to take judicial notice;[23] and the determination of any motion or entry of any order, judgment, or decree the judge would be authorized to hear, determine, or enter at term.[24]

The California pretrial judge may: consider whether the court has jurisdiction to act in the case; determine whether discovery has been completed, and if not, to fix limits for completion; order trial briefs; reestimate trial time required; assign the date and place of trial; and discuss settlement.

Michigan, like California, provides for discussion of settlement, discovery completion, and estimate of trial duration. In addition, it provides for: hearing and determination of pending defenses and motions; consideration of consolidation, separation of issues, and order of trial of issues; appointment of an impartial medical expert; and specification of damages as of conference date.

NOTES TO APPENDIX E

[1] Federal Rule 16 provides:

"In any action, the court may in its discretion direct the attorneys for the parties to appear before it for a conference to consider

(1) The simplification of the issues;
(2) The necessity or desirability of amendments to the pleadings;
(3) The possibility of obtaining admissions of fact and of documents which will avoid unnecessary proof;
(4) The limitation of the number of expert witnesses;
(5) The advisability of a preliminary reference of issues to a master for findings to be used as evidence when the trial is to be by jury;
(6) Such other matters as may aid in the disposition of the action.

"The court shall make an order which recites the action taken at the conference, the amendments allowed to the pleadings, and the agreements made by the parties as to any of the matters considered, and which limits the issues for trial to those not disposed of by admissions or agreements of counsel; and such order when entered controls the subsequent course of the action, unless modified at the trial to prevent manifest injustice. The court in its discretion may establish by rule a pretrial calendar on which actions may be placed for consideration as above provided and may either confine the calendar to jury actions or to nonjury actions or extend it to all actions."

Rule 16 is often supplemented by local rules, which conform to the district's particular needs. A great deal of variation results. Highly detailed and encompassing local provisions are found in the calendar rules of the Southern District of New York (S.D.N.Y. Cal. R. 13). All cases are required to undergo at least informal pretrial before being placed on the Ready Day Calendar. In addition the Chief Judge may set any case for pretrial at any time after joinder of issue upon written notice for good cause shown. As for the pretrial itself, the rules prescribe, among other things, a form of order to be forwarded to the attorneys which serves as either final or preliminary notice of the scheduled conference. It informs them of the necessity of a preliminary meeting between counsel to: arrive at stipulations and admissions; exchange and examine exhibits; and to exchange names, addresses, and specialties, if any, of witnesses to be called. Memoranda are then to be filed containing: a statement of the basis of federal jurisdiction; the factual contentions of each side including points on which there is agreement; specific information, the nature of which varies with the type of case involved; facts not admitted; amendments to the pleadings; issues abandoned; statement of the applicable law with citations; exhibits expected to be offered; and a list of witnesses expected to be called. Failure to attend or properly prepare for the conference subjects the offending side to possible dismissal or default, preclusion or imposition of costs (S.D.N.Y. Cal. R. 16).

[2] Alabama—Ala. Eq. R. 8
Alaska—Alaska Civ. Proc. R. 16
Arizona—Ariz. Civ. Proc. R. 16
Arkansas—Ark. Stats. (1947) Ann. §§ 27-2401–27-2403
California—Cal. Super. Ct. Rules 208-21
Colorado—Col. Civ. Proc. R. 16
Connecticut—Order on Trial, Pretrial and Assignment Procedures (As amended June 18, 1962)
Delaware—Del. Super. Ct. R. 16
Florida—Fla. Civ. Proc. R. 1.16
Georgia—Ga. Code Ann. Tit. 81 §§ 81-1013, 81-1014
Hawaii—Hawaii Civ. Proc. R. 16
Idaho—Idaho Civ. Proc. R. 16
Illinois—Ill. S. Ct. R. 22
Indiana—Ind. S. & App. Cts. R. 1-4
Iowa—Iowa Civ. Proc. Rules 135-39
Kansas—Kan. Gen. States. Ann. (1949) § 60-2705
Kentucky—Ky. Civ. Proc. R. 16
Louisiana—La. Rev. Stats. Art. 1551
Maine—Me. Civ. Proc. R. 16
Maryland—Md. Civ. Proc. R. 504
Massachusetts—Mass. Super. Ct. (Civ.) R. 58
Michigan—Mich. Ct. R. 35 § 4
Minnesota—Minn. Civ. Proc. R. 16
Missouri—Mo. Civ. Proc. R. 62.01
Montana—Mont. Civ. Proc. R. 16
Nebraska—S. Ct. Rule (no number assigned)
Nevada—Nev. Civ. Proc. R. 16
New Hampshire—N.H. Super. Ct. R. 48
New Jersey—N.J. Civ. Prac. R. 4:29

New Mexico—N.M. Civ. Proc. R. 16
North Carolina—N.C. Gen. Stats. § 1–169.1
North Dakota—N.D. Civ. Proc. R. 16
Oklahoma—Okla. S. Ct. R. 5
Pennsylvania—Pa. S. Ct. R. 212
Rhode Island—Letter from Raymond A. McCabe, Clerk of the Rhode Island Supreme Court to Project for Effective Justice, October 16, 1962
South Dakota—S.D. Code of 1939 (1960 Supp.) § 33.1003
Texas—Tex. Civ. Proc. R. 166
Utah—Utah Civ. Proc. R. 16
Vermont—Vt. Cty. Ct. R. 3A
Virginia—Va. S. Ct. of App. R. 4:1
Washington—Wash. Plead., Practc. & Proc. R. 16
West Virginia—W.Va. Civ. Proc. R. 16
Wisconsin—Wisc. Stats. Ann. Tit. 25 § 269.65
Wyoming—Wyo. Civ. Proc. R. 16

[3] Mississippi—Committee on Pretrial Procedure, Section of Judicial Administration, ABA, Use of Pre-Trial in State Courts 6 (Aug. 15, 1955).

New York—*E.g.,* Kings Co. S. Ct. R. 8

Ohio—Committee on Pre-Trial Procedure, Section of Judicial Administration, ABA, Use of Pre-Trial in State Courts 8 (Aug. 15, 1955)

Oregon—Letter from John R. McCullough, Administrative Assistant to the Chief Justice, Oregon Supreme Court to Project for Effective Justice, October 23, 1962

South Carolina—Committee on Pre-Trial Procedure, Section of Judicial Administration, ABA, Use of Pre-Trial in State Courts 10 (Aug. 15, 1955)

Tennessee—Committee on Pre-Trial Procedure, Section of Judicial Administration, ABA, Use of Pre-Trial in State Courts 10 (Aug. 15, 1955)

[4] Alabama, Alaska, Arizona, Colorado, Connecticut, Delaware, Florida, Hawaii, Idaho, Illinois, Indiana, Kentucky, Maine, Maryland, Massachusetts, Michigan, Minnesota, Missouri, Nebraska, Nevada, New Hampshire, New Jersey, New Mexico, North Dakota, Oklahoma, Pennsylvania, Rhode Island, Texas, Vermont, Virginia, Washington, West Virginia, Wyoming

[5] Arkansas, Georgia, Iowa, Kansas, Louisiana, Montana, North Carolina, South Dakota, Utah, Wisconsin

[6] California

[7] California, Michigan, New Jersey, Oklahoma

[8] Florida, Indiana, Iowa, Kentucky (for some cases only), North Carolina, North Dakota

[9] Alabama, Alaska, Arkansas, Maryland, Pennsylvania, Vermont, Virginia, Wyoming

[10] Idaho, Kansas, Louisiana, Montana, Nebraska, North Dakota

[11] California, Georgia

[12] Alaska, Iowa, Nebraska, North Carolina, North Dakota

[13] Florida

[14] See note 1 *supra*

[15] California, Michigan, North Carolina, Oklahoma, Virginia

[16] Connecticut, Georgia, Indiana, Iowa, Louisiana, Maine, Michigan, Missouri, Oklahoma, Rhode Island, Utah, Vermont, Virginia

[17] Alabama, Arkansas, California, Florida, Kentucky, Maryland, Massachusetts, Minnesota, South Dakota, Wisconsin

[18] Alaska, California, Connecticut, Iowa, Massachusetts, Michigan, New Hampshire, New Jersey

[19] Alabama

[20] Connecticut

[21] Iowa

[22] Iowa

[23] North Carolina

[24] North Carolina, *cf.* Texas

APPENDIX F. AN AUDIT OF THE EFFECTS OF TRANSFERRING "UNDERSIZED" CASES FROM THE "LARGER" TO THE "LESSER" COURTS

THE purpose of this Appendix is to inquire whether the "transfer" procedure installed in the New Jersey courts in 1953 does the work it was intended to do; and what side effects it produces. A transfer may be made at any stage of the litigation, but as used here it refers to the process by which the judge determines at the threshold of a pretrial conference whether the case involves so little money that it properly should have been brought in the district court (with a jurisdictional limit in personal injury cases of $3,000), instead of in the Superior or County court, where it was actually filed. Rule 4:3–4, which authorizes transfer at a pretrial conference, requires that it appear then "with reasonable probability that the ultimate recovery . . . will not exceed the jurisdiction of the county district court." If, after transfer, the District Court finds that the plaintiff is entitled to more than $3,000, the jurisdictional ceiling of the court is removed *pro hac vice*.[1]

Two events converged in 1959 to bring about the special Project substudy of the operation of the transfer procedure as a corollary to the pretrial conference study. The first was the following observation by the Director of the Administrative Office of the New Jersey Courts in his 1957–58 Annual Report:

It is of interest to note that settlements, dismissals and discontinuances prior to trial have fallen off over the past five years almost in exact proportion to the increase in transferrals to the County District Courts. This raises at least the suspicion that those cases which are now being transferred are cases which otherwise might never have reached the trial stage in the Superior and County Court.[2]

The second circumstance was the observation by the Project for Effective Justice, based on its studies in New York, that there was a direct relation between "size" of personal injury cases and the work burden they cast upon the courts.[3] This raised the possibility that it may be an inefficient practice to use judge time to "screen" small cases from the larger courts, because small cases settle with very high frequency if left to themselves.

Accordingly, when the controlled experiment was installed in the New Jersey Superior and County courts in the seven test counties at the beginning of 1960, provision was made for testing the impact of the transfer procedure. The basic plan was to suspend transferral for the duration of the test period, thus allowing undersized cases to remain in the Superior and County courts, where their careers after pretrial could be followed. In addition, substudies were made of cases transferred at other times, both before the controlled experiment began and after it ended. These groups were used as "controls" —that is, the settlement and trial data on them were compared with the test cases that, though undersized, were not sent down to the district court during the experimental period.

MECHANICS OF THE TRANSFER STUDY

To identify the normally transferrable under $3,000 cases that had been brought in the Superior and County courts, the following procedure was devised: As each case from the A group (set for mandatory pretrial) or the C group (set for pretrial because of lawyers' choice) came before the judge at the opening of a pretrial conference, he was called upon to estimate its recovery potential. The pertinent instructions were:

1. When a personal injury case is before you for pretrial conference, make an evaluation of the case in accordance with paragraph 2 below. However, during the period of the test, regardless of the evaluated amount of the case, no cases will be transferred at pretrial to the District Court.

2. In each personal injury case, at the beginning of the conference, please make a confidential estimate of the amount a trial court would actually award, starting with the following assumptions:
 (a) that the case were to be tried without a jury and
 (b) that defendant's liability were conceded.
Please do not disclose this estimate to the attorneys in the case.
 If the award is estimated at below $3000, check "Small" on form F, item 1 (a); if between $3000 and $7500, check "Medium"; if over $7500, check "Large."

3. If a test case is one that would have been transferred by reason of under $3000 potential except for the test, check 'YES' on Form F, item 1 (b).

Since the transfer determination is made on the basis of "reasonable probability that ultimate recovery will not exceed $3000," it is possible that some cases regarded as untransferrable by you will nevertheless be estimated as "Small" (under $3000) cases.

Only if both parties to the case voluntarily requested transfer to the district court did the pretrial judge allow a transfer. This occurred in only 114 of the approximately 1600 cases that underwent size screening, those cases being referred to herein as "voluntary transfers." The pre-experiment and post-experiment control cases that were sent to the district court by judicial order (about 600) are called "transferred by order" cases. The 597 test cases that though found to have a potential of less than $3,000 were allowed to remain in the larger courts are called "transferrable cases." The data set out below are comparisons of the litigation careers after pretrial of the three groups of cases thus classified.

The first problem is to determine whether transfer of undersized cases saves time for the Superior and County courts, and if so to estimate approximately how much time is saved. Then comes the question whether the system as a whole (including the district courts) saves or loses judge time from the transfer procedure. Following that, the results in transferred as against not-transferred cases are compared for any untoward side effects of the transfer process.

FINDINGS

Transfer of undersized cases occurs in large volume in the New Jersey courts. In the 1962–63 year, 33 per cent of the cases, or 4,629, were transferred by court order at the beginning of 14,017 pretrial conferences.[4] Of the 1,609 test cases, all of them personal injury actions, 597 (37 per cent) would have been transferred by court order but for the temporary suspension of compulsory transferrals in the test counties. But the sheer volume of transferrals is an unreliable index of the amount of work the higher jurisdiction courts would have been spared, inasmuch as it is known that the removed cases had small recovery potentials and hence were unlikely to persist to trial with high frequency. The first problem was to determine how many of the transferrable cases reached trial and roughly how much judge time they absorbed in the Superior and County courts. The first part of the answer is given in Appendix Table F-1.

Appendix Table F–1. Durability of Transferrable Cases

Settled before trial	79%
Reached trial	21%
Number of cases	574

Compared to the 21 per cent rate at which the transferrable cases reached trial, the "large" cases produced a figure of 31 per cent and the "medium" cases a figure of 25 per cent. This evidence of the "size-durability" principle at work in the New Jersey test cases is underlined if we look at the frequency of trials in small recovery cases compared to large ones. Whereas cases that recovered up to $1,000 went through trial only 6 per cent of the time and the $1,001–$3,000 cases only 8 per cent, the over-$10,000 recoveries were produced by trial 25 per cent of the time.

Despite their lower durability, some 120 transferrable cases reached trial and these absorbed significant judge time. We calculate that the median time consumed by each trial was roughly 7 hours, and assuming that the average time was about the same figure, we estimate that the total time they absorbed was about 840 judge hours.[5]

There is no doubt, therefore, that removal of the transferrable cases from the Superior and County court trial lists achieves a substantial saving in judge time expended on those cases *in those courts*. But the intriguing next question is whether, considering the time they absorb in the transferee district court, the court system as a whole enjoys a net saving. That depends on two factors, first, the rate at which the cases settle in the district court as compared with the rate in the larger courts; and second, the average time trial of these cases requires in the respective courts. A categorical answer is not possible on the second question because of gaps in essential data. However, on the basis of available evidence we can be quite sure that transfer to the district court inhibits rather than promotes settlement, as Appendix Table F–2 indicates.

Appendix Table F–2. Transferred Cases Reached Trial More Often than Cases That Were Not Transferred Although Normally Eligible

	Cases Transferred by Court Order	Transferrable Cases (Not Transferred During Test)
Settled before trial	66%	79%
Reached trial	34%	21%
Number of cases	605	574

From Appendix Table F–2 it is manifest that the transferred cases had a markedly higher durability than the cases whose transfer was suspended during the controlled test—34 to 21 per cent. Although there is no certainty that the transferred cases were statistically similar to the transferrable test cases, there is no reason to doubt that they were. The only determinant of the former group was the pretrial judge's estimate that they had a small recovery potential, and that was precisely the basis upon which the transferrable cases were selected by the pretrial judges during the controlled test.

Another uncertainty that is not as subject to a convincing answer relates to whether the district court trials in transferred cases consumed as much judge time as Superior and County court trials in the transferrable cases. There is no evidence either way on that question, for no records exist permitting an analysis of the average time consumed by trials in transferred cases. Extant district court records merely record the number of trial days, treating any fractions as whole days. Unless the district court trials are substantially shorter than trials in similar cases in the larger courts, it is clear that there is a high likelihood that the transferral of cases tends to make them more costly in judicial time. It might be wiser to transfer district court judges temporarily to the Superior and County courts and permit them to conduct trials in small cases there. This would have the added virtue of saving the judge, lawyer, and clerical time now absorbed in the process of calling a case for a pretrial conference, aborting the conference at the threshold and handling the case again in the district court. Once more it is impossible for us to estimate the loss in time involved in the procedure, but considering the volume of transferrals, it seems likely that the loss is substantial.

An interesting aside relates to the 114 test cases allowed to transfer to the district court at the parties' request despite the moratorium during the test. An astonishing 54 per cent of them reached trial,[6] perhaps because the parties were resigned to the fact that their cases could not be settled and preferred a trial in the lesser court, the plaintiff perhaps recognizing that the damages were within its jurisdictional limits. In those voluntary transfer cases the parties waived a jury more often (20 per cent) than in the cases transferred by court order (17 per cent) or in the transferrable cases (14 per cent).

Why, it might be asked, do plaintiffs persistently bring their small cases into the larger courts, there to meet with a transfer order one third of the time? It may be that plaintiffs' attorneys fear or expect

TRANSFERRING "UNDERSIZED" CASES

that their clients' injuries will become more substantial as time passes. More likely they believe the same case is worth more in a larger than in a lesser court. But the correct reason, for the majority of cases, is probably that the plaintiff's convenience dictated placing the suit in the Superior Court. By doing so, venue may be laid in one of several counties, whereas the choice is more restricted in the district court. In any event, there is no sanction upon their bringing small cases in a major rather than a minor court and they often do so.

An unexpected feature of the transfer process is that it appears to alter the outcome in a substantial percentage of the cases. Plaintiffs seemingly win more often if their case goes to a judgment in the transferee court than if it remains in the larger court; but such verdicts as plaintiffs recover in the major courts are considerably larger.

Appendix Table F-3. Defendants Won More Verdicts in Transferrable Cases than in Transferred Cases

	Cases Transferred by Court Order	Transferrable Cases (Not Transferred During Test)
Judgment for defendant	28%	53%
Number of cases	122	78

Again assuming (in the absence of evidence either way) that the transferrable cases and the transferred cases were substantially similar, we infer that plaintiffs in small cases much more frequently go away empty-handed after trials in the major courts than in the district court. This may be due to the willingness of the court and the jury to find a defendant's verdict in small cases in the larger courts.

However, when the plaintiffs do win a judgment in the larger courts the amount is much larger than in the transferred cases, as Appendix Table F-4 discloses.

Appendix Table F-4. Transferrable Cases More Frequently Recovered over $3,000

Amount recovered	Cases Transferred by Court Order	Transferrable Cases (Not Transferred During Test)
$1–$1,000	49%	32%
$1,001–$3,000	44%	32%
Over $3,000	7%	35%
Number of cases	88	37

The high rate of recovery of over-$3,000 judgments, in the transferrable cases completes the picture of a sort of jackpot justice at work in small cases in the major courts. The plaintiff often loses, but when he wins, he wins big.

Given the apparent variations in the outcome of cases depending on whether or not they are transferred to the district court, and given the apparent cost in judicial time because of the increased durability of transferred cases, we think there are good arguments for discontinuing the transfer procedure. If it thereafter develops that plaintiffs' lawyers increase their practice of filing undersized cases in the Superior and County courts, other correctives can be attempted. One of these may be to transfer district court judges to the major courts on temporary assignment and to permit them to try small cases.

NOTES TO APPENDIX F

[1] N.J. Rev. Stat. tit. 2A:6-35 (Supp. 1963) which limits damages in actions resulting from negligence to no more than $3,000 and costs in a county district court is, under the provisions of subsection (c), made inapplicable "to any action transferred to a county district court pursuant to [N.J. Rev. Stat. tit. 2A:15-4.1 (Supp. 1963)]." The latter provision is the legislative source for Rev. Rule 4:3-4 which sets up the machinery for transfer of undersized cases from the Superior and County courts.

[2] 1957-58 REPORT 10-11.

[3] The existence of a relationship between potential recovery ("size") and the stage of litigation at which a negligence case terminates ("durability") was reported in Rosenberg & Sovern, *Delay and the Dynamics of Personal Injury Litigation*, 59 COLUM. L. REV. 1115, 1127-36 (1959). The study noted that potentially "large" personal injury cases are more likely to go to trial than potentially "small" ones. Illustrative of this "size-durability hypothesis" is the finding that if the recovery was no more than $3,000, trial had commenced in only 1 of every 20 suits, but in recoveries exceeding $10,000, the trial stage had been reached 3 times in every 10 suits. *Id.* at 1130, 1134.

[4] During the 1962-63 court year the Superior Court held 4,204 pretrial conferences in the Law Division (1962-63 REPORT, Table C-1) and the County Court held 9,813 (*id.,* Table F-1), a total of 14,017. As a result, 4,629 were transferred. *Id.,* Table C-2.

[5] The calculation of median trial time is based upon Table 9 (see page 52). "Average" trial length can only be derived by inference, since available data do not provide the precise number of hours consumed by each trial.

[6] The trial-reaching rate is based on the 82 cases for which information on stage of disposition was available.

APPENDIX G. APPLICABILITY OF THE FINDINGS TO CASES OTHER THAN PERSONAL INJURY ACTIONS

IN THE interests of the clearest possible evaluation of the impact of pretrial, we limited the controlled experiment solely to personal injury cases. The excluded types of civil suits comprised roughly 30 per cent of the total case load which the New Jersey courts subject to pretrial conference. Now that we have learned what differences pretrial makes in the injury actions, we face the question of whether the findings are applicable in any degree to "other" cases. That is the problem to which this Appendix addresses itself.

The absence of quantitative data severely handicaps us in drawing conclusions about the other cases. Any statements we venture here are offered with diffidence and are coupled with the strong hope that a systematic investigation will soon be undertaken on the operation of pretrial in cases *not* involving personal injury. Ideally, the study would be built around a controlled experiment.

Meanwhile, the present study did produce some interesting non-quantitative information on other types of cases. The source was the voluminous transcript of the judges' comments at the Princeton seminars on pretrial, September 5–7, 1962, fully reported in Chapter V. At the Princeton seminars, as the judges discussed and analyzed the functioning of pretrial conferences in personal injury cases, they frequently compared them with other types, such as contract, chancery, and "prerogative writ" actions. Synthesizing the judges' remarks has produced a summary of the relevant differences they themselves perceive in the "other" cases; in how the attorneys prepare for pretrial in those cases; and in how the judges conduct conferences in them.

We shall assume that the judges' reports regarding differences in the other cases are approximately accurate, and then shall estimate (on a purely speculative basis) what effects those differences might have for our findings about pretrial in injury cases.

The first difference remarked by the judges relates to the obvious fact that there is far less likelihood that the extent of plaintiff's monetary damages will be a vigorously contested issue. In personal injury cases, how much plaintiff is entitled to recover, if defendant is liable, is usually a disputed question. In contract, chancery, and prerogative writ cases, on the other hand, damages often are liquidated, or their amount is conceded. In other cases the plaintiff often does not seek a money award as a remedy. Removing the question of "how much" as a major point of dispute may mean that there is less chance to engage in trading or negotiation, with the result that settlements are less frequently reached. One judge generalized with regard to chancery cases: "it is a little more difficult to settle [them] because there are normally no monetary damages."

A second contrast that emerges on comparing personal injury case pretrials with others is the strong view of many judges that attorneys are better prepared for pretrial in cases not concerned with negligence. One judge asserted that "everyone concedes" more time is devoted by the lawyers to preparing their pretrial memoranda in a "prerogative writ case, a chancery case, or cases of that nature." It was asserted that lawyers are "more like specialists" in cases not involving negligence issues and that personal injury cases are "the biggest headache as far as lack of preparation at pretrial." Product liability litigation was mentioned as an area of particularly poor performance by reason of the attorneys' inexperience.

Thirdly, the judge's participation in the pretrial apparently tends to be more strenuous if the case is other than a personal injury suit. For example, chancery case pretrials were said to run longer—an hour or two. An odd explanation was offered by one judge, who said that chancery suits often involve will contests in which a common issue raised is duress, but it is "a sham, a smokescreen, a fishing expedition," and detailed probing at pretrial results. In complex contract actions, one judge reported, it "sometimes takes a half hour to dictate the factual contentions." There was a consensus that judges meet with less opposition to marking documents as exhibits in "other" cases, compared to automobile negligence cases. In the latter it is "awfully difficult," even though there is frequent "going through the motions of attempting to get exhibits marked." Attorneys often declare that hospital records are unavailable and rebuff the judge's efforts to mark photographs in evidence.

In summary, comments at Princeton by the judges were to the effect that non-injury cases are basically different in their low emphasis on damage issues, in their higher level of attorney preparedness for pretrial, and in the judge's more active participation at the conferences. Accepting those comments as correctly stating material factors regarding the functioning of pretrial in negligence and non-negligence cases, what can be said of the applicability to them of the test findings on the impact of pretrial?

First, the finding that pretrial improves the trial process with appreciable frequency should apply a fortiori to other types of cases. The better prepared the attorneys are for the conference and the more active the judge's participation, the more to be expected are beneficial results, in the absence of any countervailing circumstances, and none are suggested.

Second, as to efficiency, since pretrials did not increase the frequency of settlement in personal injury cases, they are highly unlikely to do so in other types, where money damages are more likely to be fixed and less subject to dispute, bargaining, and compromise. Perhaps it can be put this way: In a personal injury case, disputes can be raised both as to whether the defendant is liable and as to the extent of plaintiff's losses, and both types of issue do usually arise in a case. It may be that the fluidity of the damages offers a chance for the parties to reflect the strengths and weaknesses in their liability positions in the amount they offer or demand. By contrast, if the amount of damages is a precise quantum, it may be that there is less basis to negotiate and the case tends to go to trial on a winner-take-all basis. Such speculations as those were uttered by judges at Princeton in accounting for the lower susceptibility of non-negligence cases to settlement.

The test findings also reported that pretrial failed to shorten trials in cases that did not settle. That finding would appear less likely to hold up in other types of cases, if we can project what the judges said at Princeton. They stressed that at pretrial conferences in contract, chancery, and prerogative writ cases the judges participate more actively and give close attention to the marking of documents into evidence. Such activities are well calculated to abbreviate trials for obvious reasons. Without knowing how widespread the document-admitting procedure is in "other" cases it is not possible to estimate

APPLICABILITY TO OTHER CASES

whether it produces a major saving in trial time, but the potential is definitely there.

An indirect influence on trial length is waiver of jury. The test finding was that frequency of jury waiver is not increased (hence, a potential saving of trial time goes unrealized) in personal injury cases that have been pretried. There is no reason to suppose that in non-negligence cases any major saving would result from jury waiver after pretrial. Firstly, in the chancery cases there is no right to a jury and the potentiality therefore does not even arise. Secondly, even in contract and other cases on the law side in which a jury is available on demand, the general tendency is to forgo the demand much more frequently than in negligence cases.

As to whether pretrial is likely to result in faster settlements than otherwise, that did not occur in the negligence cases and there is no apparent reason why it should occur to any appreciable extent in non-injury cases. To be sure, there will be instances when a pretrial conference exposes just the right issues, produces just the right stipulations, and admits the key documents; and the result is a quickened settlement. But nothing in the test findings or in the judges' comments suggests that this happens with marked frequency.

Is the outcome affected by pretrial in non-negligence cases, as it is, according to the test data, in personal injury cases? Without further insight into what influences the stepped-up recovery after pretrial in negligence cases, we can only speculate in the dark on this question. It would seem that the de-emphasis of damages as a center of dispute in the "other" cases would minimize the likelihood that a step-up in money damage awards will be experienced after pretrial in those cases. So far as altering the winner on the liability question, we observed that pretrial did not appear to do that in negligence cases and there is no reason to suppose that it does so in other actions.

In summary, it would appear that few firm statements about the impact of pretrial on non-negligence cases can be based upon the findings of this study. What evidence there is, however, points to the likelihood that pretrial conferences will have rather more favorable effects in non-injury cases.

BIBLIOGRAPHY

I. BOOKS AND PAMPHLETS

ABA, The Improvement of the Administration of Justice (1961)
ABA, Special Committee on Court Congestion, Ten Cures for Court Congestion (1959)
Calif. Judicial Coúncil, California Manual of Pre-Trial Procedure and Rules Relating to Pre-Trial Conferences (1956)
Frank, Jerome, Courts on Trial (1949)
Holbrook, James G., A Survey of Metropolitan Trial Courts—Los Angeles Area (1956)
Levin, A. Leo, & Edward A. Woolley, Dispatch and Delay (1961)
Millar, Robert W., Civil Procedure of the Trial Court in Historical Perspective (1952)
N.J. Administrative Office of the Courts, Manual of Pretrial Practice (1959)
Nims, Harry D., Pre-Trial (1950)
Pollock, Frederick, The Expansion of the Common Law (1904)
Proceedings of the Clinic on Pre-Trial Procedure Sponsored by the Comm. on Pre-Trial Procedure of the Judicial Conference of Senior Circuit Judges (1944)
Van Alstyne, Arvo, & Harvey M. Grossman, California Pretrial and Settlement Procedures (1963)
Vanderbilt, Arthur T., Minimum Standards of Judicial Administration (1949)
——The Challenge of Law Reform (1955)
Zeisel, Hans, Harry Kalven, Jr., & Bernard Buchholz, Delay in the Court (1959)

II. ARTICLES, ADDRESSES, AND MEMORANDA

Ackerson, Henry E., Jr., *Pretrial Conferences and Calendar Control: The Keys to Effective Work in the Trial Courts*, 4 Rutgers L. Rev. 381 (1950)

BIBLIOGRAPHY

——— *Medical Testimony Pretrial Conference in State Courts Urged,* 68 N.J.L.J. 21 (1945)

Adams, Chester D., *The Effectiveness of Pre-Trial Conferences Under the New Rules of Civil Procedure,* 47 KY. L.J. 198 (1959)

Alexander, James P., *Pre-Trial Procedure,* 2 TEX. B.J. 65 (1939)

Baldwin, Raymond E., *How Can We Expedite the Business of the Courts?,* 27 CONN. B.J. 1 (1953)

Ballantine, Thomas A., Address, *Pre-Trial Conference,* 81 KY. S.B.A. 81 (1955)

Belli, Melvin M., *Pre-Trial: Aid to the New Advocacy,* 43 CORNELL L.Q. 34 (1957)

Bentley, Vernon G., *How To Do Pre-Trial in State Courts,* 14 WYO. L.J. 1 (1959)

Bohannan, J. Gordon, *Pre-Trial Procedure,* 51 VA. S.B.A. 300 (1939)

Botein, Bernard, *Impartial Medical Testimony,* 328 THE ANNALS 75 (1960)

Brand, George E., *"Mighty Oaks"—Pretrial,* 26 J. AM. JUD. SOC'Y 36 (1942)

Brennan, William J., Jr., *The Continuing Education of the Judiciary in Improved Procedures,* Seminar on Practice and Procedure, 28 F.R.D. 37, 42 (1960)

——— *After Eight Years: New Jersey Judicial Reform,* 43 A.B.A.J. 499 (1957)

——— *Pretrial Procedure in New Jersey,* 21 ALBANY L. REV. 1 (1957)

——— *New Jersey Tackles Court Congestion,* 40 J. AM. JUD. SOC'Y 45 (1956)

——— *Pre-Trial Procedure in New Jersey—A Demonstration,* 28 N.Y.S.B. BULL. 442 (1956)

——— *Remarks on Pre-Trial,* 17 F.R.D. 479 (1955)

Broeder, Dale W., *The University of Chicago Jury Project,* 38 NEB. L. REV. 744 (1959)

Caplan, Oscar S., *Streamlining Our Court Procedure,* 6 JOHN MARSHALL L.Q. 178 (1940)

——— *Pretrial System in the Municipal Court of Chicago,* CASE & COM., Feb. 1941, p. 17

Carver, William, *Should Florida Adopt the Pre-Trial Procedures As Set Forth in the New Federal Rules?,* 13 FLA. L.J. 226 (1939)

Chandler, Stephen S., *Discovery and Pre-Trial Procedure in Federal Courts,* 12 OKLA. L. REV. 321 (1959)

Charlton, Robert D., *Pretrial Procedure—Should It Be Abolished in Colorado?*, 30 DICTA 371 (1953)

Chillingworth, C.E., & Joseph S. White, *Pretrial Conference in Florida*, 4 U. FLA. L. REV. 141 (1951)

Christenson, A. Sherman, *When Is a Pre-Trial Conference a "Pre-Trial Conference"?*, 23 F.R.D. 129 (1958)

Cinamon, Joseph H., *Pre-Trial and Conciliation Lists*, 12 LAW SOC'Y J. 4 (1946)

——— *More About Pre-Trial*, 12 LAW SOC'Y J. 170 (1946)

Clark, Charles E., *Objectives of Pre-Trial Procedure*, 17 OHIO ST. L.J. 163 (1956)

——— *The Evershed Report and English Procedural Reform*, 29 N.Y.U.L. REV. 1046 (1954)

Cole, Albert H., *The Rules for Civil Procedure in the United States District Courts: Pre-Trial Procedure*, 14 IND. L.J. 149 (1938)

[Comment], *California Pretrial in Action*, 49 CALIF. L. REV. 909 (1961)

[Comment], *Congested Calendars and the Pre-Trial Conference*, 35 CORNELL L.Q. 390 (1950)

[Comment], *Pre-Trial Hearings and the Assignment of Cases*, 33 ILL. L. REV. 699 (1939)

[Comment], *Settlement of Personal Injury Cases in the Chicago Area*, 47 NW. U.L. REV. 895 (1953)

Connolly, Paul R., *"Pre-Trial"—As Seen by the Defense*, PRAC. LAW. Jan. 1958, p. 30

Cooper, Frank E., *Pre-Trial Procedure in the Wayne County Circuit Court, Detroit, Michigan*, 6 MICH. JUDICIAL COUNCIL ANN. REP. 61 (1936)

Cox, Louis S., *Pre-Trial and Conciliation Lists*, 6 LAW SOC'Y J. 641 (1935)

Crary, Ralph W., *The Pre-Trial in Action*, 37 IOWA L. REV. 341 (1952)

Crawford, Earl T., *Legal Problems of the Pre-Trial Conference*, 31 CORNELL L.Q. 285 (1946)

Crawford, R.S., *Pre-Trial in Country Districts*, 3 TEX. B.J. 139 (1940)

Curd, Thomas H. S., *Pre-Trial of Lawsuits*, 46 W. VA. L.Q. 148 (1940)

Delehant, John W., *Pre-Trial Conferences in the Federal District Courts: Their Value for Counsel and for Judges*, 35 J. AM. JUD. SOC'Y 70 (1951)

——— *The Pre-Trial Conference in Practical Employment: Its Scope and Technique,* 28 NEB. L. REV. 1 (1948)
Demonstrations of the Pre-trial Conference, 11 F.R.D. 3 (1951)
Diamond, Arthur S., *English Interlocutory and Pretrial Practice and Procedure,* 47 A.B.A.J. 697 (1961)
Dobie, Armistead M., *Use of Pre-Trial Practice in Rural Districts,* 1 F.R.D. 371 (1940)
Douglas, William O., *Pre-Trial Procedure,* 26 A.B.A.J. 693 (1940)
Dow, David, *The Pre-Trial Conference,* 41 KY. L.J. 363 (1953)
Ellenbogen, Henry, *Justice Delayed,* 14 U. PITT. L. REV. 1 (1952)
English, Robert E., *A Year of Pre-Trial Settlement Conferences,* 40 CHI. B. RECORD 343 (1959)
Fee, James A., *Justice in Search of a Handmaiden,* 2 U. FLA. L. REV. 175 (1949)
——— *The Lost Horizon in Pleading Under the Federal Rules of Civil Procedure,* 48 COLUM. L. REV. 491 (1948)
Fisher, Harry M., *Pre-Trial Conference and Its By-Products,* 1950 U. ILL. L.F. 206
——— *Judicial Mediation: How It Works Through Pre-Trial Conference,* 10 U. CHI. L. REV. 453 (1943)
Franklin, Marc A., Robert H. Chanin, & Irving Mark, *Accidents, Money, and the Law: A Study of the Economics of Personal Injury Litigation,* 61 COLUM. L. REV. 1 (1961)
Freifield, Samuel, *Broader Aspects of Pretrial,* 26 J. AM. JUD. SOC'Y 24 (1942)
Friesen, Ernest C., Jr., *The Minimum Requirements of a Pretrial Rule,* 33 ROCKY MT. L. REV. 523 (1961)
——— "Techniques in Pretrial" (unpublished monograph, in Project for Effective Justice File, Columbia Law School)
Genzberger, Earle N., *Pretrial Preparation: Some Personal Observations,* 40 A.B.A.J. 1077 (1954)
Gershenson, Harry, *Pre-Trial Procedure,* 26 WASH. U.L.Q. 348 (1941)
Gourley, Wallace S., *Effective Pretrial Must Be the Beginning of Trial, Seminar on Practice and Procedure,* 28 F.R.D. 37, 165 (1960)
Grimson, Gudmundur, *Progress Report on Pretrial Conferences in North Dakota,* 30 N.D.L. REV. 85 (1954)
Hale, Quincy H., *Pre-Trial Procedure in Wisconsin,* 15 MINN. L. REV. 491 (1931)
Henderson, William B., *Pre-Trial Aids Judges to Better Administer Justice,* 23 OKLA. S.B.J. 797 (1952)

Hilton, Ordway, *Pre-Trial Preparation and Pre-Trial Conferences in a Questioned Document Case*, 27 TUL. L. REV. 473 (1953)
Hinshaw, Joseph H., *Pre-Trial Practice*, 6 JOHN MARSHALL L.Q. 25 (1940)
Holtzoff, Alexander, *Federal Pretrial Procedure*, 11 AM. U.L. REV. 21 (1962)
——*Pretrial Procedure in the District of Columbia*, 3 CATHOLIC U.L. REV. 1 (1952)
Howard, Charles M., *Pre-Trial Procedure*, 44 MD. S.B.A. 68 (1939)
Hughes, Sarah T., *Pre-Trial Progress in Texas*, 16 TEX. B.J. 131 (1953)
Hugus, Wright, *Pre-Trial in West Virginia*, 55 W. VA. L. REV. 110 (1953)
Jacobson, Aaron, *Pre-Trial in the Courts: An Opinion*, 5 CLEV.-MAR. L. REV. 61 (1956)
Jayne, Ira W., *Foreword [to Symposium]*, 17 OHIO ST. L.J. 160 (1956)
——*A Pre-Trial Statement*, 38 J. AM. JUD. SOC'Y 80 (1954)
Johnson, Kenneth M., *Antecedents of the Pre-Trial Plan*, CALIF. S.B.J. Aug. 1938, p. 19
Kales, Albert, *Short Cuts in Procedure Accomplished by Agreement*, 2 J. AM. JUD. SOC'Y 178 (1919)
Kaufman, Irving R., *The Federal Rules: Control of the Human Equation Through Pre-Trial*, 12 WYO. L.J. 92 (1958)
——*Report on Study of the Protracted Case*, 21 F.R.D. 55 (1957)
——Address, at Tenth Circuit Annual Judicial Conference, May 10, 1957 (unpublished, in Columbia Law School Library)
Kennerly, T.M., *The Pre-Trial Conference under the Federal Rules of Civil Procedure*, 18 TEXAS L. REV. 190 (1940)
Keyes, Leonard, *Beginnings in Pre-Trial*, 38 MINN. L. REV. 236 (1954)
Kincaid, Clarence L., *A Report on Pre-Trial Procedure*, 33 LOS ANGELES B. BULL. 339 (1958)
—— *Pre-Trial Procedure in California*, PHI DELTA DELTA, Dec. 1958, p. 15
—— *Pre-Trial Conference Procedure in California*, 4 U.C.L.A.L. REV. 377 (1957)
—— *A Judge's Handbook of Pre-Trial Procedure*, 17 F.R.D. 437 (1955)
—— *Pre-Trial in Our Superior Court*, 27 CAL. S.B.J. 255 (1952)
Kirschenbaum, Meyer, *Pre-Trial Procedure to Eliminate Perjury*, 63 N.J.L.J. 24 (1940)

Kloeb, Frank L., *Pre-Trial Conference in Federal Court Practice,* 9 OHIO ST. L.J. 203 (1948)

Kurtz, Irwin, *Pre-Trial Practice and Procedure in Bankruptcy Hearings,* 38 J. AM. JUD. SOC'Y 77 (1954)

Kuykendall, J. Sloan, *Pretrial Conference: A Dissent from the Bar,* 45 VA. L. REV. 147 (1959)

Laws, Bolitha, J., *A Trial Judge Looks at Pre-Trial Procedure,* PRAC. LAW. Jan. 1958, p. 17

——— *Pre-Trial—Its Purposes and Potentialities,* 21 GEO. WASH. L. REV. 1 (1952)

——— *Pre-Trial Conference,* 13 TEX. B.J. 435 (1950).

——— *Pre-Trial Procedure—A Modern Method of Improving Trials of Law Suits,* 25 N.Y.U.L. REV. 16 (1950)

——— *Pre-Trial Practice Aids Justice,* 30 ILL. B.J. 11 (1941)

——— *Plan for Pre-Trial Procedure Under New Rules in District of Columbia,* 25 A.B.A.J. 885 (1939)

——— *Pre-Trial Procedure,* 6 N.C. S.B. 31 (1939)

——— H.C. Blouton, & D. Stripps; Addresses, *Pre-Trial Practice,* 4 J. Mo. B. 279 (1948)

Lay, Donald P., *Discovery Practice in Wisconsin,* 1954 WISC. L. REV. 429

Lemley, Harry J., *A Pre-Trial Conference Statement,* 16 F.R.D. 75 (1955)

Levit, William H., *Pretrial Procedures in the Los Angeles Superior Court,* 38 LOS ANGELES B. BULL. 433 (1963)

Lorry, Wilfred R., *"Pre-Trial"—As Viewed by Plaintiff's Counsel,* PRAC. LAW. Jan. 1958, p. 23

Louisell, David W., *Discovery and Pre-Trial Under the Minnesota Rules,* 36 MINN. L. REV. 633 (1952)

McAllister, Breck P., *Pre-Trial Practice in the Southern District of New York,* 12 F.R.D. 373 (1951)

McCarthy, Walter F., *Pre-Trial in Virginia,* 40 VA. L. REV. 359 (1954)

McIlvaine, John W., *The Value of an Effective Pretrial,* Seminar on Practice and Procedure, 28 F.R.D. 37, 158 (1960)

McNaugher, William H., *The Pre-Trial Court at Pittsburgh,* 6 U. PITT. L. REV. 5 (1939)

McNeal, Harley J., *"Pre-Trial"—Some Questions and Answers,* PRAC. LAW. Jan. 1958, p. 37

Marshall, Elliott, *Pretrial Conference: An Endorsement from the Bench,* 45 VA. L. REV. 141 (1959)

Martz, Clyde O., *Pretrial Preparation, Seminar on Practice and Procedure*, 28 F.R.D. 37, 137 (1960)
Maulitz, Herbert R., *Pre-Trial Proceedings—A Plea*, 6 ALA. L. REV. 19 (1953)
Meyer, Milford J., *What Every Lawyer Should Know*, 22 SHINGLE 171 (1959)
Millar, Robert W., *A Rule for Pre-Trial Hearing*, 28 ILL. B.J. 201 (1940)
Miller, George J., *Introduction to Pretrial Conferences*, 25 FLA. L.J. 171 (1951)
Moynihan, Joseph A., *Observations on Pretrial Procedure*, 11 MO. B.J. 144 (1940)
——— *Pre-Trial Hearings*, 62 N.J.L.J. 405 (1939)
Murrah, Alfred P., *Pre-Trial Procedure*, 328 THE ANNALS 70 (1960)
——— *The Pretrial Conference: Conceptions and Misconceptions*, 44 A.B.A.J. 39 (1958)
——— *Some Bugaboos in Pre-Trial*, 7 VAND. L. REV. 603 (1954)
——— *Pre-Trial Procedure—A Statement of Its Essentials*, 14 F.R.D. 417 (1954)
——— *Pre-Trial Procedure—Some Practical Considerations*, 26 A.B.A.J. 592 (1940)
Nelson, Dorothy W., *Pre-Trial—An Effective Weapon of Advocacy*, 4 U.C.L.A.L. REV. 381 (1957)
Niles, Emory H., *Pre-Trial*, 11 MD. L. REV. 300 (1950)
Nims, Harry D., *Some By-Products of Pre-Trial*, 17 OHIO ST. L. J. 185 (1957)
——— *Some Comments on the Relation of Pre-Trial to the Rules of Evidence*, 5 VAND. L. REV. 581 (1952)
——— *Some Comments on Pre-Trial*, 28 DICTA 23 (1951)
——— *Recent Demonstrations of Pretrial Procedure, A Step Forward in the Administration of Justice*, 36 A.B.A.J. 611 (1950)
——— *Pre-Trial in the United States*, 25 CAN. B. REV. 697 (1947)
[Note], *Indiana Pre-Trial Procedure*, 22 IND. L. J. 280 (1947)
[Note], *Pre-Trial Conference*, 38 KY. L.J. 302 (1950)
[Note], *Pre-Trial Conference Adopted for Nebraska District Courts*, 26 NEB. L. REV. 110 (1947)
[Note], *Pre-Trial Conferences in the District Court for Salt Lake County*, 6 UTAH L. REV. 259 (1958)
[Note], *Pretrial Hearings*, 30 CALIF. L. REV. 212 (1942)

[Note], *Pre-Trial in North Carolina—The First Eight Years,* 36 N.C.L. REV. 521 (1958)

[Note], *Pre-Trial Practice in Pennsylvania,* 17 NOTRE DAME L. REV. 40 (1941)

[Note], *Pretrial Procedure Under the New Iowa Rules,* 29 IOWA L. REV. 82 (1943)

[Note], *The Status of Pre-Trial Practice in New England,* 35 B.U.L REV. 256 (1955)

[Note], *Time for Holding the Pre-Trial Conference,* 11 WYO. L.J. 66 (1956)

Olney, Warren, III, *An Analysis of Docket Congestion in the United States District Courts in Light of the Enactment of the Omnibus Judgeship Bill, Seminar on Procedures,* 29 F.R.D. 191, 217 (1961)

Paschal, J. Francis, *Pre-Trial in North Carolina: The First Eight Months,* 28 N.C.L. REV. 375 (1950)

Patterson, Logan E., *Pre-Trial Procedure in Practice,* 41 KY. L.J. 383 (1953)

Peacock, James C., *Pretrial and the Appellate Courts,* 24 J. AM. JUD. SOC'Y 173 (1941)

Peck, David W., *Court Organization and Procedures to Meet the Needs of Modern Society,* 33 IND. L.J. 182 (1958)

——— *The Law's Delay—What Insurance Companies Can do About It,* 1956 INS. L.J. 7

Pharr, Ralph H., *The Truth About Pretrial,* 47 A.B.A.J. 177 (1961)

Phillips, Richard H., *Breaking the Judicial Log Jam: Connecticut's Blitz on Court Congestion,* 45 A.B.A.J. 268 (1959)

——— *Pre-Trial—Optional or Mandatory?,* 15 CONN. B.J. 150 (1941)

Pickering, H. G., *The Pre-Trial Conference,* 9 HASTINGS L.J. 117 (1958)

Pinanski, Abraham E., *The Superior Court—Jury Pooling, Auditors, Pre-Trial,* 8 LAW SOC'Y J. 120 (1938)

Pre-Trial Challenges Lawyers' Influence, 23 J. AM. JUD. SOC'Y 69 (1939)

Pretrial Comes to Cleveland, 24 J. AM. JUD. SOC'Y 29 (1940)

Pre-Trial Conference Report, 40 ILL. B.J. 356 (1952)

Pretrial Is Readily Adapted to Rural Counties, 26 J. AM. JUD. SOC'Y 106 (1942)

Pre-Trial Practice Symposium, 29 ILL. B.J. 6 (1940)

Pre-Trial Procedure—A Symposium (Wanderer, Udall, Murrah), 60 COM. L.J. 251 (1955)

Pre-Trial Procedure Adopted for Boston, 19 J. Am. Jud. Soc'y 11 (1935)
Pre-Trial Procedure, Demonstrations at Annual Meeting of Missouri Judicial Conference, 15 Mo. B.J. 77 (1944)
Pre-Trial Procedure in Wayne Circuit, 16 J. Am. Jud. Soc'y 136 (1933)
Pre-Trial Procedures in the Federal Court—A Forum (Kaufman, Medina, Dawson, Ellis, Wallace), 11 The Record 180, 314 (1956)
Pre-Trial Rules, Institute of Judicial Administration Bull. 2–U22 (1953)
Pre-Trial's Part in Evaluating Damages in Personal Injury Cases (Panel Discussion: Thomas, McNeal, Sindell), 21 Ohio St. L.J. 144 (1960)
Probert, Walter, *A Survey of Ohio Pre-Trial Practices and Achievements,* 7 W. Res. L. Rev. 428 (1956)
Proceedings of the Nebraska State Bar Association, October 1949, 29 Neb. L. Rev. 341 (1950)
Propper, Leonard M., *Pre-Trial Comes to Philadelphia,* 20 Shingle 34 (1957)
Quinlan, Edward J., *Pre-Trial Procedure,* 13 Conn. B.J. 233 (1939)
Raia, Alfred E., *Application of the Pre-Trial Conference Rule,* 25 Fla. L.J. 265 (1951)
Rice, Eugene, *Pre-Trials and the Improvement of the Administration of Justice,* 6 Okla. L. Rev. 249 (1953)
Ridge, Albert A., *What Do Judges and Lawyers Want from the Mandatory Pre-Trial Conference Practice?,* 17 U. Kan. City L. Rev. 83 (1949)
Robson, Edwin A., *Streamlining Justice by Pre-Trial Procedure,* 40 Ill. B.J. 341 (1952)
Roemer, Erwin W., *Advantages to Lawyers in Pre-Trial Conferences,* 40 Ill. B.J. 345 (1952)
Rosenberg, Maurice, *Comparative Negligence in Arkansas: A "Before and After" Survey,* 13 Ark. L. Rev. 89 (1959)
—— & Robert H. Chanin. *Auditors in Massachusetts As Antidotes for Delayed Civil Courts,* 110 U. Pa. L. Rev. 27 (1961)
Rosenberg, Maurice, & Myra Schubin, *Trial by Lawyer: Compulsory Arbitration of Small Claims in Pennsylvania,* 74 Harv. L. Rev. 448 (1961)
Rosenberg, Maurice, & Michael I. Sovern, *Delay and the Dynamics of Personal Injury Litigation,* 59 Colum. L. Rev. 1115 (1959)

Ross, James R., *Suggested Application of the Pre-Trial Conference,* 30 Los ANGELES B. BULL. 7 (1954)
Ryan, Stanley M., & John C. Wickman, *Pre-Trial Practice in Wisconsin Courts,* 1954 WISC. L. Rev. 5
Sarpy, Leon, *Pre-Trial in Louisiana,* 6 LOYOLA L. REV. 105 (1952)
Schechter, Herman & Rex Rowland, *Pre-Trial Conferences and Summary Judgments in New York,* 26 CORNELL L.Q. 667 (1941)
Schulman, Sidney, *Trial Congestion and Delay—Some Proposals,* 20 SHINGLE 81 (1957)
Searl, Clifford H., *What of Pre-Trial?,* 4 SYRACUSE L. REV. 1 (1952)
Selected Bibliography, Trial of Protracted Litigation, Seminar on Protracted Cases, 21 F.R.D. 395, 533, (1957)
Shafer, Morris L., *Pre-Trial Conference in Common Pleas Courts of Pennsylvania,* 63 DICK. L. REV. 239 (1959)
Shafroth, Will, *Pre-Trial Techniques of Federal Judges,* 3 WYO. L.J. 185 (1949)
——— *Pre-Trial Techniques of Federal Judges,* 28 J. AM. JUD. SOC'Y 39 (1944)
Shields, Roy F., *Advantages to a Trial Lawyer of a Pretrial Conference, Seminar on Protracted Cases,* 23 F.R.D. 319, 342 (1958)
Shumaker, Ross W., *An Appraisal of Pre-Trial in Ohio,* 17 OHIO ST. L.J. 192 (1956)
Skinner, Thomas E., *Pre-Trial and Discovery Under the Alabama Rules of Civil Procedure,* 9 ALA. L. REV. 202 (1957)
Slough, M. C., *Trial Preparation Under Kansas and Federal Rules: A Contrast,* 4 KAN. L. REV. 58 (1955)
Smith, Ralph H., *Amazing Success of Pretrial on Special Dockets,* 25 J. AM. JUD. SOC'Y 46 (1941)
Smith, William F., *Pretrial Conference—A Study of Methods, Seminar on Procedures,* 29 F.R.D. 191, 348 (1961)
Spangenberg, Craig & Leslie R. Ulrich, *Pre-Trial from the Viewpoints of Two Lawyers,* 7 W. RES. L. REV. 418 (1956)
Stanley, Arthur, Jr., *Pre-Trial Procedure,* 19 KAN. B.A.J. 5 (1950)
Stavely, A. K., *Pre-Trial—Five Years After,* 2 U. KAN. L. REV. 360 (1954)
Stiff, Lawson K., *Pre-Trial Proceedings,* 1943 N.M. S.B. 39
Success of Pretrial Hearings Demonstrated, 21 J. AM. JUD. SOC'Y 160 (1938)
Suggs, Tom, *Pretrial Technique,* 12 TEX. B.J. 17 (1949)
——— *Pre-Trial Technique,* 6 TEX. B.J. 61 (1943)

Sunderland, Edson R., *Procedure for Pretrial Conferences in Federal Courts,* 3 WYO. L.J. 197 (1949)
——— *The Function of Pre-Trial Procedure,* 6 U. PITT. L. REV. 1 (1939)
——— *The Theory and Practice of Pre-Trial Procedure,* 36 MICH. L. REV. 215 (1937)
Sweeney, George C., *Expert Use of Pretrial Docket in Federal Court,* 23 J. AM. JUD. SOC'Y 11 (1939)
Symes, J. Foster, *A Comment on Pre-Trial Procedure,* 27 DICTA 163 (1950)
Symposium on "Trauma or Heart Disease? Pretrial Conference for Medical Testimony," 15 MD. L. REV. 110 (1955)
Taylor, T. Raber, *Pre-Trial in Colorado in Words and At Work,* 27 DICTA 157 (1950)
The Pre-Trial Conference in Iowa (Panel Discussion: Lewis, Ingersoll, Wilmarth, Davis, Gibson, Prall), 7 DRAKE L. REV. 41 (1958)
Thode, E. Wayne, *The Case for the Pre-Trial Conference in Texas,* 35 TEXAS L. REV. 372 (1957)
Thomas, S. B., *Voluntary Pre-Trials,* 28 MISS. L.J. 302 (1957)
Thomas, William K., *The Story of Pre-Trial in the Common Pleas Court of Cuyahoga County,* 7 W. RES. L. REV. 368 (1956)
Tilbury, Roger, *Pre-Trial Conference in the Kansas City Area,* 21 U. KAN. CITY L. REV. 77 (1952)
Troutman, Robert B., *Pre-Trial Conference,* 4 MERCER L. REV. 302 (1953)
Vanderbilt, Arthur T., *Improving the Administration of Justice—Two Decades of Development,* 26 U. CINC. L. REV. 155 (1957)
——— *The Five Functions of the Lawyer: Service to Clients and the Public,* 40 A.B.A.J. 31 (1954)
Vaught, Edgar S., *The Pre-Trial Conference,* 15 OKLA. S.B.J. 751 (1944)
Vetter, George M., *Pre-Trial in the Southern District of New York,* 19 THE RECORD 110 (1964)
Warren, Earl, *Delay and Congestion in the Federal Courts,* 42 J. AM. JUD. SOC'Y 6 (1958)
Weston, S. Burns, *A Trial Lawyer Looks at Pre-Trial,* 17 OHIO ST. L.J. 174 (1956)
Whaley, M. S., *Pretrial Conference,* 1 S.C.L.Q. 221 (1949)
Whitney, O. W., Jr., *Adaptability of Pre-Trial to the Less Populated Counties,* 17 OHIO ST. L.J. 171 (1956)

Williams, Claude, *Pretrial Procedures in the State Courts of Texas,* 5 So. Tex. L.J. 261 (1960)

Winters, John M., *The Pre-Pre-Trial Conference Without the Judge in Federal District Courts,* 37 Neb. L. Rev. 449 (1958)

Worley, *Pre-Trial Conference and the Rules,* 21 Tenn. L. Rev. 385 (1950)

Wright, J. Skelly, *The Pretrial Conference, Seminar on Practice and Procedure,* 28 F.R.D. 37, 141 (1960)

――― *Pre-Trial on Trial,* 14 La. L. Rev. 391 (1954)

Yankwich, Leon R., *Crystallization of Issues by Pretrial: A Judge's View,* 58 Colum. L. Rev. 470 (1958)

――― *"Short Cuts" in Long Cases,* 13 F.R.D. 41 (1951)

Zachory, Francis, *Voluntary Pre-Trials,* 28 Miss. L.J. 324 (1957)

Zavatt, Joseph C., *English Interlocutory and Pretrial Practice and Procedure,* 47 A.B.A.J. 696 (1961)

――― *Pre-Trial Practice,* 22 N.Y.S.B.A. Bull. 75 (1950)

Zeisel, Hans, *Delay by the Parties and Delay by the Courts,* 15 J. Legal Ed. 27 (1962)

――― *Social Research on the Law: The Ideal and the Practical,* in Law and Sociology 124 (Evan ed. 1962)

――― *The New York Expert Testimony Project: Some Reflections on Legal Experiments,* 8 Stan. L. Rev. 730 (1956)

――― *The Significance of Insignificant Differences,* 19 Public Opinion Q. 319 (1955).

――― & Thomas Callahan, *Split Trials and Time Saving: A Statistical Analysis,* 76 Harv. L. Rev. 1606 (1963).

III. REPORTS

1960 U.S. Administrative Office of the Courts Ann. Rep. 120

1956 U.S. Administrative Office of the Courts Ann. Rep. 226

1948 U.S. Conference Judicial Rep. 36

Prettyman Comm. Report to the U.S. Judicial Conference, *Procedure in Anti-Trust and Other Protracted Cases,* 13 F.R.D. 62 (1951)

1956 Temporary Comm'n on the Court Report, Leg. Doc. No. 18

D.D.C. Comm. on Docket Acceleration Rep. to The Chief Judge and Court (1961)

Holtzoff Comm. Report to D.C. Judicial Conference, *Pretrial Procedure,* 1 F.R.D. 759 (1940)

18 CALIF. JUDICIAL COUNCIL BIENNIAL REP. 126 (1959–60)
17 CALIF. JUDICIAL COUNCIL BIENNIAL REP. 55 (1957–58)
15 CALIF. JUDICIAL COUNCIL BIENNIAL REP. 13 (1953–54)
Comm. Report, *Pre-Trial Procedure,* 13 CONN. B.J. 164 (1939)
1962–63 N.J. ADMINISTRATIVE DIRECTOR OF THE COURTS ANN. REP.
1961–62 N.J. ADMINISTRATIVE DIRECTOR OF THE COURTS ANN. REP.
1960–61 N.J. ADMINISTRATIVE DIRECTOR OF THE COURTS ANN. REP.
1959–60 N.J. ADMINISTRATIVE DIRECTOR OF THE COURTS ANN. REP.
N.J. SUP. CT. COMM. ON PRETRIAL PROCEDURE DRAFT OF PROPOSED RULES TO IMPLEMENT REPORT (1963)
1962 N.Y. JUDICIAL CONFERENCE ANN. REP. 116
15 N.Y. JUDICIAL COUNCIL ANN. REP. 64 (1949)
Report of Committee on Judicial Administration on Pre-Trial Conference, 27 PA. B.A.Q. 29 (1955)

INDEX

INDEX

A

Acceleration of settlement, see Purposes and claims
Admissions, see Observed conferences
Adversary philosophy, 5, 11, 14
Age at closing, 54–55
Alabama, pretrial provision in, 211
Alaska, pretrial provision in, 212
All-pretried cases, see Cases
Alternate jurors, 213
Amendment of pleadings, 100–101, 111, 115, 126, 172, 176, 178, 180–82, 212
Appeals: as indicator of defective trial, 30; personal injury, proportion of civil, 20; reversed or modified, 22, 31
Arbitration, compulsory, 161 n. 68
Arkansas, pretrial provision in, 211, 212
Attendance at conference, 211–12
Attorneys: attendance at conference and trial, 22; as firm members or not, 21–22; inept, 5; judges' complaints about, 84; opinions whether pretrial makes a difference, 42–43; opposition to pretrial, 11, 12, 24; opting for a conference, 20, 29; preliminary obligations, 7, 9, 90; preparations of, 8; traditional role in litigation, 23; see also Princeton Seminar; Trial
Auditors, see Massachusetts
Authorization for pretrial, see Enabling authority
Automobile, see Cases, motor vehicle
Avoidance of pretrial, 210

B

Bentley, Vernon G., quoted, 140 n. 24
Brennan, Justice William J., Jr., 7, 8, 91
Bureau of Applied Social Research, see Columbia University

C

Calendar, cases added to the, 144 n. 11; pretrial, 18, 88
California: attorneys' memoranda in, 212; cases not pretried in, 210, 211; discovery in, 213; retrenchment of pretrial in, 12; naming of witnesses in, 213; settlement rate in, 119; subjects considered at conference in, 213; timing of conference in, 211
Cases: all-pretried, 19, 20, 27; complex, 52–53; in-part-pretried, 19; large, 121–23; lawyers' choice, 19, 27; mandatory, 19; motor vehicle, 21, 53; multiclaim, 21, 53; multiparty, 21, 53; nonmandatory, 19; not pretried, 19, 20; optional, 19, 20, 36, 48, 49, 57; personal injury, 1–2; premise, 21; public liability, 21; total in test, 18; tried-to-completion, 32; type pretried, 211; see also Nonpersonal injury cases; Personal injury cases
Check lists, 107, 108; illustration of, 128
Chicago Jury Project, 65
Claims favoring pretrial, see Purposes and claims
Colorado, settlement rate in, 119
Columbia University: Bureau of Applied Social Research, 18; planning of New Jersey study, 2, 16–17; previous study's finding on size-durability relationship, 49; Project for Effective Justice, history of, 133 n. 3
Complaint, conference scheduled from service of, 9
Compliance, 208–9; see also Methodology of the study
Conference: conduct of the, 28; determination of motions at, 213; duration, 21; entry of judgment at, 213; multi-

INDEX

purpose, 97–98; number per hour, 83; participants at, 9, 84; in personal injury actions, 114; reactions to demonstration, 73, 78, 85, 88; settlement-oriented, 9–10, 97, 114–16; subjects discussed at, 7, 9, 212–13; suggestion for timing of, 89; trial-oriented, 9–10, 97, 114–16; when held, 1, 7, 9, 107, 211; where held, 6, 82, 99; *see also* Observed conferences; Princeton Seminar

Connecticut, provisions for pretrial, 211–12

Costs, time, 56; *see also* Savings, time

Courts, responsibilities of, 1, 24

D

Damages, *see* Conference; Recovery

Delay, growth of, 45; measurement of, 45, 154 *n*. 35; *see also* Purposes and claims

Demand-supply, 45–46

Design, 18–20; *see also* Methodology of the study

Discovery, conducted at attorneys' initiative, 23; at the conference, 9, 179–80; effect on durability of, 121–22; and pretrial, 6, 9, 14; suggestions for revisions in, 90–91; termination of, 7, 83; *see also* Conference; Princeton Seminar

Discretionary pretrial, 210–11

Durability, 49; and size, 167 *n*. 9; and time devoted to discovery, 121–22; theory of, 155 *n*. 41

Duration, *see* Conference; Trial

E

Effectiveness of pretrial: and auditing procedures, 123–24; measure of, 24–25, 29–30; *see also* Purposes and claims

Efficiency, effect of pretrial on, 28–29, 47, 56–58; *see also* Age at closing; Purposes and claims; Settlement; Trial

Enabling authority: citations to individual states, 215–16; classification of, 210; New Jersey, 6, 171 *ff*.

Evidence, *see* Conference; Princeton Seminar; Trial

Experiment, controlled, *see* Methodology of the study

F

Fairness, measure of, 25–26; *see also* Settlement; Trial

Federal pretrial, 6, 12; draftsman of, 106–7; purposes of, 8; text of rule, 214

Findings 28–29

Forms, 18–19, 33, 42, 43, 95; samples of, 184–207

Francis, Justice John J., 91

Friesen, Ernest C., Jr., 79

H

History: of New Jersey pretrial study, 2, 15, 16–17; of New Jersey transfer substudy, 218; of pretrial, 1, 5, 45

Holtzoff, Judge Alexander, 107

I

Idaho, pretrial provision in, 212, 213

Illinois, pretrial provision in, 211

Information sources, *see* Methodology of the study

Interrogatories, *see* Discovery

Iowa, pretrial provision in, 212

Issues, *see* Conferences; Observed cases; Princeton Seminar; Trial

J

Judges: Active-passive role, 10–11, 177–79; duties of 10, 23, 178–79; number of participating in test, 21; opinions on fairness, 42, 43; as a pretrial factor, 70; settlement rates of, 70; time devoted to civil law matters, 161; time devoted to duties by, 57, 160–61; *see also* Observed conferences; Princeton Seminar

Judicial Seminar on Pretrial Conferences, *see* Princeton Seminar

Jury: demand for, 21, 54; waiver of, 21, 54, 229

K

Karlen, Delmar, 76

Kentucky, pretrial provision in, 211

Kincaid, Judge Clarence L., 8

L

Lawyers, *see* Attorneys

Legal theories, *see* Conference; Trial

## INDEX

Levin, A. Leo, 82
Liability: effect of pretrial on, 59–61, 118; judge and jury agreement on, 65–66; ratio of findings against, 60; *see also* Transfer

M

McIlvaine, Judge John W., 14, 155 *n.* 37
Mandatory pretrial: in New Jersey, 2, 6, 8, 12; in personal injury cases, 15; after request, 210–11; states having, 210
Manual of Pretrial Practice, see *New Jersey Manual of Pretrial Practice*
Maryland, pretrial provision in, 212
Massachusetts: auditor system in, 161 *n.* 68; pretrial provision in, 211
Methodology of the study: basis, 2; benefits of controls, 47; comparison of scores, 32; compliance, 208–9; data-gathering devices, 32; deviation from ideal, 17, 49; information sources, 2–3, 19; limitations imposed, 27–28; self-selection problem, 48–49, 62–63, 208; size-screening procedure, 63; type of case used, 17; unstructured questions, 33; *see also* Transfer
Michigan, pretrial provision in, 213
Mistrials, percentage of, 22
Motions, 6, 23–24; impact of pretrial on, 13; *see also* Mistrials; New trials
Motor vehicle, *see* Cases
Murrah, Chief Judge Alfred P., 7–8, 25–26

N

New Jersey courts: appeals in, 20; appellate views of pretrial, 9; distinction between Superior and County courts, 144; role of Supreme Court in study, 16–17
New Jersey Manual of Pretrial Practice, 8–9, 111
New Jersey pretrial rules: 6–7, 9, 79–80, 83–84, 86, 122; text of, 171–76
New trials: indicating defective trial, 30; motions for and granted, 22, 31
New York: pretrial purpose, 8; recovery rate of tried cases, 22; settlement rate, 119; size-settlement relationship, 49
New York City: pretrial in, and frequency of no recovery, 148

New York, Southern District of; pretrial in protracted cases, 10
Non-jury, 21, 53, 54, 159 *n.* 57
Nonmandatory cases, *see* Cases
Non-personal injury cases, applicability of test findings to, 226–29
North Carolina: cases precluded from pretrial, 211; pretrial provision in, 212

O

Observed conferences: administration in, 95–96, 99; admissions at, 102; discovery at, 101; document marking at, 101; judges' performance at, 95–99; judges' preparation for, 99; judges' settlement achievements at, 102–4; multipurpose type illustrated, 97–98; number of, 93, 108; number of judges in, 93, 125; objectives of judges at, 96; order, diversity of preparation at, 99–100; recording procedure for data at, 93–94, 108; sanctions at, 96; settlement-oriented illustrated, 97; stipulations at, 102; transfers ordered at, 102–3; trial preparation illustrated, 96–97; type of, 94, 108; where held, 99
Observer forms, *see* Forms
Oklahoma: avoidance of pretrial in, 210; pretrial provision in, 212; witness identification at pretrial, 212
Opposition to pretrial, 2, 11–12, 14–15, 24
Optional pretrial, *see* Cases
Optionality, 208
Order, *see* Pretrial order
Outcome of case, *see* Liability; Recovery

P

Pennsylvania: arbitration's impact on outcome, 161 *n.* 68; pretrial provision in, 212
Personal injury cases: appealed, 20, 145; conference specifically mandated in New Jersey for, 29; and mandatory pretrial, 2; as a proportion of civil litigation, 1–2, 20; subjects discussed at conference for, 114; suitability for pretrial of, 15; trial completion rate of, 52; yearly number of, 20, 56
Pharr, Judge Ralph, 58

Pleadings, 6; discussed at pretrial, 212; effect of pretrial order on, 6, 180–82
Poor man's discovery, 9, 101, 179–80
Preparation, *see* Attorneys; Judges
Pretrial memoranda, 89–90, 212
Pretrial order: amendment of, 176, 180–82; contents of, 6–7, 8, 172–73, 177; diversity in preparation of, 99–100; effect on pleadings, 6, 180–82, when prepared, 7; purpose of, 1; requirements for a, 95, 212; and settlement-oriented conference, 10; *see also* Observed conferences; Princeton Seminar
Policy, pretrial, 110–11
Pretrial test forms, *see* Forms
Princeton Seminar: attorneys, complaints about, 72, 84–87; conference formality, 72, 81–82; conferences, number scheduled, 72, 88; date of, 71; demonstration conference, responses to, 73, 78, 85, 88; discovery, 83, 90–91; evidence, 72–78; improvements, suggestions for, 88–91; issues, 77–80; judges' self-criticism, 87; order, effect of, 82; order, preparation of, 72, 82; rules, compliance with, 72, 82–84; sanctions, 80–81; settlement, 73–76; surprise, 76–78; trial preparation, 72, 77–80; where conference held, 82
Project for Effective Justice, *see* Columbia University
Purposes and claims, 1, 5–6, 7–9, 10, 12–14, 25–26, 45, 107; in New Jersey, 6–9, 29, 45, 59, 116–17; *see also* Settlement

Q

Quality, *see* Settlement; Trial

R

Recommendations: improved conferences, 110–12; type of pretrial in New Jersey, 118–23
Recovery: amount of, 22, 61–62, 117–18; analysis of disparity in, 63–66; estimated, 63; impact of pretrial on, 29, 59, 61–62; judge and jury agreement on, 65–66; percentage of cases obtaining a, 22, 60; *see also* Transfer
Relationship of pretrial to other procedures, 6

S

Sanctions, *see* Observed conferences; Princeton Seminar
Savings, time, 56–57, *see also* Costs
Selective pretrial, 120–23
Self-selection, defined, 208; *see also* Methodology of the study
Settlement, 13; elements of a good, 25–26; impact of pretrial on, 25, 29, 43, 44, 46–50; maximum rate possible, 119; and the pretrial order, 8; as pretrial purpose, 8–9, 13, 14, 107; quality of, 43–44; rate of, 22, 46–48; relationship of size to, 49, 121; state provisions for discussion of, 8–9, 212; *see also* Age at closing; Princeton Seminar; Transfer
Significance, *see* Significant differences
Significant differences, 151 *n.* 9, 208
Size, case: defined, 49, 63; estimated, 63; and settlement, 49, 121; and time costs, 219
Stage of litigation, *see* Conference
States, number having pretrial, 210
Subjects discussed at conference, *see* Conference
Summary judgment, 79, 111, 116, 126, 213
Surprise, *see* Conference; Princeton Seminar; Trial

T

Techniques, conference, 107–8
Test counties, 18; as representative of state, 143–44
Test procedures, *see* Methodology of the study
Texas, pretrial provision in, 211
Thomas, Judge William K., 107
Time, *see* Costs; Savings
Transfer, 83, 145 *n.* 13, 218–24; *see also* Purposes and claims
Trial: attorney preparation at, 28, 34–35; duration, 22, 28–29, 50–53; evidence at, 37–38; fairness, 42, 43; issue emergency at, 34–35; judge time consumed by, 46; presentation of case at, 34–35; quality, 14, 25, 28, 32–43; surprise at, 39–40; theory exposition at, 34–35; *see also* Conference; Jury; New trials, Observed conferences; Princeton Seminar
Type of action, *see* Cases

U

Universal pretrial, *see* Cases
University of Chicago, *see* Chicago Jury Project

V

Vermont, 211, 212
Voir dire examination, 213

W

Weintraub, Chief Justice Joseph, 2, 87
Work week, judges, 160–61
Wright, Judge J. Skelly, 106–07

Z

Zeisel, Hans, 142–43, 154 *n.* 35, 156 *n.* 42